SECOND EDITION

essential linguistics

what teachers need to know to teach

- ESL
- reading
- spelling
- grammar

DAVID E. FREEMAN
YVONNE S. FREEMAN

HEINEMANN
Portsmouth, NH

Heinemann
361 Hanover Street
Portsmouth, NH 03801–3912
www.heinemann.com

Offices and agents throughout the world

The authors and publisher wish to thank those who have generously given permission to reprint borrowed material:

Excerpts from *The Language Teaching Controversy* by Karl Diller. Copyright © 1978. Reprinted with permission from Cengage Learning SO, conveyed through Copyright Clearance Center, Inc.

Excerpts from "Logic and Conversation" by Herbert Paul Grice originally appeared in *Syntax and Semantics*, vol. 3 (1975). Copyright © 1975 by Emerald Group Publishing Limited. Reprinted by permission of the publisher.

Excerpts from the poem "T-Shirt" from *My Name Is Jorge on Both Sides of the River* by Jane Medina. Copyright © 1999 by Jane Medina. Published by Wordsong, an imprint of Boyds Mills Press. Reprinted by permission.

Excerpts from *Beginning to Read: Thinking and Learning About Print* by Marilyn Adams. Copyright © 1990 by Massachusetts Institute of Technology. Published by MIT Press. Reprinted by permission of the publisher.

Acknowledgments for borrowed material continue on page vi.

Library of Congress Cataloging-in-Publication Data
Essential linguistics : what teachers need to know to teach ESL, reading, spelling, and grammar / David E. Freeman and Yvonne S. Freeman. — Second Edition.
    pages cm.
  Includes bibliographical references and index.
  ISBN 978-0-325-05093-5
  1. Language and languages—Study and teaching. 2. Language acquisition. 3. English language—Grammar.   I. Freeman, Yvonne S.

P51.F694 2014
418.0071—dc23   2014009168

Editor: Holly Kim Price
Production: Vicki Kasabian
Cover and interior designs: Shawn Girsberger
Typesetter: Shawn Girsberger
Manufacturing: Steve Bernier

Printed in the United States of America on acid-free paper
7 8 9 10 11 RWP 24 23 22 21 20
November 2020 Printing

We would like to dedicate this book to our daughters, Mary and Ann. Both Mary and Ann have followed in our footsteps by becoming teacher educators specializing in language, bilingual education, and literacy. Their families language and translanguage daily on two different coasts.

In California, Mary's Salvadoran husband, Francisco, teaches bilingually in Spanish and English, and their two children, Maya and Romero, translanguage as they negotiate their home and school worlds.

In New York City, Ann's Greek American husband, Christopher, works for a multinational company. Their children, Christiana and Alexander, learn Greek from their father and Spanish from their mother. They are surrounded by people translanguaging in a multilingual city.

Contents

Acknowledgments for borrowed material continued from copyright page:

Figures 5.5 and 5.6: From *Insight from the Eyes: The Science of Effective Reading Instruction* by Eric J. Paulson and Ann Ebe. Copyright © 2003 by Eric J. Paulson and Ann Ebe. Published by Heinemann, Portsmouth, NH. All rights reserved.

Excerpt from *The Disappearing Alphabet Book* by Richard Wilbur. Copyright © 1997 by Richard Wilbur. Published by Houghton Mifflin Harcourt. Reprinted by permission of the publisher.

Poem "My Teddy Bear" from *Rhymes About Us* by Marchette Chute. Copyright © 1974. Published by E. P. Dutton. Reprinted by permission of Elizabeth Weinrich.

Excerpt from *A Cache of Jewels and Other Collective Nouns* by Ruth Heller. Copyright © 1987 by Ruth Heller. Reprinted by permission of Grosset & Dunlap, Inc., a division of Penguin Group (USA) LLC.

Excerpt from *Up, Up and Away: A Book About Adverbs* by Ruth Heller. Copyright © 1991 by Ruth Heller. Reprinted by permission of Grosset & Dunlap, Inc., a division of Penguin Group (USA) LLC.

Excerpts from *Under, Over, by the Clover* by Brian P. Cleary. Text copyright © 2002 by Brian P. Cleary. Excerpts from *To Root, to Toot, to Parachute* by Brian P. Cleary. Text copyright © 2001 by Brian P. Cleary. Reprinted by permission of Millbrook Press, a division of Lerner Publishing Group, Inc. All rights reserved. No part of these text excerpts may be used or reproduced in any manner whatsoever without the prior written permission of Lerner Publishing Group, Inc.

Figure 8.8: From *The Journey of English* written by Donna Brook and illustrated by Jean Day Zallinger. Text copyright © 1998 by Donna Brook. Published by Clarion Books, an imprint of Houghton Mifflin Harcourt. Reprinted by permission.

Excerpts from "About Wordsift" by Kenji Hakuta and Greg Wientjes on Wordsift.com: http://wordsift.com/site/about. Stanford University © 2010. Reprinted by permission of the authors.

Excerpts adapted from *Teaching Grammar in Context* by Constance Weaver. Copyright © 1996 by Constance Weaver. Published by Heinemann, Portsmouth, NH. All rights reserved.

Acknowledgments

We would like to acknowledge the many people who provided important feedback that helped us as we wrote this revision of *Essential Linguistics*. David continued to use the first edition in his linguistics classes, and the feedback from his students has been extremely useful. We have attempted to rewrite sections that students found difficult or confusing. In addition, we added to the instructions for the applications so students would better understand what they were being asked to do.

We contacted several colleagues and other educators who have used the first edition for their feedback and received a number of useful suggestions. We would like to especially thank Susan Spezzini, who carefully read and commented on the phonology chapter. Her expertise in phonology is much appreciated, and she passed on useful feedback from one of her students as well. In addition, thanks go to Steve Krashen, who gave us a key reference for the chapter on spelling.

Other educators provided us with important feedback as well. Socorro Herrera and Miki Loschky provided specific suggestions on different sections of the book and also suggested ways this book could benefit students studying for the Praxis exam. Yukari Amos gave detailed feedback on several chapters and many of her suggestions were incorporated in this revision. Jenny Spencer Green, whose students had posted creative chapter summaries of the first edition on YouTube, also provided her thoughts for the second edition. In addition, we want to thank Lydia Breiseth, Anonieta Romero, and Alfredo Mercuri, who gave us important feedback on the sections of the book comparing English and Spanish. The current revision has been enriched by the contributions of all these educators.

We also want to acknowledge the support and advice we received from our editor at Heinemann, Holly Kim Price. Our meetings and email correspondence with her encouraged us and was extremely helpful during our writing. The production team at Heinemann always does an outstanding job. We were fortunate to work again with Vicki Kasabian, a true professional and a good friend. Vicki is a meticulous editor who also knows how to choose the right fonts and format for a book so that it looks appealing. We appreciate all her efforts.

Finally, it is also important to acknowledge all those from Heinemann who have helped to produce and promote our books. With their support our books reach the hands of educators and students who benefit from all the books the Heineman team produces.

1 /wʌn/

How Linguists Study Language

As the number of English learners increases, most practicing teachers and students preparing to become teachers are required to take coursework in second language acquisition, English language teaching methods, cross-cultural communication, and linguistics. While the first three courses are usually regarded as useful and interesting, many teachers and teacher candidates are apprehensive and some are even resentful as they enter a linguistics class. They are nervous about having to take the class, and, at the same time, suspect it will be of no use. Few classes, with the possible exception of statistics, trigger such strong emotions.

- Why study linguistics?
- What are the different approaches to the study of language?
- How do linguists study language?

Of course, some students look forward to taking a course in linguistics. They regard the study of language as interesting. Unfortunately, such students are in the minority. Many students connect "linguistics" with "grammar," which, in turn, triggers thoughts of identifying parts of speech—nouns, verbs, and conjunctions. If these students were not particularly successful at determining whether a word was an adjective or an adverb in the past, they figure that now it will get even harder. They begin the class believing that, since they never were very good at grammar, this class will further expose that weakness.

Other students associate linguistics with activities like diagramming sentences. They are convinced that sentences must be hard to diagram. They aren't sure what a tree diagram is. Or perhaps they have heard from other students that they will need to learn a new writing system called phonemic transcription. This system uses unfamiliar symbols to represent sounds. All this can be intimidating. In addition, for students who are studying to be teachers and for those already working in schools, identifying parts of speech, drawing tree diagrams, and writing phonemic transcriptions appear to have little connection to their classrooms. They ask themselves and their instructors questions like "How will this knowledge help me be a better teacher?" and "How will this class give me any practical ideas I can use with my own English learners?"

Pedagogical Language Knowledge

We have written this book to help dispel these fears about linguistics. In the chapters that follow, we present the basic concepts of linguistics in everyday language. We focus on aspects of linguistics that have clear classroom connections. We provide examples and suggest activities to help educators apply concepts from linguistics to their own teaching. Our primary goal is to turn key insights from linguistics into what Krashen (2003) calls *comprehensible input.* We hope to provide teachers with the knowledge they need to make informed decisions as they help their students, both native English speakers and students learning English as an additional language, develop academic literacy.

We agree with Bunch (2013), who argues that teachers need *pedagogical language knowledge*. As Bunch explains:

> I argue that efforts to prepare teachers for working with English learners (ELs) to engage with increasing language and literacy expectations across the curriculum requires development of *pedagogical language knowledge* (Galguera 2011)—not to "teach English" in the way that most mainstream teachers may initially conceive of (and resist) the notion, but rather to purposefully enact opportunities for the development of language and literacy in and through teaching the core curricular content, understandings, and activities that teachers are responsible for (and, hopefully, excited about) teaching in the first place. (298)

Bunch notes that pedagogical language knowledge is different from *pedagogical content knowledge* that all teachers need. English teachers, for example, need to know about how to teach effective writing and how to analyze literature. This is pedagogical content knowledge, and it is different from the pedagogical content knowledge a social studies teacher would need. All teachers need to know their content and how to teach it.

In addition, they need to know the language of their content area and how to teach that language. This is pedagogical language knowledge. For example, a teacher teaching a mathematics lesson on division would need to know how to teach division (pedagogical content knowledge) and how to teach the language required to read, write, and discuss division (pedagogical language knowledge). For instance, the teacher would need to be aware of the possible confusion for an English learner of the expressions "divide into" and "divide by" and plan a lesson to help clarify the difference.

What teachers need to know

Fillmore and Snow (2000) have written a detailed paper outlining what teachers need to know about language to teach effectively, especially when teaching English learners. They organize their report by considering the different roles a teacher plays and the language needed for each role. Figure 1.1 summarizes the language demands for the different roles.

In addition to discussing teachers' roles and responsibilities, Fillmore and Snow list a number of things teachers should know about language. These include knowledge of the basic units of language (phonemes, morphemes, words, phrases, clauses, discourse); how the lexicon is acquired and structured; an understanding of dialects or language varieties; academic English; English spelling; what makes a written text easy or difficult to understand. This is a daunting list, but it does reflect the kind of knowledge that is the basis for pedagogical language knowledge.

Teachers of English learners do not need the same detailed knowledge of linguistics that a teacher of linguistics would need. However, they do need to understand basic concepts of linguistics to develop pedagogical language knowledge so

Why do we need knowledge of linguistics?

Teacher as Communicator	Teachers need to understand their students. This requires an understanding of alternate discourse patterns. Teachers also need to know how to provide comprehensible oral input.
Teacher as Educator	Teachers need to understand language development. This allows teachers to distinguish between cognitive problems and second language problems. In addition, teachers need to teach students to read and write in the different content areas.
Teacher as Evaluator	Teachers often group students for instruction. English learners may have different ways of using language and of interacting than middle class native English speakers do. In evaluating students, then, it is important to understand the differences between ways students from different backgrounds use language.
Teacher as Educated Human Being	A knowledge of linguistics should be part of the general knowledge that any educated person develops. Teachers need to understand how language works, the history of their language, and differences between their language and that of their students.
Teacher as Agent of Socialization	For many English learners, schools represent a different culture than their home culture. Teachers are the agents who help socialize children into a new culture. Teachers need to understand children's home cultures and languages in order to help them accommodate to the school culture. Children can make this accommodation without losing their home culture and language.

Figure 1.1 *Roles of the teacher* (Adapted from Fillmore and Snow, 2002, with permission from the Center for Applied Linguistics)

that they can meet the language needs of their students. Further, in the case of teaching adults a second language, it is helpful for teachers to know enough grammar to be able to explain why some ways of saying or writing something in the language are considered to be standard or conventional forms and some ways are not. The teacher does not need to directly teach the grammar, but having some knowledge of grammar gives a teacher credibility. Often, if older students have studied the grammar of English and are familiar with its rules, they lose confidence if their teacher does not know the grammar.

In addition, some researchers, such as Long (2001), have argued that while teaching discrete grammar items in isolation is not useful, teaching grammar in the context of meaningful activity can improve students' facility with the language. Teachers could either point out errors and provide corrective feedback during an activity, or they could plan a lesson that focuses on a common error they have observed.

For example, if students are having trouble with irregular past-tense forms, such as *brought*, and use a form such as *bringed*, the teacher could simply point out the error and provide the correct form, or the teacher could plan a lesson that would require students to use irregular past forms. For instance, the teacher could say, "I want each of you to tell me about one thing you brought to class today." Some knowledge of linguistics would be helpful in planning such lessons.

The research on providing corrective feedback and on planning lessons that elicit forms students have trouble with has not been conclusive. Often, exercises like asking students to tell what they brought to class are not meaningful, and it appears that engagement in meaningful use of a language is the key to language acquisition.

Whether or not a teacher decides to teach grammar directly, the more he knows about how language works, the more effectively he can use language to help his students learn. As Halliday (1984) wrote, "A child doesn't need to know any linguistics to use language to learn; but a teacher needs to know some linguistics if he wants to understand how the process takes place—or what is going wrong when it doesn't" (9).

Three Aspects of Language Development

The reason that Halliday emphasizes the importance of teachers knowing about linguistics is that subject matter content is always developed through language. It is nearly impossible to separate the knowledge of a subject and the knowledge needed to read, write, and talk about that subject. For example, it would be hard to learn mathematics without knowing what the words *triangle* or *multiplied by* mean. As Halliday (1984) points out, we learn language, we learn through language, and we learn about language.

Teachers armed with linguistics knowledge can help all their students *learn language*. Whether her students are six years old or twenty-six, whether they speak English as the native language or are learning English as an additional language, a teacher is responsible to help all students develop their language abilities. A first-grade teacher expands her students' language knowledge by representing their experiences in writing during a language experience activity. A middle school language arts teacher helps his students discover the organizational structure of the short stories they read. A high school biology teacher shows her students how to use contextual clues to understand new science vocabulary. Teaching any subject involves teaching the language—the vocabulary and the organizational structures—common to that content area.

The second aspect of language development is *learning through language*. Go into most classrooms and what do you hear? The teacher is talking, the students are talking, the room is full of talk. Why is this? It's because one way that humans learn is through oral language. In the case of deaf children, the mode of communication is sign rather than oral language, but language is just as much present. If you look around the classroom, you will also see written language. There are books, lists on the board, student papers on the wall, and words on computer monitors. Everywhere you look, there is written language. Students continually learn through language, both oral and written, inside and outside classrooms. And teachers continually teach their students through language.

Students also *learn about language*. Sometimes they learn that the language they came to school speaking is not valued in that setting. Sometimes they learn how to make subjects and verbs agree. Or they may learn that when two vowels go walking the first one does the talking. Every day, students learn about language. In classrooms this language study should be scientific. For example, students might work together to discover why many English words end in a silent *e* and then develop a rule for keeping or dropping the *e* before adding a suffix. This approach to language study is most common in classes where the teacher has studied linguistics. Such a teacher has her students engage in linguistic investigations following the same approach that linguists use.

The greater a teacher's understanding of basic language structures and processes, the easier it is for that teacher to make good decisions when teaching tough topics like phonics, spelling, and grammar. A teacher with an active interest in language will arouse a similar interest in students who may be surprised to find that *hippopotamus* means "river horse," that the reason commas and periods go inside quotation marks is that typesetters didn't want to lose those little pieces of punctuation as they laid out type for printing, and that the rule about not ending a sentence with a preposition was created in a period of history when teachers decided to try to base English grammar rules on Latin rules. The more that teachers understand language, the more effectively they can help their students develop their knowledge of language.

Why Study Linguistics?

In this book we focus on connections between linguistics and teaching, specifically teaching English learners and teaching literacy. We will show how knowledge of linguistics can help teachers work more effectively with English learners as well as with native English speakers. However, there are several other reasons for studying linguistics.

One very good reason for studying linguistics is that language is what makes us distinctly human. Lederer (1991) puts it in the strongest terms, "The birth of language is the dawn of humanity . . . before we had words, we were not human beings" (3). Pinker (1994) argues that humans have a language instinct. Chomsky (1975) claims that language is innate, that it grows in the human mind the same way hair grows on our heads.

controversial?
agree

Most linguists agree that language is uniquely human; it is what distinguishes us from other living creatures. Other creatures can use signs to communicate, but only humans have syntax, the ability to combine symbols to create new symbolic meanings. Syntax expands language capacity and enables humans to communicate in unique ways. For example, there is a difference in meaning between these two sentences:

(i)   The dog bit the man.
(ii)   The man bit the dog.

Notice that the same elements (dog, man, bit) occur in each sentence. However, English speakers use word order to convey meaning, and here the change in the word order results in a change in meaning. This illustrates how syntax enables English speakers to combine symbols in different ways to convey different meanings.

Human communication is qualitatively different from animal communication. A dog might be able to communicate to its owner (or to another dog) that she is hungry, but she can't tell her master what she did yesterday or what she hopes to do tomorrow. However, the claim that only humans have language is debatable. It's a topic students might want to investigate. Do dolphins or chimpanzees have language? How is their communication different from communication among humans? Is language what distinguishes humans from other creatures? Linguistics ① is the scientific study of language, and the study of linguistics gives teachers and students the tools to investigate questions such as these.

LINGUISTIC

A second reason to study linguistics is that language study is interesting. Students are fascinated to discover that sandwiches got their name from the Earl of Sandwich, who spent his days (and nights) playing cards. He also loved to eat meat, but he didn't want to get grease on the cards, so he wrapped the meat in bread, and the sandwich was born! Newspaper columns, radio shows, books, and Internet websites feature information about language. Richard Lederer's (2012) books on language are best sellers. Many of his lines (*Why do we park in the driveway and drive on the parkway?*) make their rounds on the Internet as friends forward emails with lists of interesting language tidbits. However, even though language is a fascinating subject, the only exposure many students get to language study during their elementary and secondary years is through worksheets and exercises that bore them to tears and serve little practical purpose in improving their reading or writing. What students need is a new approach, and teachers who study linguistics can awaken students' interest in language and engage them in linguistic investigations.

A third reason for studying linguistics is that a well-educated person should know something about language. Unfortunately, it is usually only when students study foreign languages that they begin to learn how their own language works. Language study should be introduced early in school, and the approach to language study should be scientific. This book is designed to help teachers build the knowledge they need to provide a scientific approach to language study for their students.

A final reason to study linguistics is that "the study of language is ultimately the study of the human mind" (Akmajian, Demers, and Harnish 1979, 5). Although linguists are interested in the structure and functioning of language, their goal in trying to understand how language works is to gain insights into how the human mind works. Even though scientists cannot examine the workings of the mind directly, they can study language, the unique product of human minds. Language reflects the inner workings of the mind. As Chomsky (1975) puts it, "language is a mirror of mind in a deep and significant sense. It is a product of human intelligence, created anew in each individual by operations that lie far beyond the reach of will or consciousness" (4).

Approaches to the Study of Language

Linguistics, broadly defined, is the scientific study of language. People have always been fascinated with language. Over time, different approaches have been taken to the study of language. Derewianka (2007) identifies three models of grammar that have been developed. She refers to these models as "grammar as structure, grammar as mental faculty, and grammar as functional resource" (843).

As Derewianka points out, all grammars of English can be traced back to Greek roots. Plato argued that sentences represent propositions made up of a *subject* (what we are talking about) and a *predicate* (what we are saying about the subject). So in a sentence such as "Third-grade students must pass high-stakes tests" the subject is "third-grade students" and the predicate is "must pass high-stakes tests." The sentence, as a basic unit, represents a proposition that the speaker or writer makes. According to Derewianka (2007), "Plato was interested in the truth value of propositions, not in grammatical analysis as an end in itself" (843–44).

Aristotle took a slightly different approach to the study of language. He categorized language into its structural parts. Like Plato, he was not so much interested in defining these parts as in determining how they function in rhetoric (effective or persuasive speaking or writing), poetics, and reasoning. It was Dionysius Thrax who produced the first systematic grammar. He identified most of the parts of speech that linguists use today.

These early scholars raised important questions about language that continue to be studied. Derewianka lists the following questions:

1. What are the basic consituents of a sentence and how are they organized into structures?
2. Is there a universal grammar that reflects human cognition?
3. How does language function to help us achieve our rhetorical purposes? (844)

All three questions are important for an understanding of language and how it functions. At the same time, as linguists have studied these questions, their findings have had important implications for how we teach a second language and how we teach literacy.

Language as structure

One question that linguists have studied is "What are the basic parts of a sentence and how are they organized into structures?" This line of study has led to a greater understanding of the parts of a sentence and how these parts are combined or structured in different languages. Most linguists would agree that the basic parts of a language may include words and phrases that correspond to the traditional English parts of speech (nouns, verbs, adjectives, adverbs, articles, prepositions, conjunctions, and pronouns). Not all languages have all of these parts. Some languages do not have articles. In some languages, the words we refer to as *prepositions* come after the noun, so they are called *postpositions*. In such languages the English phrase "under the table" would become "the table under." Despite these and other differences, the world's languages generally have words that serve the same functions as the types of words in traditional English grammar.

The words in a language are combined to form phrases, clauses, and sentences. The study of language structure involves identifying the way words are organized into these larger units. For example, in some languages sentences begin with a subject followed by a verb and an object. In other languages, the verb comes at the end. In some languages, the order of the words is quite fixed while in other languages, endings on the words indicate whether they are subjects, objects, and so on, making the order of the words more flexible. The task for linguists who view language as structure is to determine the parts and how they are organized into larger units. This is the study of syntax.

A number of reference grammars for English have been produced. These grammars describe the parts and the structure of English in detail. These reference grammars represent important scholarly work, but since they can only be accessed through major libraries, they are not often used by teachers. Some recent reference grammars have been developed by analyzing large corpuses of text, usually several million words. Computer analysis of written and spoken language allows linguists to describe how a language is currently being used.

Implications for teaching a second language and teaching literacy

Work by linguists to develop accurate descriptions of languages, the parts and how they are structured, has strongly influenced language teaching. The traditional approach to teaching a second language has been to teach the grammar and vocabulary of the new language. Teaching a language this way seems like a logical approach. It involves breaking down the language into its parts and then teaching each part. So, for instance, a teacher might teach students that some words are nouns, some are adjectives, and so forth. Once students can identify the parts of speech, they study how to put the parts together to produce conventional oral and written language.

While the traditional approach to teaching language is logical, it generally does not enable people to communicate in that language. Often, students who know the grammar of the language still do not know how to use the language to make themselves understood or to understand others. The failure of the traditional grammar-based approach should not be surprising. Many people who are native speakers of a language do not "know" its grammar—that is, they cannot identify parts of speech, the tenses of verbs, or other things, such as subject–verb agreement. Generally, it is only when they try to teach the grammar that they learn it. The fact is that we acquire our native language without first learning the grammar. Why, then, do we need to teach a second language by teaching the grammar? If people acquire a second language in much the same way that they acquire their first language, then explicit teaching of grammar is not needed.

This logical approach also applies to teaching people to read and write. In traditional reading methods, written language (which is a kind of second language for everyone) is broken down into its parts (letters, words, paragraphs, and so on) and the parts are taught one by one. Usually, students are taught the sound or sounds each letter makes, how to blend sounds, and how to use that information to sound out words. Once the written language is transformed into oral language, the assumption is made that students should be able to recognize the words and know their meanings. Then they can put the meanings of the words together to figure out the meaning of a text. The problem with this "logical" approach is that students taught using this method often struggle to make sense of what they read. Again, this suggests that written language can be acquired and does not need to be taught as a step-by-step process. In Chapter 2 we examine more carefully how people acquire a first language, and in Chapter 3 we look in more detail at how second languages and written language are taught and learned.

Language as mental faculty

A second line of research in linguistics that has had implications for second language teaching comes from the work of Chomsky and his followers. Chomsky is interested in the relationships between language and cognition. He has argued that people acquire their first language naturally because the human brain is wired for language. He sees language as a mental faculty unique to humans.

Chomsky and other linguists argue that humans are born with a *language acquisition device*, a set of mental structures that enable them to use language input to form subconscious rules for how language works. Over time, humans develop an internal grammar, a set of rules they can use to understand and produce one or more languages. The internal grammar includes a syntactic component along with a knowledge of phonology, morphology, semantics, and pragmatics.

In later work, Chomsky referred to the language acquisition device as *Universal Grammar*. He has argued that all humans are born with the ability to acquire a language. However, since languages differ, what babies need to figure out is how the language or languages they hear work. For example, babies seem to be born knowing that the language they hear will be made up of units that include subjects and predicates (although they certainly could not explain it that way). This was the insight Plato discussed.

In English most sentences have a subject, a verb, and an object. A typical sentence in English would be "Juan studied mathematics." First comes the subject, then the verb, and finally an object. Babies seem to know that sentences have subjects, verbs, and objects. If they hear English or Spanish they learn that the order of these three components is subject, verb, object. If they hear other languages, they may hear a different sequence. In some languages, such as Japanese, the order is normally subject, object, verb. The universal knowledge all humans have is that all sentences have subjects, verbs, and objects. The specific knowledge they develop involves the syntax, the order of the components.

Chomsky's claim is that humans are born with an ability to develop language naturally. This claim is generally accepted when applied to young children acquiring a first language or even to acquiring more than one language at an early age. The question is whether older children and adults have the capacity to acquire additional languages in the same way that young children acquire their first language or languages.

Implications for teaching a second language and teaching literacy

If people are born with an innate ability to acquire language, as Chomsky argues, then teaching a second language involves tapping into that ability. As we discuss in detail later, the approach to teaching that is consistent with a view of language as a mental faculty is one that de-emphasizes direct teaching of grammar and instead focuses on providing comprehensible language input. The teacher's job is to make language understandable, not to teach the grammar of the language. This is best done when the focus of lessons is on the academic content being studied instead of on the language itself. However, in order to make language understandable, a teacher needs to know about language and how language works. Then the teacher can make modifications in speech or writing to help aid students' comprehension.

Krashen (1982) developed a theory of second language acquisition based on Chomsky's work. According to Krashen, the traditional approach to teaching a second language by teaching the grammar and vocabulary does not result in people being able to comprehend and produce a second language. Instead, Krashen argues, students need comprehensible input, messages they can understand, in either oral or written form. Comprehensible input allows the language acquisition device to develop the internal rules needed to understand and produce the new language.

Krashen's theory of second language acquisition has strongly influenced teachers. Most current methods of second language teaching focus on ways to make lessons understandable, and grammar is de-emphasized if it is taught at all. Since English learners in K–12 settings need both English and academic subject-area knowledge, teachers can teach both language and content simultaneously. Current methods focus on helping students develop academic English, a register of English used in schools to read, write, and discuss different academic content-area subjects.

Chomsky's linguistic theories have also had implications for teaching both native English speakers and English learners to read and write. Rather than teaching the discrete parts of written language, teachers use methods to make written texts understandable. For example, a teacher might read a picture book with a repetitive pattern to students as they follow along. Over time, students acquire the ability to read and write texts on their own. At first, the teacher provides a great deal of help. Over time, she gradually releases the responsibility for reading and writing to students. This approach to literacy is similar to the approach used to teach a second language.

Language as functional resource

A third line of research in linguistics that has had a strong influence on teaching a second language comes from the work of Halliday (1994) and others, such as Martin (2001) and Derewianka (2007), using an approach called *systemic functional linguistics*. These linguists investigate the question "How does language function to help us achieve our rhetorical purposes?" That is, how do we use language to comprehend and express ideas? Halliday sees language as a resource for making meaning. He is interested in understanding how the process takes place. Halliday's influence was first seen primarily in Australia, but in recent years, it has had a strong influence in the U.S. and other countries.

While Chomsky takes a biological approach to language acquisition, Halliday takes a social approach. As a result of engaging in social interactions, humans develop the language they need. People constantly make choices as they use languge, and these choices are influenced by the context.

Halliday identifies three aspects of the context that shape language interactions: the *field*, the *tenor*, and the *mode*. The field refers to the ideas being expressed, the topic of a conversation or a paper. The tenor refers to the relationship between the speaker and listener or the reader and writer. People choose different kinds of language depending on their relationship with the person they are talking with. Finally, the mode refers to the ways speakers or writers shape their texts (oral or written) to make them cohesive and coherent. These three aspects, the field, tenor, and mode, make up the language register that is used in a particular context.

To take a simple example, if two friends are discussing a movie they attended, the field would be the subject of the movie. The tenor would be shaped by the equal relationship of friends. The mode would be oral language that is coherent because the different comments relate to the movie and cohesive because there would be links among the different comments. The two friends would constantly make language choices based on these contextual factors. The context shapes the language, and, at the same time, the language is an important part of the context.

Halliday's approach to language development is consistent with Vygotsky's (1962) claim that learning takes place through social interactions. As Derewianka puts it, "Language learners are not simply processors of input or producers of output but speaker/hearers engaged in a collaborative process through which they build grammatical, expressive, interactional, and cultural competence" (2007, 851).

Implications for teaching a second language and teaching literacy

Halliday's work has had an increasing influence on how second languages are taught. Teachers have focused on helping students develop the genres (types of oral and written texts) needed for school through careful scaffolding. For example, a teacher of history might involve his students in an analysis of the kinds of history texts they are expected to be able to discuss, read, and write. A mathematics teacher might work with students to help them understand how word problems are structured.

Teachers using a functional approach follow a model referred to as the *curriculum cycle* (Derewianka 2007). The cycle has four phases. In the first phase, the teacher works with the students to build knowledge of the field of study. So if students will be reading about the Missouri Compromise, the teacher would engage them in activities to understand the historical context of the Compromise and the language needed to discuss, read, and write about this historical event.

In the next phase the teacher provides students with a sample of a text about the Missouri Compromise. Together, the teacher and students read the text and discuss it to construct a clear understanding. Then the teacher works with the students to deconstruct the text, looking carefully at how the author used language.

In the third phase, the class works together to construct a response to the text, such as an explanation of what occurred. During this phase, the teacher helps the students focus on the kinds of language needed to write a historical explanation.

For example, students would need different kinds of words and phrases to express cause and effect.

In the final phase, students work independently to produce a text of their own on this topic or a closely related topic. Throughout the curriculum cycle, the teacher scaffolds instruction and helps students focus on both the history content and the language used to express this content.

Gibbons (2002, 2009) provides many examples showing how teachers with English learners can implement this approach. For example, in one fourth-grade class, students first work in small groups to conduct experiments with magnets. The language they use is not precise. They do not use technical terms, such as *magnet*, *attract*, or *repel* during this activity. Following the small group experiments with magnets, the teacher explicitly teaches the key words (*magnet*, *attract*, *repel*) that students need to discuss their experiments. She does this using a magnet and demonstrating the terms *attract* and *repel* as she places different materials near the magnet.

After this explicit teaching, one student reports back from each small group what they have learned about magnets. During the oral reports, the teacher scaffolds the students' language, helping them to incorporate technical terms into their speech. Finally, the teacher has the students write about what they learned in their science notebook.

Throughout the lesson, the teacher pays attention to both the content students are learning and the language they need to talk and write about the science content. The teacher is not just providing the students with comprehensible input. She is working with them to build their language resources so that they can make choices of language that fits the context. For example, in a written report on magnets students should use technical language that is formal and establishes them as an authority on the topic.

This view of language as a functional resource is consistent with García's (2009) claim that people do not *have* one or more languages. Rather, they build up a linguistic resource that they can draw on as they *do* language. In fact, García uses *language* as a verb and refers to people using language as people who are *languaging*. Language enables us to function, to do things in the world. It is an active process, and the task for students is to use language (to language) appropriately in the different contexts of schooling. For example, the language demands of math are different from those of language arts, and a good history report is different from a report in science.

Halliday's approach to language as a functional resource is the linguistic theory that supports a model of reading developed by Goodman (1996), Smith (1985), and others. Methods of teaching reading and writing based on this model include scaffolding to make written language comprehensible. Reading instruction follows a gradual release of responsibility model (Pearson and Gallagher 1983) and includes read-alouds, shared and guided reading, and independent reading. Students read and write for real purposes in a workshop setting. This approach to teaching reading fits well with a view of language as a resource that develops in social interactions.

These three approaches to the study of language—language as structure, language as mental faculty, and language as functional resource—continue to be studied by linguists. Insights from linguistics influence the way second languages and literacy are taught. Knowledge of linguistics equips teachers with the pedagogical language knowledge they need to work effectively with English learners and students developing reading proficiency.

How Do Linguists Study Language?

Linguistics is the scientific study of language, and linguists study language in the same way that other scientists study their fields. Science always starts with a question. For example, a linguist studying a new language might ask, "What are the meaningful sounds in this language?" To investigate a question, a scientist forms a hypothesis and collects data to test the hypothesis. The linguists' goal is to describe the new language.

Akmajian, Demers, and Harnish (1979), who are Chomskyan linguists, explain how a linguist studies language scientifically. Several steps are involved in building a theory to describe a language. When a linguist attempts to describe a new language, the first step is to break the speech stream up into units. It's not hard for people to listen to another person who speaks their own language and write down the words that person utters. The speech of that language is perceived as being divided into discrete units. But when we try to determine the units in a language we don't speak or understand, the job of picking out meaningful units is a challenge. When we lived in Lithuania, we wanted to learn a few words of the language. However, as we listened to people speak, we had a very hard time deciding where one word ended and the next one began. We invite you to try this yourself with a language you don't speak. See if you can divide the language up into words. It's not easy because the physical speech stream is continuous. Speakers don't pause between words.

Let's imagine that the linguist has collected some data, and when she looks at her field notes, this is what she finds:

Doesyournewhusbandcookwell

First, the linguist must decide how to divide up the stream into discrete units that occur in a sequential order. She might do this by trying to find repeated sequences. After considerable work, the linguist might hypothesize that in this language, the units are these:

Does your new husband cook well

The second task in describing a language is to figure out the differences among the units of speech. They don't all seem to be alike. This leads to forming a hypothesis about categories of words in the language. For example, in English words may be classified as nouns, verbs, conjunctions, and so on. Each of these labels represents a category. Working with this sentence, the linguist might categorize the units this way:

Does   your   new   husband   cook   well

AUX   DET   ADJ   N   V   ADV

She uses AUX for an auxiliary, or helping, verb and DET for a determiner, such as an article or a possessive pronoun.

The third step in describing a language is to decide how the speech units can be grouped together. For example, in this sentence "your new husband" might be one group and "does cook well" might be another. The groups of words each play a specific role, so the fourth step would be to determine the function of each group. Here "your new husband" serves as the subject of the sentence, and "does cook well" is the predicate.

The final step in describing this language would be to find what linguists call *dependencies*. In this sentence *does* depends on "your new husband." The subject and verb have to agree in number. If the subject were "your new husbands" then the auxiliary verb would be *do*, the form used with plural subjects.

Readers shouldn't be worried if they are rusty on their auxiliary verbs, subjects, and predicates. This book doesn't include a test on parts of speech or the parts of a sentence. This example simply illustrates how linguists go about the scientific study of a language. They collect data and form hypotheses about the linguistic units, categories, groupings, functions, and dependencies. They use scientific methods to describe various aspects of a language. Of course, languages are very complex, and no linguist would claim to have described any language completely. Science is always a work in progress.

How Do Schools Teach Students About Language?

In most elementary and secondary schools, language study is not approached from a scientific perspective. Linguists work to describe language so that they can study it. However, historically, grammar teachers have prescribed, not described. They have laid down the rules for students to learn and follow. Teachers have told their classes that subjects and verbs must agree, and they have given students worksheets to practice this skill. Many students have learned that they can't end a sentence with a preposition. Teachers of grammar, from the earliest days, have used this prescriptive approach.

We want to encourage teachers to take a descriptive approach to language study because prescriptive approaches to natural phenomena like language simply don't work. The laws of physics ensure that if I drop my pencil, it will fall to the ground, not fly up into the sky. This will occur no matter what rules about gravity great physicists proclaim. In the same way, prescriptive teachers can tell students not to split infinitives, but that won't inhibit a writer who wants "to boldly go" where no person has gone before. In fact, great writers seldom follow the rules in grammar books. In response to a critic who suggested that he rewrite a sentence to avoid ending it with a preposition, Winston Churchill is reputed to have commented, "This is the sort of nonsense up with which I will not put!"

As an alternative to the teaching of grammar rules, a teacher with some linguistic knowledge might choose to involve students in linguistic investigations. For example, students might examine books written by well-known writers to see if they ever end sentences with prepositions. Students could collect examples of such sentences and discuss how the sentence would sound if it were rewritten with the preposition coming earlier. In the course of this investigation, students would need to learn to distinguish between a preposition (He ran *up* a big hill) and a particle (He ran *up* a big bill). A *particle* is a word that is used to form a two- or three-word verb. They might even discover that what Churchill's critic objected to was a final particle, not a preposition after all. *Put up with* is actually a three-word verb.

When teachers understand basic linguistic concepts, they can make informed decisions about how to teach language to their students. Knowledgeable teachers can teach their students about language using a descriptive approach. They also have the knowledge base to determine how to approach topics like phonics, vocabulary, or spelling. We encourage teachers to explore topics in linguistics with their students. We have organized this book to provide the essential linguistics teachers need to boldly go where many teachers have not gone before.

Organization of This Book

One goal for this book is to provide teachers with the linguistics concepts they need to help their students become more proficient in their use of both oral and written language. A second goal is to suggest ways that teachers can help their students take a scientific approach to learning about language, to conduct linguistic inquiry. The two goals are related. Students who investigate how language works can apply insights from their study to their own reading, writing, and oral language development.

To help teachers apply what they are learning about linguistics to their classroom practice, we begin with a chapter on first language acquisition. In Chapter 2 we consider how researchers from different fields of study have approached the topic of language acquisition. Chapter 3 extends the discussion to the acquisition of second and written languages. We argue that people acquire a second language or written language in the same way that they acquire a first language. The following chapters examine different aspects of language.

Chapter 4 looks at the sound system of English. We explain what phonemes are and describe the English phonological system. With the increased emphasis on phonemic awareness and phonics, it is important for teachers to develop a thorough understanding of English phonology in order to make informed decisions about the best way to teach reading and to teach a second language. In Chapter 5 we consider the implications from phonology for teaching a second language and for teaching reading.

Chapter 6 traces the history of writing development and describes the system of English orthography. Teachers with a good knowledge of orthography can better decide how to help their students with spelling. Chapter 7 focuses on morphology, the word system of English. We consider how words are structured and how new words are formed. In Chapter 8 we explore the implications from morphology for teaching a second language and for teaching reading. In this chapter we discuss vocabulary development and vocabulary teaching. Chapter 9 deals with the structure of sentences. We describe how a linguist develops a theory of syntax. We then explain how to analyze the structure of sentences. In Chapter 10 we consider the implications from syntax for teaching a second language and teaching reading. We explain strategies for using syntactic cues while reading. We also discuss the syntax of academic language and describe ways teachers can help students read and write academic texts.

Our hope is that readers of this book will keep asking, "How can this knowledge from linguistics inform my teaching?" Teachers are constantly teaching language, teaching through language, and teaching about language. The better they understand English phonology, orthography, morphology, and syntax, the easier they will find it to make good choices about how to structure lessons to enable their students to become proficient language users.

Conclusion

In this chapter we addressed three questions:

- Why study linguistics?
- What are the different approaches to the study of language?
- How do linguists study language?

There are several reasons for teachers to study linguistics. In the first place, teachers need to develop pedagogical language knowledge. This is knowledge about how to teach the language students need to discuss, read, and write about the different content areas. Teachers play a number of different roles, and a basic knowledge of linguistics enables them to build the pedagogical language knowledge they need to succeed in these roles.

As Halliday (1984) points out, we learn language, we learn through language, and we learn about language. Teachers need to understand how students learn first and second languages. Teachers also need pedagogical language to help students learn through language. In addition, a knowledge of linguistics helps teachers teach students about language.

Three other reasons for studying linguistics are that language is what distinguishes humans from other species, so we should understand something about the nature of language and how it works. This study can be presented in an interesting way by teachers who know linguistics. Further, in the same way that well-educated people know about the arts, social science, science, and mathematics, they should also know about language. Finally, as Chomsky (1975) points out, language is a mirror of mind. By studying language closely, linguists can gain insights into how the human mind works. All of these are reasons for studying linguistics.

Derewianka (2007) discusses three approaches to the study of language that have developed over time. The first approach is the model of grammar as structure. Beginning with Aristotle, scholars have studied language to determine the basic parts and how they are organized into different structures. The view of language as structure is reflected in the teaching of traditional grammar in schools.

The second model of grammar is grammar as mental faculty. This model draws on the theories developed by Chomsky and other linguists. These linguists are interested in describing the internal rules that people develop that allow them to comprehend and produce language. This model has led to acquisition-oriented methods of teaching a second or foreign language and of teaching literacy.

The third model, based on work by Halliday and linguists working in his tradition, views language as a functional resource. These linguists study how people use language to accomplish different purposes as they interact with others. This model has been used recently to analyze academic texts to enable students to understand how such texts are constructed and to read and write academic texts in different subject areas.

Linguists study language using a scientific method. To describe language linguists follow a series of steps that include breaking the language down into discrete units, categorizing the units, grouping the units into constituents, and then finding dependencies among the consituents. This descriptive scientific method contrasts with the traditional prescriptive grammar often taught in schools.

APPLICATIONS

1. What has been your experience with grammar? Think back through your school career. How were you taught grammar? Write down what you remember and prepare to share with classmates.

2. We described three approaches to the study of language in this chapter. Create a chart like the one below. List the key ideas related to each of the three approaches.

Language as Structure	Language as Mental Faculty	Language as Functional Resource

3. Look at a textbook used to teach grammar to native speakers or to second language speakers. What approach to teaching grammar is used? Is it descriptive or prescriptive? Now consider whether the approach to grammar in the textbook is consistent with a view of language as structure, language as mental faculty, or language as functional resource. Be prepared to share your answers in class.

2 /tu/

First Language Acquisition

At every level, teachers are teaching their students language. A kindergarten teacher might be concerned about whether her children are developing their sounds. A fifth-grade teacher might wonder how to help his students comprehend their science textbooks. An eighth-grade teacher might face the challenge of integrating a student with very limited English and limited formal schooling into his social studies/language arts block. A high school math teacher might question the best way to help her students develop the academic vocabulary needed to do word problems in mathematics.

- What are the different theories of first language acquisition?
- What insights into first language acquisition have researchers from different fields provided?

Even though the school may not refer to these teachers as language teachers, that is what they are. The task they have in common is helping their students gain the language proficiency they need to succeed in school. The teachers' understanding of how students develop language will guide their curricular decisions. In this chapter, we review the research on first language acquisition that comes from different fields of study. We invite readers to reflect on their own beliefs about language development as they study the different perspectives on language acquisition presented in this chapter.

The focus in this chapter is on how young children develop one or more languages. We use the term *acquire* to refer to this process. We wish to distinguish between acquiring a language and learning a language. *Acquisition* refers to a natural process that occurs without conscious effort or any kind of direct teaching. Young children begin to comprehend and produce language well before they receive any sort of instruction.

Learning, on the other hand, refers to the process that occurs in school when we consciously attend to information that is presented to us and attempt to master some subject. For example, people learn history, they don't just pick it up naturally. It takes some conscious effort. There is general agreement that humans acquire their first language. In fact, children exposed to more than one language may acquire two or more languages. In this chapter, we look at how young children acquire language. In the next chapter, we will turn to the question of whether a second language can be acquired later in life and if the process of developing literacy more closely resembles acquisition or learning.

First Language Acquisition

When children begin to develop language, they start by babbling. Soon they utter their first word. Not long after that, they begin to produce two-word sentences like "Tommy go" or "Drink milk." And it isn't long before these two-word expressions evolve into full sentences. Parents hang onto every sound infants make. They marvel at how quickly their child learns to understand and speak. But parents aren't really surprised at the development of language in their child because most children accomplish this incredible feat.

Children exposed to two or more languages develop these languages following the same path as children developing one language. In cases where children are simultaneously developing more than one language, it is hard to determine which is the first language. We use terms such as *mother tongue* or *heritage language*, but in some cases the languages being developed may not be the mother's language or even the family's language.

Children seem to acquire the languages they are exposed to, no matter who speaks those languages. As García (2009) points out, it is better to think of language as something we do rather than something we have. Children exposed to more than one language build up the ability to communicate in all the languages that they interact in.

García refers to children who come to school speaking a language other than the language of instruction as *emergent bilinguals* (EBLs). Thus, if a student comes to a school speaking Spanish, and instruction is only provided in English, that student should be referred to as an emergent bilingual rather than as an English learner (EL). The term, emergent bilingual, is more positive and emphasizes the ability humans have of expanding their language resources and their communication potential. We will generally use the term emergent bilingual instead of English learner when referring to children acquiring a second or third language.

Early Theories of First Language Acquisition

Early theories of language acquisition were based, for the most part, on common sense. Two theories, *imitation theory* and *reinforcement theory*, although now discredited, reflect commonsense beliefs. *Behaviorism*, based on scientific studies in psychology, combined elements of imitation and reinforcement theories.

Imitation theory

One early theory of first language acquisition, now no longer accepted by linguists, was that children learn language through imitation (Bergmann, Hall, and Ross 2007). According to this imitation theory, the child hears a word or phrase and then attempts to repeat it. Little by little, children's imitations resemble adult speech. Language acquisition, then, is seen as a process of memorizing the language spoken by others.

This theory does reflect the fact that children do imitate others as they attempt to communicate. In addition, this theory correctly predicts that the child will speak the language of the community, no matter what the child's background. An Hispanic child brought up in a home where everyone speaks English will learn English, not Spanish.

However, there is ample evidence to refute the imitation theory. In the first place, children produce words or sentences that do not reflect the speech of the adults around them, such as *bringed* or *Daddy buy candy* or *Christiana gots me car!* Many words and sentences that young children produce could not be the result of imitation. In addition, imitation theory has no explanation for how children and adults can both create and understand new sentences. Despite these serious limitations, when asked, many people would say that children learn language by imitation.

Reinforcement theory

A second early theory of first language acquisition that is no longer accepted is reinforcement theory. This theory holds that children develop language through positive reinforcement of standard language forms, and they are corrected when they produce nonstandard forms. So, the child who points to a dog and says, "That is a dog" is praised. The parent responds, "Yes, that is a dog. You can pat the dog." On the other hand, if the child points at a dog and says, "That a dog," the parent, according to reinforcement theory, responds, "That *is* a dog. Say, 'That is a dog.'"

Like imitation theory, reinforcement theory only accounts for some of what goes on as children acquire language. Parents and other caretakers often do not reinforce standard speech, and they only occasionally correct nonstandard forms.

Many things that children say are not reinforced or corrected. And, as parents are aware, corrections seem to do little to change children's speech. Even after being corrected, they often continue to produce nonstandard forms.

In most cases, caregivers respond to what the child is trying to say rather than to the grammatical correctness of the child's actual message. So, if a child says, "That a dog" while pointing to a cat, a parent would most likely respond, "No, that's not a dog. It's a cat." Reinforcement theory also is based on the assumption that children will spontaneously produce correct forms of language that can be reinforced. Studies of child language, however, reveal that children produce many nonstandard forms.

Behaviorist theory

Although neither imitation theory nor reinforcement theory alone was considered a credible account of first language acquisition by psychologists and linguists, the behaviorist view of language development, which combines elements of imitation theory and reinforcement theory, was generally accepted. Skinner's book *Verbal Behavior* (1957) was very influential. He held that all learning, including language learning, happened as a process of stimulus and response. According to the behaviorists, children's language learning begins when a child imitates a sound he has heard and a parent or other caregiver reinforces that action positively. For example, if the child, in the babbling stage, utters something like "da da" and the father is nearby, he might pick the child up, smile, and begin talking to the child. This positive reinforcement would lead the child to respond by producing this sound again. This general process of positive reinforcement of responses to stimuli eventually leads to full adult language proficiency.

not to full adult lang. prof. i.m.o.

This is a simplified account of the behaviorist view. Behaviorists believed that language is learned like anything else. Learning depends on the response of the individual to the environment. Whatever is reinforced is repeated. In this view, children have the potential for language, and, given the right circumstances, become proficient language users. The behaviorist view also fits the general idea that language is learned by imitation. Children try to imitate the sounds that adults make. When their attempts are rewarded, they repeat them and eventually learn to make certain sequences of sounds.

During the period that behaviorism was the accepted theory of how humans learn and develop, *structural linguistics* was the accepted theory in the field of linguistics. Structural linguists attempted to describe language by looking at sentence patterns, particularly focusing on patterns in oral language. Behaviorism and structural linguistics together formed the basis for beliefs about language development. Children, it was thought, acquired language by learning regularly occurring sentence patterns through a process of stimulus and response.

The behaviorist view prevailed for a number of years. However, researchers found that behaviorism could not adequately account for learning in general. One of the most detailed critiques of behaviorism came from Chomsky (1959), who wrote a review of B. F. Skinner's book *Verbal Behavior* (1957). Skinner, the foremost proponent of behaviorism at that time, had written *Verbal Behavior* to account for human language learning. However, Chomsky showed convincingly that language was too complex to be learned through Skinner's behaviorist model.

In addition to Chomsky's critique, careful studies of children acquiring language revealed a number of problems with the behaviorist view. Studies indicated that learning is not only the result of the environment acting on the individual. Instead, the new view was that humans are born with innate cognitive abilities, and learning is the result of the child acting on the environment much like a scientist making and testing hypotheses.

Reason 1   Lindfors (1987) lists several of the problems with the behaviorist theory of language acquisition. First, if learning is the result of the environment acting on the child, and if learning environments vary, how can one account for the uniformity of the language development sequence in children? Children brought up in very different circumstances all seem to learn to speak at about the same time, and they all go through the same stages. Behaviorist theory would predict different developmental paths for children raised in different circumstances, but this is simply not what happens. Although it is true that some children are exposed to a more language-rich environment and may develop a larger vocabulary and more complex language than children with less exposure, all children do acquire language in the same order.

Reason 2 Secondly, if learning is the result of imitation and reinforcement, then why wouldn't other intelligent beings, like apes, also learn to speak? A great deal of study continues to be carried out with apes, dolphins, and other animals, and while some animals seem to be able to develop certain language functions, there is a qualitative difference between human language and the communication systems found among animals. The failure of scientists to teach animals to speak using a behaviorist approach undermines claims for behaviorist learning theory.

Reason 3 A third problem is that close examination of children's language development shows that children don't simply imitate adults. If they did, they would never produce sentences like "I goed home yesterday" because they would never hear sentences like that. At the same time, careful observation reveals that adults seldom correct children's grammar. Instead, as mentioned earlier, they respond to the truth value of what the child says, to the message, not the form of the message. So if a child says something like "I goed home yesterday," a parent might respond, "Yes, and then you watched TV."

Transcripts of child–adult interactions show that corrections are not common. And even when parents do correct the form of the child's speech ("You mean you *went* home yesterday") it does little good, as most parents can attest. This is because children are building underlying rules as they figure out how language works. The child who says "goed" is starting to develop a rule for how English speakers indicate past tense. At an early stage, children may correctly produce irregular past-tense verb forms like *went* simply because they have heard others use them. However, as soon as children begin to understand that language is rule governed and has patterns they overgeneralize the rule for past tense, applying it to irregular verbs and producing forms like "goed." Still later, they realize that some verbs do not follow the pattern of adding *-ed* to form the past tense, and they begin to use irregular past tense verbs correctly.

Reason 4 → A fourth problem with the behaviorist view is that it can't account for the speed with which almost all children master a complex linguistic system. Children learn language much more quickly than they learn other things. Even though they are not exposed to extensive examples of language and are given only minimal correction, they seem to figure out the system in a very short time. A theory of stimulus and response cannot account for this remarkable accomplishment.

Current Views of First Language Acquisition

The foremost linguist in the United States, Noam Chomsky, developed a theory referred to as *generative grammar*. Chomsky was interested in describing language in terms of a small set of rules that could be applied to generate all the sentences of a particular language. Since there is no limit to the number of different sentences that can be expressed in any language, Chomsky reasoned that there must be a finite set of rules capable of generating an infinite number of sentences.

Chomsky has attempted to develop a theory of grammar that is psychologically real. "According to Chomsky, to say that a grammatical hypothesis is psychologically real is to attribute to it the same characteristics that one attributes to a physical theory by saying that it is physically real. Chomsky urges that the same scientific realism that is appropriate for physics is appropriate for psychology" (Sober 1980). Chomsky goes on to explain that for a hypothesis to be psychologically real, it must be psychological in nature and true. Studies of language combine psychology and linguistics, so a theory of grammar is psychological in nature, not physical.

To determine whether or not a theory is true, Chomsky asks, "Is this hypothesis the best explanation of observable behavior? If so, it is true" (Sober 1980). The linguistic theories that Chomsky and other linguists have developed are their attempts to provide explanations of language that are true in that they account for the acquired rules people use to produce and comprehend language.

By the time they reach school, most children have mastered many of the features of their language and can use it effortlessly to comprehend and produce sentences. As Chomsky (1975) comments, "A normal child acquires this knowledge [of language] on relatively slight exposure and without specific training. He can then quite effortlessly make use of an intricate structure of specific rules and guiding principles to convey his thoughts and feelings to others, arousing in them novel ideas and subtle perceptions and judgments" (4). Humans continue to learn vocabulary throughout their life, but many of the basic structures of phonology and syntax are acquired early.

The rejection of the behaviorist position on language learning and the development of generative theories of linguistics led to renewed interest in child language acquisition. In the last fifty years or so researchers from fields such as developmental psychology, sociology, anthropology, education, and linguistics have conducted studies to determine how children acquire language. Language is complex, and determining just how it is that children develop the capacity to understand and speak the language that surrounds them is no simple task.

Researchers have focused on different aspects of language acquisition. Developmental psychologists have concentrated more on the child and the child's capacity for learning. Since language is the means by which humans communicate with one another in social settings, sociologists and anthropologists have studied the environmental setting to determine how the social context influences language development. Educators have looked at factors that influence children's language development and affect school success. New studies in brain science have expanded the understanding of how children develop language. Linguists have looked closely at just what it is that children acquire when they acquire language. Although studies in these areas overlap and provide complementary information, it is helpful to look at them separately. In the following sections, we consider research in child language acquisition that has been centered on each of the three areas: the child, the environment, and language.

Insights from Developmental Psychology: Focus on the Child

According to Rice (2002), "any satisfactory model of language development must be compatible with how children learn; their ability to perceive, conceptualize, store, and access information; and their motivations" (21). The question of how language learning is related to developmental psychology, then, might be, "Do children learn language in the same way they learn other things, such as how to tie their shoes or how to build with blocks, or do children have a special cognitive capacity for language learning?"

Much of the research in child language acquisition has focused on the early language that children produce. Since researchers can't directly observe what goes on in the brain, and since they can't ask one- or two-year-olds to reflect on how they are learning language, scientists have to rely on children's linguistic output. Researchers who have observed children over time and have transcribed children's speech have identified certain stages in normal language development. This work is very intensive, and the studies are longitudinal. We describe several key research studies that have looked at child language development.

Brown (1973), for example, studied three children over time. He found that their earliest utterances referred to things of interest to the children (*Mommy*, *ball*). He discovered that there were strong parallels between children's language development and the stages of cognitive development identified by Piaget (1955). For example, at an early stage infants focus on objects and actions, and their early speech reflects this in sentences like "Me ball" or "See baby."

As researchers continued to collect data, they found that language and cognition seemed to develop separately, although the two are related. As Rice comments,

> There is not a clear temporal order of cognitive insights first, followed by linguistic achievements. Instead, language and related nonlinguistic competences appear at the same time. The relationship between language and cognitive development seems strongest at the early stages, but cognitive development and language development, although related, take different courses as children grow . . . children at first draw heavily on concepts as a way to master language and later use language to learn new concepts. (22)

Other researchers have continued to conduct detailed studies of early language development. In her book on language development, Lindfors (1987) includes a number of transcripts that show how children move from babbling to one-word utterances to two-word sentences and beyond. Although early studies, such as Brown's, were of middle-class white children, subsequent studies have looked at different ethnic and economic groups across a number of languages. The findings have been consistent with the earlier studies, suggesting that children's language development is the same despite differences in language and culture.

Many studies of child language development have focused on the interactions between mothers or other caregivers and children. Researchers have analyzed the speech of adults as they interact with children using a kind of language, a register, often referred to as *motherese*. Interestingly, adults adjust their language and speak to children in ways that they would never speak to adults. What mother would say to a friend, "Time to go bye-bye"? Children hear this kind of language from their caregivers, and yet, over time, they develop speech that corresponds to adult norms.

Studies of child language development show consistency across children and across languages. During the first year, children develop the physical capacity for speech and begin to babble. Pinker (1994) notes that children's babbling undergoes a change at about seven or eight months. At this age, children begin to produce syllables with a consonant–vowel structure, like "ba" or "dee." At about one year, children start to produce individual words. Researchers have found that nearly all children produce the same types of words. According to Pinker, about half the words are for objects (food, body parts, clothing, vehicles, toys, household items, animals, and people). The words name the people and things that are important to children. Brown's study showed a similar result.

Even though children may only produce one-word utterances at this stage, the single words may represent complex ideas. A word like *bottle* might mean something like "I want my bottle" or "My bottle is empty." On the surface, it appears that language develops from simple forms to more complex forms—from single words to complete sentences. At a deeper level, though, what is happening is that children are discovering how to express ideas more fully. At this early stage, the whole idea is represented in a single word. As time goes on, children add more words to express the idea in a form others can understand more easily. Children start with the most important words: nouns to represent objects and verbs to represent actions. Over time they fill in with adjectives and adverbs to describe objects and actions (*red* ball, walk *fast*). The last words to come in are the grammatical function words like prepositions, conjunctions, and articles. For this reason, early speech is often referred to as *telegraphic*. Like an older child or an adult texting, a child includes only the key words to express a message.

The next stage of language development comes at around eighteen months. At this stage, children start to put together two-word utterances. In English, simple sentences need at least two words ("Fish swim"), so children at this point are producing sentences and beginning to show an understanding of syntax. That is, they are showing an understanding of how words go together to form sentences. Pinker reports on studies that indicate that children at this stage understand the difference between sentences like "Big Bird is washing Cookie Monster" and "Cookie Monster is washing Big Bird." Infants are seated where they can view two video screens. On one screen Big Bird washes Cookie Monster, and on the other Cookie Monster washes Big Bird. A voice comes over a central speaker saying, "Oh look! Big Bird is washing Cookie Monster. Find Big Bird washing Cookie Monster." The researchers then record where the children look. Even before they can produce two-word utterances, at an age between one year and eighteen months, infants consistently look at the video corresponding to the voice prompt. This shows that very young children are developing syntax. They recognize the difference in meaning between two sentences like "Big Bird is washing Cookie Monster" and "Cookie Monster is washing Big Bird," a difference based on the order of the words.

At about eighteen months children's vocabulary also begins to grow very rapidly. Pinker (1994) states that at this age "Vocabulary growth jumps to the new-word-every-two-hours minimum rate that the child will maintain through adolescence" (267–68). Children's ability to learn vocabulary so rapidly along with the ability to recognize and then produce sentences that reflect an understanding of syntax supports the idea that the capacity for language development is either innate or the reflection of a special cognitive-processing capacity for language. Children don't learn other things nearly as rapidly as they acquire language, and this ability seems to apply to almost all children.

Acquisition of signed language

In a series of studies, Petitto (2003) has shown that infants exposed to sign language go through the same stages as babies exposed to oral language. Using a sophisticated, computer visual-graphic analysis system, Petitto and colleagues are able to record information from babies exposed to sign language and get the same kinds of detailed results that linguists get by recording oral language on a spectrograph machine.

Petitto observes, "In order for signed and spoken languages to be acquired in the same manner, human infants at birth may not be sensitive to sound or speech *per se*. Instead, infants may be sensitive to what is encoded within this modality. I propose that humans are born with a sensitivity to particular distributional, rhythmical, and temporal patterns unique to aspects of natural language structure" (1). In other words, it is certain characteristics of natural language that humans are able to learn, not just one modality of language. As Petitto states,

> One novel implication here is that language modality, be it spoken or signed, is highly plastic and may be neurologically set after birth. Put another way, babies are born with a propensity to acquire language. Whether the language comes as speech, sign language, or some other way of having language, it does not appear to matter to the brain. (2003, 1)

Petitto's research shows that any form of input that has the properties of natural language can be used to develop a form of language needed for communication.

In more recent studies Petitto has used a new technology called *functional Near Infrared Spectroscopy* (fNIR) that allows her to look at the brain tissue of young infants to see how the brain tissue develops when exposed to sign language and when exposed to speech. Her findings confirm her earlier studies.

> What was believed to be only sound processing tissue, instead processes both signed and spoken languages. Rather than being exclusively set to sound, parts of what was previously labeled "auditory tissue" is set to highly specific temporal patterns at the heart of all human language, be it language on the hands or the tongue. (Polk 2012, 1)

Petitto's research also shows that biologically the human brain performs better when it is exposed to more than one language. As Petitto says, "It's almost as if the monolingual child's brain is on a diet and the bilingual child's brain stretches to the full extent and variability that Mother Nature gave it to use language and exploit human language" (Polk 2012, 3). This finding has important implications for education and supports the implementation of dual language bilingual programs. In the past, it was thought that exposing a child to more than one language would confuse the child (Baker 2011), but as Petitto's research has shown, exposure to two or more languages actually helps humans to reach their language potential.

Studies in child language development have concentrated on the early stages. The problem that researchers face is that beyond the two-word stage language growth is incredibly rapid and complex. As Pinker writes, "Between the late twos and the mid threes, children's language blooms into fluent grammatical conversation so rapidly that it overwhelms the researchers who study it, and no one has worked out the exact sequence" (1994, 269). Children's sentences become longer and more complex as their language approximates adult speech.

Many developmental psychologists view the development of oral or signed language as the result of general cognitive processes. However, language learning differs from other kinds of learning in two ways: most normal children develop language, and they do this very rapidly without instruction. This has led some developmental psychologists to suggest that humans have a special capacity for language. Slobin (in Lindfors 1987), for example, asks, "Does the child have strategies which were specifically evolved for the task of language acquisition, or can one account for this process on the basis of more general human cognitive capacities? . . . I suspect that both general cognitive principles and principles specific to language are at play in the child's construction of his native language" (108). The question of the nature of the child's ability to make meaning continues to be debated among developmental psychologists, but many would agree that children seem to have some sort of special cognitive ability for language learning. Language acquisition seems to be a case of both nature and nurture.

Summary: Developmental psychology

Studies in developmental psychology have contributed a great deal to the understanding of how children acquire language. Early studies attempted to link cognitive stages and stages of linguistic development. However, subsequent studies suggest that cognition and language develop along related but independent paths. Most studies have focused on the early stages of language development. These studies suggest that the stages of early language development are the same for all children, no matter what their language or culture. Most studies have been limited to children up until about age two because beyond that point language develops so rapidly that it is almost impossible to document and analyze. Some of the most recent research, using new technology, has revealed that language development may be the same whether the language is oral or gestural. Children learning oral language go through the same stages as children learning sign.

Developmental psychology looks at individual psychological factors involved in language acquisition. However, because we are social beings, humans use language to communicate with others. Studies in sociology and anthropology have focused on the social nature of language development.

Insights from Sociology, Anthropology, and Education: Focus on the Environment

Children develop the ability to understand and produce language because language is essential for social interaction. Hearing children develop the ability to talk, and deaf children develop the ability to sign. The modality is not important. What is important is the capacity for communication. In fact, children don't simply learn the grammar and vocabulary of a language, they learn how to use language appropriately in different social settings. They develop what Hymes (1970) termed *communicative competence*, the knowledge of what to say to whom under what circumstances. Language always occurs in a social context, and the meaning of many utterances depends on the context. For example, "Excuse me" could be an apology, but it could also be a means of getting someone's attention. The meaning depends on the situation.

In linguistics, the work of Halliday (1994) and others has focused on the relationship between the social context and the language. The language we use is influenced by the context, which, as we discussed in Chapter 1, Halliday analyzes in terms of the field (what we are talking about), the tenor (our relationship with the person we are talking with), and the mode (the features of the text we are producing).

Social interaction theory

A theory of first language acquisition that fits with Halliday's approach to linguistics is *social interaction theory* (Bergmann, Hall, and Ross 2007). This theory holds that children acquire language as they interact with older children and adults. Proponents of social interaction theory hold that "children prompt their parents to supply them with the appropriate language experience they need. Thus, children and their language environment are seen as a dynamic system: children need their language environment to improve their social and linguistic communication skills, and the appropriate language environment exists because it is cued by the child" (318).

Social interaction theory emphasizes the role of social interaction in language development. Unlike behaviorist theories that held that children respond to environmental stimuli, social interaction theory claims that it is the child who creates the environment needed for development by prompting the parent or other caregiver to produce the language the child needs. Studies of children and adults have shown that adults often repeat things that children say rather than children always responding to adults. One of our grandsons is just turning two. He loves blueberries. He calls them "lu-lus." When he is cranky and his parents need to get him to cooperate, they bribe him often with "Does Alej want some *lu-lus*?" They use his word to better communicate with him. At another time, Alej kept pointing to the table and saying a word none of us could understand. We kept picking things up and naming them. Finally, we picked up the peanut butter and said, "Peanut butter." That made him happy. He had elicited the word for the food he wanted.

Caregiver speech is quite different from normal adult speech. It is slow and high pitched. There are many repetitions in adult speech to children. It also contains simplified syntax and simple vocabulary. All these characteristics help children understand what the adult is saying. According to social interactionists, this manner of speaking is prompted by the child. As Halliday points out, speakers adjust their language based on their relationship with the person they are speaking to, and in the case of caregivers and young children, the children may well be prompting the adult to alter the normal speech pattern to make the language more accessible.

Wells' Bristol study

Sociologists consider the effect of the community on children's language development. Wells (1986) in his longitudinal Bristol study in England followed the native language development of thirty-two children from about fifteen months of age through their elementary years in an attempt to discover what kinds of language support families, community, and schools provide. Children in the study wore backpacks that contained tape recorders programmed to record at different intervals. Neither the parents nor the children knew when they were being recorded. Wells gathered extensive data from the recordings. He focused his analysis on identifying those factors that facilitated language development.

A key finding of the study was that caregivers who controlled and corrected young children as they were developing English inhibited, rather than aided, language development. Children who were corrected frequently did not use more error-free language. Instead, their language did not develop as well, and they did not succeed to the same degree academically, as children whose parents and others focused on understanding and extending the children's meaning.

Wells suggests that the best support adults can give young children is to "encourage them to initiate conversation and make it easy and enjoyable for them to sustain it" (50). Four specific suggestions from Well's work are:

- When the child appears to be trying to communicate, assume he or she has something important to say and treat the attempt accordingly.
- Because the child's utterances are often unclear or ambiguous, be sure you have understood the intended meaning before responding.
- When you reply, take the child's meaning as the basis of what you say next—confirming the intention and extending the topic or inviting the child to do so him- or herself.
- Select and phrase your contributions so that they are at or just beyond the children's ability to comprehend. (50)

Wells discusses implication for teachers in classrooms. Teachers should encourage children to explore their understandings and use language for making meaning rather than asking students to respond to their specific questions looking for formulaic answers. In addition, teachers of emergent bilinguals should work to understand what the student is trying to say and help the student communicate instead of correcting the student's grammar or pronunciation.

Heath's study

Anthropologists have investigated how children growing up in different speech communities develop the ability to function in those communities. Heath (1983), for example, looked at differences in the language development of children in three different communities in the same area of the Carolinas. Roadville was a white, working-class community. For four generations, people from Roadville had worked in the textile mills. Residents of Trackton also worked in the textile mills.

Trackton residents were blacks who had previously been farmers. Children from both Roadville and Trackton attend school with mainstream whites and blacks. The mainstream children were the children of the managers of the mills, the Townspeople. Heath showed differences among the ways Roadville, Trackton, and Townspeople children used language to communicate.

For example, Roadville mothers considered it their duty to prepare their young children for school, so there was a lot of focus on learning to talk "right." While Roadville children were often read to and taught to respond appropriately in school, they were not encouraged to be creative or to question and analyze. Roadville children were taught only to speak when spoken to and always to tell the truth, especially in their storytelling.

Trackton children, on the other hand, were encouraged to be imaginative and entertaining in their speech. Trackton children learned how to break into a conversation and hold the floor by their creative use of language. Verbal play (playsongs, one-liners, challenges) was a regular feature in Trackton language use. The Trackton children developed creative oral language, but literacy practices were limited to environmental print they were exposed to for functional purposes.

Heath pointed out many differences between these groups' ways with words and also showed the problems that both the Roadville and Tracktown groups had in interacting appropriately in the school setting, where a different norm for appropriate language use existed. In school, the Roadville children had difficulty in using language creatively. They had been taught at home not to make up stories that were not true. On the other hand, the Tracktown children made up stories when it was not appropriate to do so and also were not accustomed to labeling objects or answering questions when it was clear to them that the teacher already knew the answer.

It was the children of the third group, the Townspeople, who met the expectations of the teachers in the schools. Their parents engaged their children in reading and writing activities that more directly mirrored the expectations of the schools, such as using written sources to find information.

Heath found that teachers needed to understand the language practices of the Roadville and Trackton children in order to draw on the language strengths those children brought to school. Only when teachers understood the home language practices of the different families were they able to help the children succeed academically in school.

What Heath suggests is that teachers take a sociocultural view of their students' strengths and value their funds of knowledge (Moll 1994). Moll and colleagues have looked at the literacy practices of Latinos in their homes to understand what literacy young bilingual children bring to school. He suggests that teachers should investigate language use in the homes of their students in order to draw on what students already know about language when they come to school.

Goodman and Goodman's account of language development

Educators have focused on how language acquisition is affected by schooling. Goodman and Goodman (1990) describe language development as the result of a tension between invention and convention. Children try out different ways of expressing their ideas. They invent words and phrases. As they use language in different contexts, they modify their inventions in light of the responses they receive from the community.

For example, when children begin to write, they often invent spellings of words. Over time, they modify their inventions to match social conventions so that others can read what they write more easily. If teachers insist on correct spelling from the beginning, they may discourage children from trying to write. However, if teachers never correct children's spelling, then others will have trouble reading what children write. When children use writing for authentic communication, when it is important to them that their readers understand their message, they begin to use spellings that are more conventional. For example, when students are paired with a pen pal, they have a real audience for their writing, and they make a real effort to use spelling that their pen pals can read.

The key is for teachers to keep a balance between invention and convention. Goodman and Goodman (1990) use the example of a satellite orbiting the Earth. As long as the outward force of the satellite (invention) matches the downward pull of gravity (convention), the satellite stays is orbit. Finding that balance is not easy. Students need to be encouraged to create, but at the same time, they have to learn conventional ways of telling stories or writing reports that communicate effectively with their listeners or readers.

Summary: Insights from sociology, anthropology, and education

Sociologists, anthropologists, and educators have made important contributions to our understanding of first language acquisition. Researchers from these fields have focused on how the social context influences language acquisition. Social interaction theory suggests that children play an important role in cueing adults during conversational exchanges so that adults provide the language the child needs for language development.

Wells' study shows that the way that parents and other community members respond to young children has a strong impact on their later academic performance. Rather than correcting the form or the content of what children say, parents and others should follow the children's lead and help them develop what they want to communicate. The study by Heath shows that children brought up in different language communities develop different "ways with words." This has implications for children's school success. Goodman and Goodman argue that two forces that affect language development are invention and convention and that teachers should find a way to balance these forces, encouraging children to invent language, and, at the same time, modify their language to conform to social conventions.

Studies of child language development by sociologists, anthropologists, and educators complement the investigations of developmental psychologists. While psychologists focus more on the child and the developmental stages the child goes through during language development, sociologists, anthropologists, and educators consider the social contexts that influence children's language development. Linguists, with a focus on language rather than on the individual or the community, have also contributed to our understanding of first language acquisition.

Insights from Linguistics: Focus on the Language

In their studies of first language acquisition, linguists have focused on the nature of language, on what it is that children acquire. As we discussed in Chapter 1, there have been three different approaches to the study of language: language as structure, language as mental faculty, and language as functional resource. The last two approaches have contributed the most to our understanding of language acquisition. Chomsky, who sees language as a mental faculty, argues that humans acquire language because of a biological predisposition to learn languages. Halliday, who views language as a functional resource, holds that humans acquire language in the course of social interactions. These two positions can be seen as complementary. Humans do seem to learn languages in a way that is different from how we learn anything else. At the same time, our motivation to learn language and our competence in using language comes from our desire to interact with others in different social contexts, and social interactions shape our language development.

What are the implications of linguistic theory for child language acquisition? In the first place, it suggests that children don't simply learn language by imitating adult utterances and then being rewarded for correct responses. Instead, children must use what they hear to develop a set of rules that allows them to understand and produce a wide variety of sentences that fit the social context, including original utterances they have never heard before. How can they do this so quickly with no direct teaching?

Universal Grammar

Chomsky's answer to the question of how children acquire language is that children have an innate capacity for language, what he at first called a language acquisition device. This language acquisition device is a specialized area of the brain designed for language. According to Chomsky, humans do not simply have a special cognitive capacity for figuring out language. Rather, humans are born with the basic structures of all human languages already present in the brain. Chomsky calls this innate knowledge of language *Universal Grammar*. Children are not born with knowledge of English or Japanese or any other human language. Instead, they are born with knowledge of those things that are common to all human languages.

Chomsky's claim that most of language is innate is based on certain facts: (1) most children acquire a first language rapidly and without formal instruction, (2) they do this with only a limited amount of evidence, and (3) they do it with only limited feedback. Support for Chomsky's claim that language is innate comes from Lenneberg (1967), who studied the biological foundations of language development. Lenneberg claimed that language is part of our biological nature and should be studied just as we might study anatomy. He viewed language as a mental organ in humans with biological properties, which grows in the mind/brain of the child in the same way that (other) biological organs grow (Boeckx and Longa 2011). He noted correlations between stages in language development and stages in physical maturation. As Lindfors comments, "Lenneberg's work linking language acquisition to biological maturation supported the innatist claim that genetic inheritance for mental abilities was not simply a general ability to learn but, rather, that it included a specific predisposition for language acquisition" (1987, 105).

Lenneberg listed six criteria for biologically controlled behavior (Bergmann, Hall, and Ross 2007). These include:

1. The behavior emerges before it is necessary.
2. Its appearance is not the result of a conscious decision.
3. Its appearance is not triggered by external events (though the surrounding environment must be sufficiently "rich" for it to develop adequately).
4. Direct teaching and intensive practice have relatively little effect.
5. There is a regular sequence of "milestones" as the behavior develops, and these can usually be correlated with age and other aspects of development.
6. There is likely to be a "critical period" for the acquisition of the behavior.

When we contrast acquiring a language with learning to play the piano, for example, it seems evident that acquiring a language fits Lenneberg's criteria for an innate, biologically controlled behavior, but learning to play the piano does not. Babies start to make sounds and speak while they are still being cared for and before they need to speak to accomplish their purposes (they can cry to show they are hungry and don't need to say, "Milk"). Babies don't decide to learn how to talk in the same way a child might decide to learn to play the piano. While babies need to be surrounded by language, the appearance of stages of speech are not triggered by specific experiences with language. Instead, babies follow a sequence of development that appears to be universal. Direct teaching and practice are not necessary for language to develop. There may be a critical period for learning language, but since there are so few children who do not develop language, this is difficult to decide. We will discuss the concept of a critical period in the next chapter when we consider second language acquisition.

Lenneberg recognized that for speech to develop, children had to be surrounded by a speaking community, so language development depends on more than innate factors. Nevertheless, his work strongly supported the innatist position that children are born with a special ability to learn language.

According to Boeckx and Longa (2011), who work in the field of biolinguistics, Lenneberg's work complements that of Chomsky:

> Chomsky stressed the importance of certain basic facts such as the creative aspect of language use and the poverty of the stimulus the child receives during language acquisition to call for the study of the innate factors underlying language growth and to bridge the gap between the tacit knowledge of language users and the primary linguistic data. Lenneberg provided arguments that were much closer to "wet" biology [experiments using plants or cells]. (1)

Chomsky's observations about linguistics suggest that language is innate; that is, it has a biological basis, and this is the same claim that Lenneberg makes based on his studies in biology.

If, as Chomsky argues, language is innate, the task facing the child is not to learn how language works, starting from scratch. Instead, since children are born with an implicit knowledge of language in general, they have to figure out how the particular language or languages they hear function. For example, all languages have something like prepositions, words that show relationships among things ("The book is *on* the table"). In languages like English these words that show position come in front of the noun, so they are called **pre**positions. In other languages, these words follow the noun, so in those languages, a child would encounter sentences with the pattern ("The book is the table *on*"). In such languages, these words are called ***post***positions because they come after (*post-*), not before (*pre-*).

Children are born with the built-in knowledge that the language they hear will have a word to show position. What children must figure out is whether the position word precedes the noun or follows it. This is a much easier task than starting without any knowledge and having to learn that there are some words that show position and also having to learn where those words go in the sentence.

It is much the same as someone who knows how to drive. If that person with this built-in knowledge of driving rents a car, he or she doesn't have to learn how to drive all over again to operate the new car. Instead, the driver just has to figure out how this particular car works. Is the windshield wiper on the turn signal or on another lever? How do I dim the lights? Which side is the gas tank on? Even though there are a number of things to learn, it is not nearly as difficult a task as learning how to drive in the first place. The knowledge that is already built in makes learning to drive the new car much easier.

If children have a Universal Grammar, this hardwired knowledge, then it is not surprising that most children acquire the language or languages that surround them. Chomsky has referred to the process of deciding the details of particular languages as parameter setting. Learning a language could be thought of as somewhat like setting up a computer or a new phone. The computer or phone already has built-in operational capacity, but a new user needs to go to the settings and put in the specific functions the person needs. For example, the new user will set up usernames and passcodes, add in contacts, and set up email. In using a word processor, the user needs to decide on margins and line spacing among other things. The computer and the phone have the capacity built in, but the new user needs to set up how he or she wants the computer or phone to function.

Learning a language, then, is a process of using the input from the language or languages a child hears to adjust the settings in a way that allows communication. The process of parameter setting occurs at a subconscious level. Children are hardwired to acquire language, but they still have to adjust the settings to accommodate the language or languages they hear.

How children form linguistic rules

Children do get evidence of how language works from the models provided by the language of adults and others around them, but linguists who have studied language have consistently noted that there would not be enough evidence in the input for children to formulate the rules of language if the process they were using was the same as the cognitive process for other kinds of learning. For example, if an adult wants to teach a child how to tie his or her shoes, the adult has to provide very specific demonstrations and give clear instructions. Even when adults do that, children take a long time to learn how to tie their shoes. Adults don't give specific information to children about how language works, but children seem to figure it out quickly.

In addition, if an adult is trying to teach a child how to tie his or her shoes, the adult will give the child feedback. The adult will correct a child who goes about the process incorrectly and then show how it should be done. None of this happens with language. Adults seldom correct young children. Instead, they respond to what the child is trying to say—to the message, not the form. So if a child says, "Him brought his car," most adults would respond by saying something like "Oh, I'm glad *he* brought his car" not with "You mean *he* brought his car, not *him* brought his car." In other words, adults seldom provide explicit feedback showing children which form is wrong and how to correct it. And, as most parents know, even when adults do give this kind of explicit correction, children seem to ignore it. As Wells' (1986) study demonstrated, children develop language much better when adults help them communicate their intended meanings, not when they try to correct what they say or how they say it.

Studies of child language acquisition show that children develop the rules of language quickly, they acquire the language despite receiving only a limited amount of input, and they do it without much correction. All this suggests that children must have a built-in capacity for language. They seem to learn language in a way that is different from the way they learn other things.

Implicit and explicit rules

When linguists write about children developing rules, they are referring to implicit or subconscious rules. Linguists do not claim that children are born with explicit knowledge of language. Children may be born knowing that the language they hear will contain something like nouns and verbs, but they cannot name the parts of speech or underline all the nouns in a sentence. The innate knowledge children have allows them to understand and produce sentences, but it doesn't allow them to explain how they do it. Trying to make this implicit knowledge explicit is the job of linguists. Humans are born with an innate capacity for language, but explaining how language works is a real cognitive challenge. This is why so many students struggle in linguistics courses! Children quickly acquire language, but children must study to learn about language. Language, like other abilities, such as walking or breathing, is something we can do even though we don't know exactly how we do it.

Humans know how to do other things that they can't explain. For example, I know how to turn on and off the lights in my house. It's something that was easy for me to learn how to do, and almost anyone living in a house with electricity can turn the lights on and off. But I can't explain to you very well what happens when I turn the switch that results in light or darkness. I can do it, but I can't explain it. My knowledge of electricity is similar, then, to a child's knowledge of language. The child can use language, but the child can't explain how he or she does it. In school, children can communicate using nouns and verbs even though they can't under- line nouns and verbs on a worksheet.

The implicit nature of linguistic rules is not limited to children. Many adults just know whether or not something sounds right, even though they can't explain how they know. For example, they know that it sounds fine to say, "I wonder when he's at home." But it would seem strange to say, "I wonder where he's at noon." It is perfectly acceptable to use a contraction, *he's* in the first sentence; however, the second sentence would sound much better without the contraction: "I wonder where he is at noon."

Contractions are acceptable in conversational English, but not always. We have a rule in our minds, one we can't explain, that tells us that it is acceptable to use a contraction in the first sentence, but we would never use the contraction in the second sentence. People can use rules they have acquired even if they can't explain them. The predisposition to acquire such rules is best accounted for by saying this capacity is something humans are born with.

Children's errors

Perhaps the strongest evidence for Chomsky's claim that language is innate comes from the fact that there are certain kinds of errors that children never make. If learning language were like learning anything else, researchers would expect learn- ers to make many different errors in the process of testing possible hypotheses. A child learning to tie his or her shoes might twist the strings in a number of different ways. Each attempt could be viewed as a test of the child's hypothesis about the right way to knot the shoe.

Close examination of language learners' errors shows something quite differ- ent. When children produce errors, the errors often represent an overgeneralization of a rule. The child who says *bringed* is applying the usual rule for past tense to an irregular verb. Children do make mistakes like this. But there are many other mis- takes a child could logically make in testing hypotheses about language. The fact that children never make certain kinds of errors suggests that the child is born with some innate knowledge of the rules of language, and the child's language attempts never violate those basic rules. The child may make mistakes with the parts of language that are unpredictable, like irregular verbs. But children don't make mistakes in some areas where mistakes would be expected.

To take one example, as noted earlier, children learn how to form questions. A good example comes from our grandson, Romero. At age three Romero asks, "What it is?" He knows questions can start with *wh* words like *what*, but he hasn't yet learned to change the order of the subject and verb to the conventional form for questions, "What is it?" Children don't immediately form questions that reflect conventional adult usage. Instead, they go through a series of approximations, producing some questions adults would never use. However, during this process there are some linguistic forms for questions that children never produce.

For example, given a statement like "The person who is sitting at the table is a linguist," an older child can form the question, "Is the person who is sitting at the table a linguist?" That may not seem like an extraordinary feat, but this transformation from a sentence to a question is complicated. If the rule is something like "Move the helping verb (*is*) in front of the subject," how does the child know which *is* to move? Consider these logical possibilities for this sentence:

Moving the first *is* results in sentence (i):

(i) Is the person who __ sitting at the table is a linguist? (the __ indicates where *is* was before it was moved)

To produce the conventional sentence, the child must move the second *is*:

(ii) Is the person who is sitting at the table __ a linguist*!*

If children acted like scientists, they would test these two hypotheses to find out which one is right. One might expect, then, to hear children produce two kinds of questions, those like (i) and those like (ii). Children could tell which one is conventional by the way people respond. If people seemed puzzled by (i) but answered (ii) with no hesitation, then the child would refine the hypothesis and develop an internal rule, something like "Move the helping verb of the main clause in front of the subject to form a question." However, researchers who study children's language never find examples of questions like (i) even though it is a logical possibility. This suggests that children do not develop their understanding of language, their internal grammars, following purely logical cognitive procedures of hypothesis testing the way that scientists do. If they did, children would be expected to produce all sorts of utterances that they never produce.

Pinker (1994) provides additional examples from a number of areas of child language acquisition. For example, children seem to figure out how to divide up speech into words even though there is no physical separation of words in the speech stream. The few errors children make are considered cute because they are so rare. Pinker gives several examples including one in which a child responds to the adult statement, "We are going to Miami" with "I don't want to go to your ami."

Pinker reports on a study by Stromswald, who analyzed sentences containing auxiliaries (words like *do*, *is*, *will*) from the speech of thirteen preschoolers. The auxiliary system in English is very complex. According to Pinker (1994), "There are about twenty-four billion logically possible combinations of auxiliaries (for instance, 'He have might eat,' 'He did be eating') of which only a hundred are grammatical ('He might have eaten,' 'He has been eating')" (272). Stromswald looked at possible errors children could make that would be logical generalizations based on the English system. Pinker lists examples like the ones shown in Figure 2.1.

Stromswold analyzed some 66,000 sentences from the preschoolers and found no errors that would be logical generalizations but that aren't grammatical in English (like those in the chart) for nearly all the possible patterns that she identified. Research like this strongly supports the claim that children are born with certain built-in linguistic concepts. It would be very difficult to account for the absence of logical errors in any other way.

Evidence from children's errors (or lack of certain errors) supports Chomsky's claim that humans are born with a general language ability or Universal Grammar and his claim that language development involves parameter setting, deciding which of a small number of options a particular language follows. However, claims by Lenneberg and Chomsky that language grows in the mind/brain the same way we grow an arm have been questioned. It appears that the child plays an important role in eliciting and processing language in the environment. While certain aspects of language may be innate, other aspects are developed through social interaction with speakers or signers of a language.

Pattern: Adult English	Pattern: Adult English	Similar Pattern	Error That Might Tempt a Child
He seems happy.	Does he seem happy?	He is smiling.	Does he be smiling?
He did eat.	He didn't eat.	He did a few things.	He didn't a few things.
I like going.	He likes going.	I can go.	He cans go.
He is happy.	He is not happy.	He ate something.	He ate not something.
He is happy.	Is he happy?	He ate something.	Ate he something?

Figure 2.1 *Children's possible errors*

Active construction of a grammar theory

The theory of language acquisition that most linguists support is the *Active Construction of a Grammar theory*. This theory "holds that children invent the rules of grammar themselves" (Bergmann, Hall, and Ross 2007, 316). What is innate is the ability to invent rules. However, the Active Construction of a Grammar theory differs from Chomsky's claim of innateness because it assigns a more active role for the language learner. The child has the innate ability to find patterns in the language that surrounds him and to create rules to account for these patterns.

Children make hypotheses about possible rules based on what they hear and then refine their hypotheses as they receive additional data. For example, a young child might form a rule for the progressive (or continuous) tense. At first the child produces the correct verb form with the *-ing* ending, "I going to the park." As the child hears more language, she adds the form of the verb *be* that was missing in her earlier statement and starts to produce sentences such as "I'm going to the park."

While children appear to have the innate ability to find patterns in language, not all aspects of language follow patterns. For example, irregular verbs such as *sing* and *think* don't follow the regular pattern of adding *-ed* to form the past tense. In addition, vocabulary is not completely systematic and predictable. There is no regular connection between sounds of words and their meanings. Even though there are patterns within vocabulary—as we will discuss in a later chapter—that enable children (and adults) to develop vocabulary knowledge fairly rapidly, learning vocabulary is different from acquiring the syntax or basic structure of a language.

The Active Construction of a Grammar theory states that children have an ability to find patterns in a language and develop subconscious rules that allow them to comprehend and produce language that follows the patterns. However, children need to learn exceptions to the rules. They also need to continue to be exposed to more advanced vocabulary and grammatical forms to more fully develop their language proficiency, especially as they encounter new language registers in schools and other contexts outside their home or community.

Summary: Insights from linguistics

Studies in linguistics have provided important insights into first language acquisition. Linguists have focused on the nature of language and have used evidence from language to develop theories of language acquisition. Chomsky and other linguists working in his tradition have demonstrated that many aspects of language are innate. They base their claim that language is a kind of mental organ on the fact that all normally developing children develop one or more languages. Children can develop rules because they are born with Universal Grammar, a set of rules common to all natural languages. Based on the input they hear, children adjust the general rules to fit the specific language they hear. Chomsky refers to this as parameter setting. Children develop a finite set of rules that allow them to generate an infinite number of sentences. They do this with minimal input and little or no correction. Studies in biology by Lenneberg support Chomsky's claim that language develops naturally in the mind.

The *rules* that Chomsky refers to are implicit rules, not explicit rules. An explicit rule might be that subjects and verbs must agree in number. If the subject is singular, speakers or writers use the singular form of the verb. Explicit rules are often taught directly in school and then practiced. Implicit rules, on the other hand, seem to develop subconsciously. They allow speakers to comprehend and produce language, but speakers usually can't explain the rule. An example of an implicit rule in English is to use a pronoun that agrees in person and number with the noun it refers to.

Linguistic studies of children's errors show that many errors are the result of overgeneralizing patterns in a language. For example, most noun plurals are formed by adding the sound represented by the letter *s*. Children apply this rule to nouns with irregular plurals like *foot* to produce *foots*. Studies of children's errors show that there are some errors they never make. These are the errors that must violate the rules of Universal Grammar.

Although Chomsky claims that language is innate and develops naturally with exposure to linguistic input, many linguists assign a more active role to language learners. The Active Construction of Grammar theory holds that what is innate is the ability to recognize patterns in language input and to form rules based on those patterns. Children are active agents in eliciting the input they need to form and test their rules. They play an active role in the language acquisition process.

The insights from studies in linguistics add to the understandings that come from developmental psychology, sociology, anthropology, and education. One other area of research that has contributed to our understanding of first language acquisition is research on the brain.

Language and the Brain

One way to consider the idea that humans have an innate capacity for language is to say that all human languages are reflections of some properties of the human mind. Linguists study language because it provides a window on the mind. Although linguists cannot see what exactly goes on in the brain, they can study language. What they learn about language gives them insights into the mind. The best evidence that humans are born with an innate knowledge of things like nouns and verbs is that all human languages have something like nouns and verbs. Thus, language must reflect certain properties of the human mind.

Scientific study of the brain has undergone tremendous advances with new technology. As early as 1861, Paul Broca identified an area in the left frontal lobe that was responsible for language. Damage to that area impaired language functioning. This area of the brain came to be known as Broca's area. About ten years later, Carl Wernicke discovered that an area in the posterior of the left hemisphere affected speech comprehension. Subsequent studies have confirmed that most language processing takes place in the left hemisphere.

However, the brain is complex. Many brain studies involve patients who have had damage to a portion of the brain. In some cases, other areas of the brain seem to be able to compensate for the damaged area. Thus, although language functions seem to be located in specific areas, the brain is sufficiently interconnected so that other areas can take on certain functions. Despite the advances in brain research, much is still not known. Even though scientists can identify the sections of the brain that process language, that knowledge does not tell them how language is acquired or how it develops. For that reason, applications of brain research in education must be analyzed carefully.

Connectionist theories of language acquisition

Although much still remains to be learned about how the brain works to develop language, brain research has led to theories of language acquisition. Connectionist theories attribute language acquisition to the ability of the brain to form neural connections. According to connectionists every time children hear a word, they connect that word to other words and phrases they have heard. They make associations between sound sequences and objects they see.

For example, if the child hears the word *toy* and sees a toy, the child starts to form a neural connection. As he hears *toy* in situations where there are other toys, the connections are strengthened. Over time, the child builds up a mental representation for *toy* and for the other words and phrases he hears.

Connectionism relies on statistical frequency. The more often a particular word is associated with a class of objects, the stronger the neural networks become. Rather than forming rules, children rely on statistical frequency to form strong connections between language and the world around them.

Connectionist theory may account for how the brain works to form associations. This position does not rule out that there could be both neural connections and rules. However, connectionist theory by itself cannot account for children's ability to generate complex language.

As Bergmann and colleagues (2007) point out:

> It is possible that children form rules and also make use of statistical data. That is, it is possible that acquisition of grammatical rules proceeds according to a hybrid model and that children actively construct a grammar by establishing and exploiting neural networks. (317)

Further advances in brain research should contribute more to our understanding of how children acquire language. However, at this point, connectionist theories by themselves do not seem to account for how children develop the ability to comprehend and produce complex language.

Conclusion

In this chapter, we addressed two questions:

- What are the different theories of first language acquisition?
- What insights into first language acquisition have researchers from different fields provided?

Studies in first language acquisition from different perspectives provide important insights into the process humans go through as they acquire a language. Early behaviorist theories of learning coupled with structural approaches to linguistics suggested that learning is essentially a process of stimulus and response. According to behaviorists, when children attempt to imitate the language they hear they receive a response. Responses that are positively reinforced are repeated until a child produces adultlike forms of the language.

Current studies in the areas of developmental psychology, sociology, anthropology, and education, as well as studies in linguistics, have contributed to new understandings of the process of first language acquisition. These current views are based on cognitive theory rather than behaviorist theory. Developmental psychologists have examined the cognitive aspects of linguistic development. Recent studies involving children acquiring sign suggest that the language modality (oral or visual) is not what is important. Instead, humans are able to find patterns in different modes of communication and use this knowledge to understand and produce messages. Children can make meaning through different modalities, and they can adjust their meaning making to different social situations. Studies by sociologists and anthropologists show differences among the ways groups within a society use language for communication. Children acquire communicative competence, the ability to use language that is appropriate for the group into which they are socialized. This knowledge should inform the teaching of language in schools.

Studies in generative linguistics and brain research have also contributed to the understanding of first language acquisition. Children are able to develop a set of rules that lets them understand and produce sentences they have never heard before. This shows that language learning is not simply imitation. The fact that children can develop these rules with minimal input and virtually no correction suggests that humans are born with an innate capacity for acquiring language. Studies have shown that children never make certain kinds of errors that would be logical to make. This evidence further supports the claim that children must have some built-in linguistic knowledge. They are faced with a formidable challenge of figuring out how their language works, but they don't start from scratch. Instead, they seem to already know how languages work in general, and their task is to figure out the workings of the language or languages they hear each day. And children do just this with great success!

Although there is continued debate over just how much of language is built in and how much is learned, most researchers in first language acquisition agree that humans are uniquely adapted for language acquisition. While input from caregivers is essential for the process of language acquisition to take place, no explicit teaching is necessary. Children come to school knowing the language of their community. Even when the language of instruction is the same as the community language, they still need to develop the registers of language used in school.

While there is general agreement that spoken (or signed) language is primarily acquired, there is a debate over whether it is possible to acquire a second language in the same way that first languages are acquired. Similarly, there is controversy over just how children acquire written language competence. In the next chapter, we turn to these debates in the areas of second language acquisition and written language acquisition. The view of second and written language acquisition has direct implications for how teachers teach.

APPLICATIONS

1. Current views of language development are shaped by insights from different fields. Complete a table following the model below to summarize the key points that come from each discipline. Bring this table to class and create a combined table for all class members.

developmental psychology	sociology, anthropology, education	linguistics

2. We have discussed several theories of first language acquisition in this chapter. Make a table like the one below. You will need to expand the cells. For each theory, list the key points and then list evidence for and evidence against the theory.

Theory	Key points	Evidence for	Evidence against
Imitation			
Reinforcement			
Behaviorist			
Social Interaction			
Active Construction			
Connectionist			

3. Children's errors reflect at least two things: (1) that they don't always imitate adults, and (2) that they overgeneralize rules. If you can interact with a young child, write down some of the children's errors and then identify structures or words children could never have heard from adults. Write down any examples you find that are the result of rule overgeneralization.

4. Heath studied the language of children from different social groups who all went to the same school. If your school has children from different social or linguistic groups, observe their interactions at school. Does their school language reflect the influence of home language practices? If these practices are different from conventional school practices, how do teachers respond to and evaluate the language of those students?

5. There have been many recent studies of language and the brain. Find and read one article on this topic and be prepared to share what you read with your classmates.

3 /θri/

Second and Written Language Acquisition

- What are the principal theories of second language acquisition?
- Can school-age children and adults acquire a second language?
- Is written language acquired or learned?

E ven though researchers debate about how much of language is innate and how much is learned, most researchers agree that young children acquire their first language. In fact, they can acquire two or three languages if they are exposed to more than one language. They do this rapidly and without formal instruction. It appears that children don't have to be taught language the way they are taught to tie their shoes.

Although many people would contend that second and written languages must be learned through explicit teaching, some researchers (Goodman 1996; Smith 1985; Edelsky 1986; Krashen 2009) argue that second and written languages are acquired in the same way that oral or signed language is acquired, through receiving comprehensible input. In the case of written language, caregivers or teachers read to and with children to make the written language understandable, and the children are able to develop literacy as a result of this support.

Second Language Acquisition

First language acquisition is almost universal, and in many parts of the world, second and third language acquisition is common. However, especially in the U.S., questions arise over whether second languages can be acquired, especially by school-age children and adults. Once a person has developed one language, can that person acquire a second language in the same way as the first? Some evidence suggests that second languages are not acquired in the same way as first languages. For example, older emergent bilinguals often struggle to develop the same level of

English proficiency as native speakers, especially with pronunciation. In addition, most students who study a second or foreign language in high school or college fail to achieve a high degree of fluency in the language. Is that because of the methods used to teach language, or is it because people acquire a first language naturally and then have to learn subsequent languages in the same way they learn other subjects in school?

For those of us who live in the United States, the idea that there are many people who speak, read, and write additional languages may seem strange. Sociologist François Grosjean (2010) defines bilingual people as those who "use two or more languages (or dialects) in everyday life" (4). Grosjean reports that a survey conducted in 1976 showed that only about 6 percent of the people in the U.S. reported speaking English and a second language. However, the 2000 census showed that almost 18 percent of the population speaks more than one language. This is a considerable increase, but the U.S. is much less bilingual than other countries.

Studies of twenty-five countries in Europe showed that more than 56 percent of the population reported using more than one language on a regular basis, and of those, 28 percent reported using a third language regularly. Grosjean comments:

> bilingualism is a worldwide phenomenon, found on all continents and in the majority of countries in the world. In some, such as the Asian and African countries for which we unfortunately do not have good data, the percentages found in Europe and North America are most probably surpassed. (16)

In fact, many researchers have concluded that more than half the world's population is bilingual, so this suggests that under the right circumstances school-age children and adults can acquire a second or third language.

Written Language Acquisition

What about written language? Can children acquire written language in the same way they acquire oral or signed language? There are clear differences between oral language and written language. As Halliday (1989) has shown, what appears in a book is not simply oral language written down. Written language is more lexically dense than oral language, and oral language is more grammatically complex than written language.

In addition, oral languages are considered natural since they result from some innate or cognitive capacity of humans. All humans develop oral or signed language unless they have serious neurological impairments or unless they are brought up under unusual conditions that do not include access to linguistic input.

Written language, on the other hand, is considered a secondary system that in some ways represents oral language. Written languages were created by people and cannot be said to reflect an innate capacity. Not all humans develop literacy. So whether or not written language can be acquired is debatable.

In this chapter we address these questions about second language and written language acquisition. Insights from linguistics suggest that both second languages and written language may be acquired rather than learned. This has important implications for teaching since the role of the teacher is quite different depending on whether the teacher believes that students must learn language or whether students can acquire language.

Two Views of Second or Foreign Language Acquisition

There are two views of how people develop a second or foreign language. One view is that first languages are acquired, but additional languages must be learned. Traditional methods of second and foreign language teaching follow from the belief that second languages are learned. The second view is that a second language can be acquired in the same way that a first language is acquired. Even though traditional language teaching practices prevail in many classrooms, current linguistic theories support methods based on an acquisition view. Figure 3.1 lists some of the differences between classrooms in which the teacher takes the view that second languages are learned and classrooms where the teacher believes that second languages may be acquired.

Learning View	Acquisition View
Goal: Teach language directly so students can produce correct language forms.	**Goal:** Teach both academic language and subject matter content.
Order: First teach the language and then teach the content.	**Order:** The language is taught along with the content.
Method: Break language into component parts and teach each part. Keep the focus on the language.	**Method:** Use various techniques to make the linguistic input comprehensible since language is acquired through meaningful use.
Classroom activities: Students do drills and exercises to practice language.	**Classroom activities:** Students engage in activities designed to help them acquire language as they study subject matter content.
Attitude toward error: Teachers correct errors to help students develop good language habits.	**Attitude toward error:** Errors are natural, so teachers keep the focus on meaning and help students understand and express ideas.

Figure 3.1 *Two views of language teaching*

Goals and methods: Learning view

The goal of instruction is to produce students who speak and understand the language. This is best accomplished by teaching each part of the language—the pronunciation, grammar, and vocabulary—directly and systematically. Teachers break each language area into parts to make learning easier. For example, early lessons might all be in present tense to teach that part of language. Later lessons might introduce past and future tenses. Students must learn the new language before they can study content subjects in the new language.

Goals and methods: Acquisition view

The goal of instruction is to enable students to use language for a variety of academic purposes. Students should be able to understand, speak, read, and write the language in different subject areas. For example, they should be able to read a math word problem and write a history report. To accomplish this goal, teachers provide students with a great deal of language input and use various techniques to make the new language comprehensible. These might include using gestures, pictures, and realia, or reading a book with a predictable pattern and clear pictures of key words. Students learn language as they engage in activities that involve them in the content.

Classroom activities: Learning view

Students practice language by engaging in oral drills and written exercises. They translate passages from the target language to their native language and vice versa. They might also learn dialogues and practice them in pairs or small groups. Each drill, exercise, or dialogue would reinforce grammar and vocabulary the students are learning.

Classroom activities: Acquisition view

Students often work in pairs or small groups. Their instruction is scaffolded in various ways to make the language of the content comprehensible. For example, they may work in pairs using different resources to compare and contrast herbivores and carnivores. They learn academic content as they develop their second language. At first they rely heavily on context clues to make sense of instruction. Gradually, they build up their ability to participate in lessons in the different subject areas. They also learn the language of the classroom for social purposes, so when the teacher says, "Open your book" or "Take your seat" the students know how to respond.

Attitude toward error: Learning view

Since the emphasis is on developing correct language forms, teachers correct errors immediately. They often do this directly. This helps students to avoid developing bad habits of grammar or pronunciation. Much of the class focus is on producing correct language forms.

Attitude toward error: Acquisition view

All students make errors. However, if their intent is to express their ideas, they will modify their language to make it more understandable to their listeners or readers. Teachers help students say what they want to say and also give them strategies so they can continue to communicate when they don't have the linguistic resources yet. For example, teachers may provide sentence frames to help students express complex ideas. For beginning students, the teacher might write up on the board, "The color is _____," "The shape is _____," "The texture is ____" for the students to use as a scaffold in their speaking or writing.

Orientations Toward Language Teaching

The two views of language development that we have described, the learning view and the acquisition view, reflect two different orientations toward language teaching. An orientation is a set of assumptions about language and learning that guide teacher practice. In the following sections we review different orientations toward language teaching and the methods associated with each orientation. We begin with two older orientations, grammar based and communicative, and then move to two orientations, empiricist and rationalist, that are the basis of more current methods.

Grammar-based orientation

The *grammar-based* orientation, an early approach, was founded on faculty psychology and traditional grammar. Faculty psychology held that different kinds of knowledge were located in different parts of the brain. For instance, math would be in one area and science in another. The belief was that it was important to exercise these different parts of the brain. According to Diller (1978) this orientation was based on the following assumptions about learning a language:

- Learning a language means learning the grammar and the vocabulary.
- Learning a language expands one's intellect.
- Learning a foreign language enables one to translate great works of literature.

- Learning the grammar of a foreign language helps one learn the grammar of one's own language. (10)

The method associated with this orientation is the *grammar translation method*. Students study the grammar and vocabulary of a language, such as Latin or Greek, with the goal of translating literature from the language to their home language.

Communicative orientation

A second early orientation was the *communicative orientation*. Here the goal was to communicate with speakers of a language rather than to translate great works of literature. This orientation was based on the idea that since children can acquire a first language naturally, the classroom should focus on providing intense interaction in the second language. This orientation was based on the following assumptions:

- The native language should not be used in the classroom.
- Students should make direct associations between the target language and the meaning.
- Language is primarily speech, but reading and writing should be taught from the beginning.
- The purpose of language learning is communication.
- Learning a language involves learning about the culture. (Diller 1978, 14)

The communicative orientation gave rise to the *direct method* of teaching. In a direct method class, no translation is allowed. The goal is for students to make associations between language and meaning, usually while studying about the culture and history of the target language. Berlitz classes are based on the direct method.

Cummins (2007) has pointed out that the "no translation" tenet of the direct method has been widely applied to dual language bilingual classes. He and other researchers, such as García (2010) argue that language acquisition and bilingualism are promoted by the use of both the first language and the second language in classrooms. Nevertheless, the direct method continues to be used in many second and foreign language classes.

Empiricist orientation

Two current orientations to language teaching and learning are the *empiricist orientation* and the *rationalist orientation*. The empiricist orientation is based on behaviorist psychology and structural linguistics. The assumptions that underlie the empiricist orientation include the following:

- Language is speech, not writing.
- A language is a set of habits.
- Teach the language, not about the language.
- A language is what its native speakers say, not what someone thinks they ought to say.
- Languages are different. (Diller 1978, 19)

The emphasis on oral language comes from the work of structural linguists, who viewed written language as a secondary form of language. The idea that a language is what native speakers say is a reaction to an emphasis on grammar in earlier methods. This reaction against teaching grammar also accounts for the idea that teachers should teach the language rather than teach about the language.

The assumption that languages are different comes from the work of structural linguists, who developed descriptions of different languages. They believed that one effective way to learn a new language was by contrasting languages. *Contrastive analysis* (Lado 1957) is a process of systematically showing differences between the phonology, morphology, and syntax of two languages.

The *Audio-lingual Method* (ALM) was based on the empiricist orientation. In this method, students practice dialogues from which drills are developed to help them form habits. Students, for example, do substitution drills with a sentence like "I like ice cream." The teacher says, "Oranges." Students in chorus then say, "I like oranges." The idea behind this is that students learn the syntactic structure, "I like . . ." and can then apply it to other situations. These substitution drills use everyday vocabulary that students were learning, but the vocabulary is not connected to specific academic content. In contrast, sentence frames described previously are used to scaffold language for students as they learn academic content.

Other drills are designed to have students practice areas where languages contrast. For example, English can start words with consonant clusters beginning with *s*, such as *school* or *special*, but Spanish does not start words with *s* followed by a consonant, so in an ALM class, Spanish speakers would practice saying English words that start with *s* followed by a consonant. The emphasis is on oral language development.

Another method based on the empiricist orientation is the *Notional Functional* approach (Wilkins 1976), which is based on teaching notions such as time and space and functions of language, such as apologies or introductions. Lessons are introduced with dialogues designed to help students develop these notions and functions rather than to practice grammar. So a lesson might be on time expressions or on making apologies rather than on present tense or forming the plural of nouns.

Suggestopedia was developed by the Bulgarian psychiatrist Lozanov (1982) and is also based on an empiricist orientation. Lozanov emphasized the importance of creating a relaxed setting and used techniques, often including rhythmic music, to help students relax and believe that they could learn a new language effortlessly. While several of the techniques, especially creating a positive and supportive classroom environment, are important, this method has never been widely used.

These methods, based on an empiricist orientation, reflect a learning view of second language acquisition. Over time, methods based on an empiricist orientation have been superseded by methods with a rationalist orientation.

Rationalist orientation

Most current methods of second and foreign language teaching are based on a *rationalist orientation*. This orientation comes from Chomsky's work in generative grammar and the research in cognitive psychology. The assumptions of the rationalist orientation include:

- A living language is characterized by rule-governed creativity.
- The rules of a grammar are psychologically real.
- People are especially equipped to learn language.
- A living language is a language in which we can think. (Diller 1978, 21)

The theory discussed earlier, Active Construction of a Grammar, is the basis for the idea that language is characterized by rule-governed creativity. Chomsky attempted to develop rules that were psychologically real. These rules would be the best description of the subconscious rules speakers develop and use to produce and comprehend language. Chomsky's innatist view that people are born with Universal Grammar forms the basis for the claim that people are especially equipped to learn language. The idea that a living language is one in which we can think is a reaction against a behaviorist claim that languages are habits developed through stimulus and response. In the development of ALM drills, for example, it didn't matter so much that students could understand the sentences they were producing. The purpose, instead, was on forming correct habits with language patterns.

Three methods with a rationalist orientation that have been used primarily with adults are the Silent Way, Community Language Learning, and Problem Posing. Gattegno (1972) developed the *Silent Way*. In this method, students are held responsible for their own learning, and the teacher is, for the most part, silent. The teacher models an expression only once, and then students must work to reproduce the expression. One feature of this method is the use of Cuisenaire rods that represent words, morphemes, sounds, and so on. Color associations are also used in the Silent Way. Colored charts are used to teach sounds, words, and sentences. Gattegno's idea is that students can develop language by taking responsibility for their learning rather than by being taught rules.

Another method used primarily with adults is *Community Language Learning,* developed by Curran (1976). In this method the teacher facilitates interaction among the students in the same way that a counselor would work with a counseling group. The teacher helps translate what the students want to say from the student's native language into the language students are learning. Conversations among students are taped and then used as a text for learning.

A third method, developed by Freire, is *Problem Posing* (Wallerstein 1987). Freire developed this method to teach literacy to adults, and the method has been adapted for teaching a second language. In this method the teacher listens to the students to find out their concerns and problems. Then the teacher poses the problem by presenting it in what Freire termed a *code.* The code could be a song, a poem, or a picture. This code is designed to enable students to look objectively at the problem. As applied in a second language class, a problem might be inadequate housing and the code could be the picture of a run-down apartment complex. Students use the second language to discuss the problem and find ways to solve it. The goal of the lessons, then, is to equip students with the language needed to discuss their problem and find solutions.

Other methods based on a rationalist orientation have been used in K–12 settings to teach emergent bilinguals. These include Total Physical Response, the Natural Approach, the Cognitive Academic Language Learning Approach (CALLA), and the Sheltered Instruction Observation Protocol (SIOP). These last two methods involve content-based language instruction, and they are used in contexts where the goal is to learn language and academic content.

Total Physical Response (TPR) was developed by Asher (1977), whose research observing young children helped him form hypotheses that included the importance of listening, the importance of a physical response in learning, and the importance of lack of stress in learning. He suggested that people learn better when they respond with their bodies. In TPR, the teacher gives commands, such as "Raise your left hand," and students respond by acting out the command. TPR has been expanded, and lessons include a series of related commands as well as dialogues, role-play, and storytelling. In most cases, TPR has been used with beginning level students as a technique as a part of another method rather than as a complete method.

The *Natural Approach,* developed by Krashen and Terrell (1983), focuses on techniques to make the input comprehensible. For example, teachers might use gestures, pictures, or real objects to convey meaning in a second language. Students move through a series of stages from preproduction to intermediate fluency. At each stage, the teacher uses different techniques. For instance, at an early stage, the teacher might ask *yes/no* questions and at a later stage *wh-* questions, such as those beginning with *when* or *where*. This approach has been widely implemented and has been modified to include more of a focus on teaching academic content rather than teaching basic everyday language.

The *Cognitive Academic Language Learning Approach,* developed by Chamot and O'Malley (1989), was designed specifically to teach academic content to older students who had developed social communicative skills in English or had developed academic content knowledge and literacy in their first language and some proficiency in English. Three components comprise CALLA: grade-appropriate content, academic language development, and instruction in learning strategies. CALLA emphasizes students' cognitive academic language development. CALLA is still used and has been the basis for much current teaching in which the focus is on acquiring language in the process of studying academic content.

The *Structured Instruction Observation Protocol* (SIOP) is the most widely used method in K–12 schools in the U.S. for teaching emergent bilinguals both language and academic subject matter content. SIOP is based on extensive research. The Center for Applied Linguistics (CAL) lists the following eight components of effective lessons for emergent bilinguals:

- lesson preparation
- building background
- comprehensible input
- strategies
- interaction
- practice/application
- lesson delivery
- review and assessment

> (Reprinted with permission from the website of the Center for Applied Linguistics: www.cal.org/siop/about)

Teachers using SIOP integrate these components into their lesson plans. SIOP lessons have been developed for different age groups and different subjects.

As this brief review of orientations and methods indicates, most current second language teaching is based on a rationalist orientation and a view that students can acquire a second language. In the following sections, we summarize the theories of second language acquisition that underlie the acquisition view of language development.

Krashen's Theory of Second Language Acquisition

Krashen's theory of second language acquisition (1982, 2003) forms the basis for much of the teaching methodology in ESL, EFL (English as a Foreign Language), bilingual, and mainstream classes for emergent bilinguals. This theory, based on Chomsky's work in linguistics, consists of five interrelated hypotheses.

The Learning/Acquisition Hypothesis

Krashen makes a distinction between two ways of developing a second language. The first, which he calls *learning*, is what many students experience in high school or college foreign language classes. Learning is a conscious process that involves studying rules and vocabulary. Students who attempt to learn a language break the language down into manageable chunks and try to memorize and practice the different parts of the language with the goal of being able to use the language to communicate. A student might study vocabulary lists or verb conjugations. Students would practice using this knowledge in a class with different exercises and drills and then be tested on what they learned.

The second way of developing language is what Krashen calls *acquisition*. In contrast to learning, acquisition is subconscious. Students acquiring a language may not even be aware that they are picking up vocabulary or sentence structures. Acquisition occurs as students use language for a variety of purposes. For example, students can acquire a language at the same time that they are learning some academic subject-area content if the teacher uses techniques to help make the instruction understandable. While learning is usually restricted to the school context, acquisition can take place in or out of school. Acquisition is what happens when someone goes to another country and "picks up" the language in the process of day-to-day living and interactions with native speakers of the language. Figure 3.2 summarizes the key differences between acquisition and learning.

Learning	Acquisition
• Conscious	• Subconscious
• We are aware we are learning.	• We are not aware we are acquiring.
• It's what happens in school when we study rules and grammar and then are tested on what we learned.	• It's what happens in and out of school when we receive messages we understand.

Figure 3.2 *Learning and acquisition*

The Natural Order Hypothesis

Krashen (1977) reviews research that shows both first language and second language are acquired in a natural order. Simply put, some aspects of language appear in the speech of language learners before other features. For example, babies acquiring English first produce sounds with vowels (usually the low, back "ah" sound) and later add consonants beginning with consonants formed with the lips like "p" or "m." This helps explain why the first word of many infants is something like "mama," much to the delight of the mother, or "papa," much to the delight of the father. Sounds like "r" come later. That's why young children might say "cwaka" and "wabbit," instead of "cracker" or "rabbit." Other parts of language also appear in a natural order. Statements come before questions. Positive statements come before negatives, and so on.

Researchers also found that there is a natural order of second language acquisition. The natural order of English as a second language acquisition differs slightly from that of first language, but there is a definite order. Dulay and Burt (1974) studied Spanish and Chinese speakers acquiring English. They looked at the order in which certain morphemes appeared. They noted that the plural "s" in a word like "toys" showed up in children's speech earlier than the third person "s" of present tense verbs in sentences like "He plays." Whether researchers look at the acquisition of phonemes, morphemes, or syntax, they find an order of acquisition that is the same even for children whose first languages are different. The order depends on the language being acquired, not on a transfer of features from the first language.

The Monitor Hypothesis

This hypothesis helps explain the role of learning in the process of language acquisition. Acquired language forms the basis for the ability to understand and produce the language. The phonology, morphology, and syntax are acquired. Acquisition is what enables native English speakers to tell what "sounds right" in the language. They may not be able to explain why "He is married to her" sounds better than "He is married with her," but because native speakers have acquired the language, they can make these kinds of judgments about what sounds right.

Learning also plays a role in language competence. The rules that people learn can be used to monitor spoken or written output. People can use learned rules to check what they say or write. In order for monitor use to be effective, language users must have time, they must focus on language form, and they must know the rules. Even in the first language, most people monitor their speech in formal situations such as giving a speech to a large group of people. However, there are effective and ineffective ways to use the monitor.

In the flow of rapid conversation, speakers generally don't have time to check what they are saying and correct themselves. In addition, monitoring involves focusing on how something is being said rather than on what is being said. It is almost impossible to concentrate on both the ideas and the correct pronunciation or grammar at the same time. The more a speaker thinks about the message, the less the speaker can concentrate on the language. Further, to use the monitor effectively, one must know the rules. Is it "different from" or "different than"? Unless the speaker knows the right answer, he or she can't monitor the output very well.

Effective monitor users steer a middle course. Overusers try to correct everything, and the result is halting speech or even a hesitation to enter a conversation. Underusers charge ahead but at times their errors make their discourse incomprehensible. Optimum use of the monitor involves checking to avoid major errors all the while keeping the focus on the message.

Spoken language is more difficult to monitor than written language. Editing during the writing process represents an ideal situation to apply the monitor because there is time and one can focus specifically on the correctness of the language to be sure that sentences are complete and words are spelled conventionally. However, if writers monitor while they are drafting, the focus on form may interrupt the flow of their ideas. It is better to do the editing after the ideas are down on paper.

The Input Hypothesis

How does acquisition take place? According to Krashen, the key is comprehensible input, messages that students understand. A teacher's job is to find ways to make the input comprehensible. Not all input leads to acquisition. Krashen says that students acquire language when they receive input that is slightly beyond their current level. He refers to this as $i + 1$ (*input plus one*). If students receive input that is below or at their current level ($i + 0$) there is nothing new to acquire. However, if the input is too much beyond their current level ($i + 10$), for example, it no longer is comprehensible.

Providing comprehensible input is not an exact science. Teachers can't possibly ensure that everything they say or write will be exactly at the $i + 1$ level for every student. The students in a class are all at different levels of proficiency. Nevertheless, as long as students understand most of what they hear or read in a new language, they will acquire the language. Different students will acquire different parts of the language depending on their current level.

To ensure that the input is comprehensible, teachers can use pictures, gestures, tone of voice, and hands-on activities. Teachers can also avoid using idioms, they can pause often to slow down the rate of speech, and they can recycle vocabulary by planning curriculum around themes so that certain words come up repeatedly in the natural process of studying the theme through different academic content areas. These techniques give students comprehensible input at the i + 1 level. Krashen is an especially strong advocate of reading for language acquisition. He cites research showing that free voluntary reading provides excellent comprehensible input and is the source of our knowledge of vocabulary, grammar, and spelling (Krashen 2004).

The Affective Filter Hypothesis

How do affective factors such as nervousness, boredom, or anxiety influence language acquisition? If language is acquired when a person receives comprehensible input, that input has to reach the part of the brain that processes language. Boredom and anxiety are affective factors that can serve as a kind of filter to block out incoming messages and prevent them from triggering acquisition.

As a result, even though a teacher may present a very comprehensible lesson, some students may not acquire the language of the lesson because their affective filter operates to block the input. Students cannot acquire language that never reaches the language acquisition device. On the other hand, when the filter is open, when students are relaxed and engaged in a lesson, even messages that are not easy to comprehend will trigger the acquisition process. This is why, for example, students often acquire language when singing or when involved in engaging hands-on activities, such as cooking or experimenting with magnets.

Together these five hypotheses constitute Krashen's theory of second language acquisition. People acquire a second language in a natural order when they receive comprehensible input and have a low affective filter. People can use learned knowledge of a language to monitor their output.

The Role of Output

Krashen argues that acquisition occurs when learners receive comprehensible input, messages that they understand. Other researchers have given importance to output as well as input. Ellis (2005) refers to theories such as Krashen's as reception based. Theories that include attention to output he classifies as production based. "Reception-based theories contend that interaction contributes to second language

"theory"
underneath
aka the
"action"

acquisition via learners' reception and comprehension of the second language, whereas production-based theories credit this process to learners' attempts at actually producing the language" (Johnson 1995, 82).

Long (1983) developed the *Interaction Hypothesis*, a theory of second language acquisition (SLA) that is production based. Long claims that learners make conversational adjustments as they interact with others and that these adjustments help make the input they receive comprehensible. As Johnson (1995) points out, "Like Krashen, Long stresses the importance of comprehensible input but places more emphasis on the interaction that takes place in two-way communication and the adjustments that are made as a result of the negotiation of meaning" (83). Long's theory of SLA is similar to social interaction theories of first language acquisition.

Swain (1985) presented research showing that language learners need the opportunity for output. She noted that students in French immersion classes did not reach nativelike proficiency in French. These students were in classes where teachers did most of the talking. Peer interaction was limited, and when interaction occurred, students spoke only with others learning French rather than with native speakers of French. Based on her observations of these students, Swain proposed that second language acquisition depends on output as well as input. According to Scarcella (1990) Swain's comprehensible output hypothesis

> suggests that students need tasks which elicit talk at the student's i + 1, that is, a level of second language proficiency which is just a bit beyond the current second language proficiency level. She claims that such output provides opportunities for meaningful context-embedded use for the second language, which allows students to test out their hypotheses about the language and "moves the learner from a purely semantic analysis of the language to a syntactic analysis of it." (70)

Swain's claim is that when we receive input that we understand, we focus on meaning or the semantic level. However, in talking, we need to string words, phrases, and sentences together, and that requires attention to syntax. Our syntactic analysis is probably not conscious, but producing output requires us to access parts of the language system different from those we use to comprehend input.

Production-based theories of SLA recognize the importance of input but add output as an important component. Long argues that output is needed for social interaction and that output leads to greater comprehensible input. Krashen's argument is that output can't help us acquire new vocabulary or grammatical structures. We can't learn a new word simply by talking. In addition, Krashen (2008) reviews the research studies on output and finds that the evidence for the effects of output on language competence is extremely weak.

Schumann's Theory of Second Language Acquisition

Krashen's theory of second language acquisition accounts for the psychological process of language development. Other researchers have considered the broader social context. Schumann (1978), for example, studied one adult immigrant, Alberto, whose English acquisition was very limited. Schumann found that a number of social factors helped explain the low level of acquisition. Alberto lived in a situation in which there was a considerable social distance between him and members of the mainstream society.

Schumann identified several factors that contribute to social distance. For example, distance is greater when there is only limited integration of the two cultural groups, when the minority group itself is large enough to be self-sufficient, when the group is very tight-knit, when the group has characteristics very different from those of the mainstream culture, when the majority group has a negative attitude toward the minority group, and when the learner only intends to stay a short time in the country.

One example might help illustrate social distance. The Hmong, a nomadic people from Laos, came to the U.S. after the war in Vietnam to escape persecution for helping the United States. The first generation settled mainly in Minnesota and central California. Their numbers in these enclaves were so large that they were able to support one another, buy from stores that catered to them, and live with minimal contact with the mainstream. All these factors contribute to social distance, and the greater the social distance between the minority group and the mainstream, the less likely that minority group members will acquire the language of the mainstream culture.

At first, then, many adult Hmong acquired very little English. As the next generations attended U.S. schools and came in closer contact with the U.S. culture, this social distance decreased; second- and third-generation Hmong not only learned English, but many lost their ability to speak Hmong fluently.

Schumann also considered psychological factors, such as motivation, attitude, and culture shock. Students with low motivation and a negative attitude toward members of the mainstream culture are less apt to acquire the language of the mainstream, especially when students are going through culture shock as they adjust to living in a new country.

Many Hmong teens arriving after the war were adjusting to the huge change in lifestyle from an agrarian society to the modern life of cities in the U.S. They felt resentment because of the persecution of their people and the lack of understanding they perceived from both teachers and other students. Many dropped out of school and/or joined gangs. Psychological factors can create psychological distance, which, combined with social distance, helps explain a low level of acquisition.

Schumann's concepts of social and psychological distance are consistent with Krashen's theory. Social distance limits opportunities for students to receive the comprehensible input needed for acquisition. Psychological distance serves to raise the affective filter and prevent input from producing acquisition.

Grosjean reports on a model of second language acquisition developed by Fillmore (1991), who explains that to acquire a second language, a person should follow three steps: (1) join a group and act like you know what is going on, even if you don't; (2) give the impression, with a few well-chosen words, that you can speak the language; and (3) count on your friends for help (Grosjean 2010, 186). This model fits Schumann's theory very well and is good practical advice.

However, programs continue to be developed that, contrary to current research, separate emergent bilinguals from native English speakers and attempt to teach language directly. For example, one program that has been developed segregates emergent bilinguals for four hours of each school day. This program takes a learning perspective. Students are taught grammar, pronunciation, and vocabulary directly. There is little research to support this program, but it has been widely implemented in Arizona and California (Clark 2009).

Another example of the ineffectiveness of separating emergent bilinguals comes from Valdés (2001). Her work has shown that many middle school and high school students are segregated from native English speakers much of the day, and, as a result, they fail to develop the academic English required for school success. If these students also have limited contact with native speakers outside school, then they will not develop the language of everyday communication either.

The Critical Period Hypothesis

There is general agreement among researchers that second languages can be acquired, although some instruction may be beneficial, and the social context plays an important role. But is there an age limit on acquisition? Is there a critical or sensitive period after which individuals cannot acquire a language and must learn it? Generally, this critical or sensitive period is put at around birth to six years of age.

Researchers from a number of fields have debated this issue for both first and second language acquisition. In the case of first languages, there have been instances of children who have been brought up under very unusual circumstances that included isolation from other humans. Such children have often exhibited considerable difficulty in developing language later in life. However, in almost every case, the children have experienced physical and psychological trauma that may account for their later language learning difficulties.

Although cases of someone failing to develop a first language are rare, there is a general belief that children are better language learners than adults. Children are able to speak a second language with little or no foreign accent, but adults usually retain an accent. This has led researchers to investigate the possibility that there is a critical or sensitive period during which language can be acquired. Once past that period, people are not able to acquire a second language.

There are two reasons that children appear to be better language learners than adults. In the first place, adults have more to learn. If an adult goes to a new country and learns to speak the language like a competent six-year-old, most people would rate the adult as deficient in the language. Adults are expected to have a much more developed vocabulary, and adults frequently use complex syntax. Nobody expects this of a six-year-old.

Not only do adults have more to learn, they usually have less time to learn it. Most adults who go to live in a foreign country go there to work. Often, at work adults can speak their native language. Outside work, adults often socialize with others who speak their language. For many adults living in a foreign country, opportunities for the use of the foreign language are limited. Children, though, have fewer responsibilities and many more chances to interact with children who speak the language of the new country. As a result, children receive more comprehensible input and have more opportunities for social interaction in the new language than adults do.

Before examining the idea of a critical or sensitive period more closely, it is important to point out that the discussion is generally limited to accent or pronunciation. Even though adults are good language learners, they usually retain an accent. Grosjean (2010) points out that "Having a 'foreign' accent in one or more languages is, in fact, the norm for bilinguals; not having one is the exception" (77).

Does this mean there is a critical period for the acquisition of phonology? Researchers from different disciplines have investigated this question, and although no definitive answers have emerged, there are several possible explanations. The three most common explanations as to why most, although not all, adults speak a second language with a foreign accent are based on neurological factors, cognitive factors, and affective factors.

Neurological factors

Studies of the brain have shown that different areas of the brain are associated with different functions. Brown (2007) notes that "There is evidence in neurological research that as the human brain matures certain functions are assigned—or 'lateralized'—to the left hemisphere of the brain and other functions to the right hemisphere. Intellectual, logical, and analytic functions appear to be largely located in the left hemisphere while the right hemisphere controls functions related to emotional and social needs" (53). Language is one of the functions located in the left hemisphere.

Lateralization of the brain begins at about age two. Not all researchers agree about when lateralization is complete. However, many researchers such as Lenneberg (1967) have concluded that by puberty the different functions of the brain have been lateralized to the two hemispheres.

Children who acquire a second language before puberty usually speak the new language without an accent. Older learners, however, generally speak the second language with an accent. Since people who learn a second language after puberty generally retain an accent, researchers have hypothesized that people are no longer able to acquire some aspects of language, such as the phonology, once the brain is lateralized and language is located in the left hemisphere. They hypothesize that the critical period for the acquisition of phonology is the period prior to changes in the brain associated with lateralization.

answer to "critical period"

Cognitive factors

Young children who develop a second language with nativelike pronunciation have not yet reached what Piaget identified as the formal operational stage. This stage begins for most children at around age eleven, and it is the point at which more abstract thought is possible. Perhaps the ability for more abstract thought changes the way people go about the task of learning a second language.

Younger children in the concrete operational stage may be able to acquire the language without needing to analyze the structure of the language. Older learners may not be able to suppress formal thought processes. To use Krashen's terms, younger children have not reached a point where learning a language is possible (learning involves knowing and applying abstract rules about language), so they develop a second language through a process of acquisition. Older learners have difficulty turning learning off. They use cognitive processes to analyze language, and, as a result, they have more difficulty acquiring a language.

Affective factors

The fact that most adults retain an accent may be due more to affective factors than to neurological or cognitive factors. For one thing, adolescents or adults learning a second language may be more self-conscious than children. Older learners may be hesitant to try out a new language for fear of appearing incompetent.

Guiora and colleagues (1972) suggest that each person has a language ego. A person's language forms an important part of that person's identity. The way someone talks helps define who he or she is. Learning a new language, at a subconscious level, may threaten the language ego. By retaining an accent a person keeps part of his or her identify. A British English speaker, for example, who speaks Spanish with a British accent, sends the message that he or she is still a person from England. The idea of a language ego is related to general attitudinal factors. Older learners who acquire a second language and speak with little or no foreign accent are often people who admire and identify with people who live in a country where the language is spoken.

Wooowww!

A great deal has been written about a critical or sensitive period. For an excellent review, see Brown (2007). However, it is important to recognize that the critical period applies primarily to pronunciation. Adults can acquire a second language, and some adults also develop a nativelike accent. In some cases, though, adult learners also make persistent errors in vocabulary and syntax when they speak in the second language.

Fossilization

The presence of certain kinds of errors that persist in the speech of adult second language learners is referred to as *fossilization*. For these learners, some errors seem to have become a permanent part of their new language. In many cases, these older learners are highly educated, and they may have spent years in the country in which the language is spoken. Instruction doesn't seem to solve the problem.

A good example of fossilization comes from an older Japanese student. This student studied and taught English in Japan. He came to the United States and completed a master's degree in teaching English. He has lived in the United States for several years. Yet, consider some excerpts from an email he sent:

> I miss a cozy, sunny weather in Fresno. I have to put on a heavy down jacket, a glove, and a cap. The strong, chilly wind attacks me. I am in the process to get used to a mean weather.

Even though this student has advanced vocabulary and syntax, his writing has a number of errors. He could probably explain the rule for each error, but when he uses English, errors like this keep coming up. Fossilization is characteristic of the language of many older people who have acquired a second language. Perhaps the best explanation for this phenomenon is that people like this student have acquired enough of the language to communicate any idea. The language serves their needs very well. Although they may say that they want to speak English perfectly, at a subconscious level at least, they may feel that their English is good enough.

Summary: *Second language acquisition*

Two views of second language development are the learning view and the acquisition view. Those who hold a learning view claim that second languages are learned in the same way that other subjects are learned. In contrast, those who take an acquisition view argue that second languages are acquired in the same way as first languages.

These two views of language acquisition have led to different orientations and methods of second language teaching. Two early methods, the grammar translation method and the communicative method, clearly reflect the two views. The grammar translation method is based on the assumption that languages are learned while the communicative method is based on the idea that languages are acquired.

Two orientations toward language teaching also reflect the two views. The empiricist orientation, based on behavioral psychology and structural linguistics, included several methods, such as the Audio-lingual Method, which reflect a learning view. The rationalist orientation, based on cognitive psychology and generative linguistics, led to methods with an acquisition view.

Krashen's theory of second language acquisition is the basis for much content-based language teaching. This theory consists of five hypothesis. Together these hypotheses claim that language is acquired (not learned) in a natural order when learners receive comprehensible input and have a low affective filter. Learned rules allow a person to monitor output. Schumann's research shows that the social context can affect the level of language acquisition. Acquisition is optimal when the social and psychological distances are small.

Some researchers have argued that there is a critical period after which a person cannot acquire a second language. Neurological, cognitive, and affective factors have been used to support the claim that there is a critical period for language acquisition. However, the critical period may only apply to pronunciation. Older learners can acquire a second language under the right conditions, but they may retain a foreign accent. In addition, the speech and writing of some older second language learners may fossilize. That is, they may continue to make certain kinds of errors despite instruction.

Two Views of Written Language Development

There is little disagreement that developing high levels of literacy is the key to academic achievement. However, there is a great deal of disagreement about the best way to teach reading and writing. In the same way that there has been a debate about whether second languages can be acquired or whether they need to be learned, there is also a debate about literacy development. Some researchers hold that literacy must be learned. Others argue that literacy can be acquired in the same way that a first language is acquired.

Teachers who hold the view that people must learn to read and write break the tasks down into their component parts and teach each part. They follow a logical instructional sequence moving from the parts to the whole. The sequence involves learning letters, connecting letters with sounds, and combining letters to construct words. Words are then combined into sentences and longer stretches of text.

On the other hand, teachers who take an acquisition view of literacy development begin by reading to children and writing with children. The role of the teacher is to make written input comprehensible and to encourage children to express their ideas in writing. Over time, the teacher gradually releases the responsibility to the students (Pearson and Gallagher 1983). The progression moves from reading aloud to shared reading, guided reading, and independent reading. The same sequence applies to writing instruction.

In the following sections, we look more closely at these two views of literacy development: a learning view and an acquisition view. For each view we consider implications for teaching students to read and write.

Learning: A logical approach

Teachers who take a learning-based approach to teaching reading begin with small parts and build up to an understanding of whole texts. One of the first steps is for students to develop phonological and phonemic awareness, the understanding that written words represent sequences of sounds. Students learning to read in alphabetic languages such as English also need to learn the letters of the alphabet and the sounds associated with the letters. Then they can blend the sounds to change the written characters into oral (or signed) language. The assumption is that any word a student can pronounce is a word the student can understand. Students then combine sequences of words to read sentences and whole texts. Each part of this process is taught, learned, and tested.

Phonics is the most commonly used method to teach reading. By applying phonics rules, such as "when two vowels go walking, the first one does the talking," readers can determine the pronunciation of a string of letters and change the written marks to words in their oral vocabulary. Even when they can apply phonics rules to correctly pronounce words in English, emergent bilinguals often have trouble comprehending texts because the words may not be part of their oral vocabulary. The result is that they become *word callers*. They may sound as though they are reading fluently, but they may not understand the words they are reading.

issue with phonics

There are two problems with applying phonics rules. Some common words such as *the* or *of* do not follow regular phonics rules, so readers also need to develop a set of *sight words*. These are words students recognize automatically. Teachers might use flash cards to help students develop their sight words. The teacher shows a card, and students say the word. In addition, long complex words are difficult to decode using phonics rules. Students can identify longer words by breaking them down into their component parts. For example, they can divide a word into its prefix, root, and suffix. Students can combine the meanings of word parts to determine the meaning of a long word like *transportation* or *reconceptualize*. Teachers sometimes tell students to find the little words inside the big word. This approach to word recognition is called *structural analysis*.

Teachers who take a learning view often use decodable or leveled books. Decodable books are those that contain only words with sound–letter correspondences that children have been taught along with a few common sight words. The resulting texts are not always interesting to read since it is difficult to write books that contain only certain sounds. Most readers have seen books with lines such as "The fat cat sat on the mat." In a book with a line such as this, the short *a* sound is featured for practice.

In classes where teachers take a learning view, one popular practice is round-robin reading. Children sit in a circle and take turns reading aloud. The teacher or other students correct errors. Despite research showing that round-robin reading is not an effective method for teaching reading (Opitz and Rasinksi 2008) it is a common practice in learning classrooms.

Acquisition: Goodman's theoretical model of reading

Goodman (1996) developed a theoretical model of the reading process. This work was based on studies in psycholinguistics and then expanded to include social factors. For this reason, the model is often referred to as a sociopsycholinguistic model. The model is consistent with an acquisition view of literacy development.

Although the claim is that children can acquire literacy in the same way that they acquire their first language, it is important to note that the teacher plays a crucial role in the process. Without the teacher's careful guidance, it would be difficult for a student to develop a high level of reading proficiency. The teacher's job is to make written input comprehensible. Instruction follows a gradual release of responsibility model that includes read-alouds, shared and guided reading, and independent reading. During this process the teacher does most of the reading at first and then gradually shifts the responsibility for reading to the students.

The goal of reading from a sociopsycholinguistic perspective is to construct meaning. All models of reading have meaning construction as the goal. However, in an acquisition classroom readers are focused on making meaning, not on identifying the individual words in order to make meaning. To construct meaning, readers use their background knowledge and cues from three linguistic systems: graphophonics, syntax, and semantics. Readers go through a process of visually sampling the text, predicting what will come next, making inferences, confirming or disconfirming their predictions, and integrating the new information with what they already know. This process occurs rapidly. Readers combine cues from the text with their own knowledge of the world to make sense of what they are reading. Every text has a certain meaning potential, and different readers construct different meanings depending on their background knowledge and their purpose for reading.

Since the goal of reading is to construct meaning, then readers should use all available information, including background knowledge and cues from all three cueing systems. The graphophonic system is one source of information readers can use. This system includes a reader's knowledge of orthography, phonology, and phonics. Letters and sounds serve as an important source of information to be combined with information from other sources. Proficient readers learn to sample the visual display and to use visual and sound information as they make and confirm predictions. However, they also use their background knowledge and cues from the syntax and semantics of the written language. In the following three chapters, we examine the components of the graphoponic system in detail.

Readers in an acquisition-oriented classroom also make use of their knowledge of morphology to construct meaning. Studying the structure of words is an important part of the language arts curriculum, especially if the word study is undertaken from a linguistic perspective. Proficient readers use their knowledge of word structure to construct meaning. We consider the wording system, or *morphology*, of English in Chapters 7 and 8.

Readers also use syntactic cues. We examine syntax in Chapters 9 and 10. *Syntax* refers to the order of words in a sentence. Knowledge of syntax helps readers make predictions. For example, if a sentence begins with the words, "He persuaded . . . ," a reader can predict that the name of a person will come next, such as "He persuaded María," and this will be followed by a phrase indicating what he persuaded María to do or believe. As readers become more familiar with the syntax of English, they can make better predictions. One of the challenges of academic language is that the syntax of school discussions and texts is different from that of everyday communication. Students can learn the syntax of academic language in the process of reading, writing, and engaging in class discussions.

In classes in which teachers have a sociopsycholinguistic or acquisition view of reading, instead of participating in round-robin reading, students read a variety of texts that represent different genres silently. They also choose books they want to read independently. Reading aloud is reserved for activities such as readers theatre. Teachers help students develop strategies to use during silent reading. These strategies are designed to improve comprehension. Teachers often talk with students about different things they can do if they come to a part of a text that they don't understand. Students need a variety of strategies that they can use flexibly to construct meaning.

The learning and acquisition views of reading are reflected in very different classroom practices. In subsequent chapters, we will look closely at the phonology, orthography, morphology, and syntax of English. As teachers better understand these linguistic systems, they can make more informed decisions about which view of reading to adopt and how to go about helping all their students, including their emergent bilinguals, become proficient readers. Figure 3.3 contrasts key elements of the two views of reading.

Learning and Acquisition Views of Writing

In the same way that there are two views of reading, there are also two views of writing. These two views again correspond to the distinction we have made between learning and acquisition. From a learning point of view, writing, like reading, must be taught directly. From an acquisition perspective, writing is acquired as students use written language for real purposes. Teachers from both points of view include writing in their language arts curriculum, but several aspects of their instruction are different.

Learning View of Reading	Acquisition View of Reading
Instruction starts with the smallest parts and builds up to the whole. Students are taught phonological and phonemic awareness, letter names and sounds.	Instruction focuses on meaning construction through the use of background knowledge and cues from three systems.
Teachers teach phonics rules, sight words, and structural analysis to identify words.	Teachers follow a gradual release of responsibility model, which includes read-alouds, shared and guided reading, and independent reading.
Teachers use decodable and leveled books to improve students' reading skills.	Teachers use a variety of texts representing different genres. Students choose texts to read.
Students read aloud in round-robin style and teachers correct errors.	Students read a variety of texts silently using comprehension strategies they have been taught.

Figure 3.3 *Learning and acquisition views of reading*

Writing in a learning-oriented classroom

In a traditional classroom where teachers take a learning perspective, writing is broken down into its component parts and taught one part at a time. For example, teachers of young children show them how to form letters. Students learn to write words, sentences, paragraphs, and then whole stories or reports. In many traditional classes, students learn how to produce a five-paragraph essay that follows a clearly defined structure. Usually, students are given the topics for writing, and they are expected to complete the writing in a fairly short time.

Teachers in traditional classrooms emphasize the importance of producing writing that follows conventions in handwriting, spelling, punctuation, and organization. Often, handwriting and spelling are major components of the writing program for young children. Students memorize lists of words and are tested each week on their spelling. To help students learn to produce correct writing, teachers correct each piece a student writes. In many traditional classes, the form of the writing becomes much more important than the content. Students who focus on form may not even try to use new words or sentence patterns for fear of making errors.

Writing in an acquisition-oriented classroom

In classrooms where the teacher takes an acquisition view, the process of writing is emphasized. Teachers may start with language experience stories, having students dictate while the teacher writes about some experience the class has had. Then the teacher and students read back what the teacher has written. The teacher may also call a child up to the flip chart or writing tablet to "share the pen" and write in one or two of the words. Following this shared writing, teachers guide students as they write. Eventually, students begin to write on their own. This process follows the same release of responsibility model (Pearson and Gallagher 1983) that is followed during reading instruction. Instruction begins with the teacher doing most of the work. Over time, the teacher releases the responsibility for writing to the students.

In such classrooms, teachers often use a workshop approach. Following the work of Graves (1994), Calkins (1991), Atwell (1998), and others, teachers have students work together to brainstorm ideas for writing, produce drafts, conference with other students, edit, and then share their work with the class. The focus of instruction is on both form and content.

Teachers provide many opportunities for students to produce different kinds of writing—a story, a letter to a friend, a list of books they have read. Rather than giving students topics, teachers help students understand that there are many situations in which they can express their ideas most effectively by using written language. For example, students who investigate a topic during a theme study might accompany their oral report with a written handout for classmates.

Teachers set aside time on a regular basis for writing. During writers workshop they teach minilessons to help students express their ideas more effectively. Teachers who take an acquisition view realize that students must read frequently. The reading provides the input needed for written output. As they read, students come to understand the different organizational structures writers use to communicate ideas.

Process writing teachers believe that writing will move from individual invention to conventional forms (Goodman and Goodman 1990). For example, students may begin by spelling most words the way they sound. Over time, they begin to produce more conventional spellings. Teachers help students keep the focus on the content of what they are writing, not just the form. At the same time, as writers share their writing with classmates and the teacher, they realize that some ways of spelling words or punctuating sentences confuse their audience, so they start to use more conventional forms to communicate more effectively.

When students have written something they want others to read, they are motivated to put their writing in a form that follows social conventions. Teachers give minilessons on all areas of writing, including spelling and punctuation. Rather than giving students lists of words to memorize, they help them discover the patterns in the spellings of English words. Conventional writing is a goal of a process classroom, but teachers emphasize that the content of the message is more important than the form.

Figure 3.4 summarizes the two views of writing.

Learning View of Writing	Acquisition View of Writing
Writing is broken down into component parts that are taught directly.	Writing is acquired as children use writing for real purposes.
Teachers teach handwriting, letter formation, words, sentences, paragraphs, and whole texts.	Teachers follow a gradual release model of language experience, shared and guided writing, and independent writing.
Teachers assign topics and correct students' writing.	During writing workshop students share their writing and learn to write drafts, conference, edit, and revise their work.
The focus of writing instruction is on form.	The focus of writing instruction is on both form and content.

Figure 3.4 *Learning and acquisition views of writing*

Summary: Learning and acquisition views of reading and writing

A teacher's view of whether written language is learned or acquired determines, to a great extent, the classroom practices the teacher follows. If teachers believe that reading and writing are learned, they divide reading and writing into their component parts and teach each of the parts directly and systematically. Reading is accomplished by recognizing words, so teachers teach phonics rules, sight words, and structural analysis. Writing consists of producing words, so teachers focus on handwriting, spelling, punctuation, grammar, and conventional organizational forms, such as writing complete sentences, coherent paragraphs, and the five-paragraph essay or a story with a clear beginning, middle, and end.

When teachers view reading and writing from an acquisition standpoint, they do a number of things to make written language comprehensible. They read and write with students and teach students strategies they can use to comprehend and produce texts. They create workshop type classroom structures where students work together to read and write. These teachers believe that written language, like oral language, develops best when students focus on both the message and the form of written language. They recognize that reading provides the input needed for writing output. They provide many opportunities for students to read and to produce and share their writing.

Conclusion

We began this chapter by posing three questions:

- What are the principal theories of second language acquisition?
- Can school-age children and adults acquire a second language?
- Is written language acquired or learned?

In our discussion of each question, we pointed out that there is a debate over two views of language development. One view is that language is learned. Teachers who hold a learning view break language into its component parts and teach them directly. They correct errors to help students develop good language habits. They keep the focus on correct language form and pay less attention to the content. How students say or write things is more important than what they say or write. This approach applies to both second languages and written language.

The second view is that language is acquired. Teachers who hold an acquisition view attempt to make language comprehensible. They use different techniques to help students understand what they read or hear. The focus always stays on making meaning. Students develop conventional language forms once they have messages they wish to communicate.

The two views of second and written language acquisition have led to different orientations. An *orientation* is a set of beliefs about how people learn and the methods teachers should use. An early orientation was grammar based. The method for language teaching associated with this view is the grammar translation method. This method was based on faculty psychology and traditional linguistics. A second early orientation was the communicative orientation. A method associated with this orientation is the direct method. This method emphasizes the use of the target language to develop proficiency in everyday communication.

Two more recent orientations toward language teaching are the empiricist orientation and the rationalist orientation. The empiricist orientation is based on behavioral psychology and structural linguistics. Methods, such as ALM, are designed to help students form correct language habits through stimulus and response style drills and exercises. The rationalist orientation is based on cognitive psychology and generative linguistics. A number of methods have been developed that are consistent with this orientation. Methods, such as CALLA and SIOP, are content based. Teachers attempt to teach both language and content together by making linguistic input comprehensible.

1 Theory Krashen's theory of second language acquisition has been the basis for most current teaching methods. Krashen claims that people acquire a language in a natural order when they receive comprehensible input slightly beyond their current level of proficiency and their affective filter is low. Learned rules can help monitor language output. Schumann's research emphasized that importance of the social context for learning. The social and psychological distances between the speakers of a second language and the target language can affect the rate and degree of language learning.

While there is agreement that young children can acquire a second language, there is debate about whether or not there is a critical period for language acquisition. Neurological, cognitive, and affective factors may affect language acquisition for older children and adults. Most noticeably, older learners often do not speak a second language with nativelike pronunciation. In addition, some aspects of language development may become fossilized.

The debate over whether written language must be learned or can be acquired has also led to different methods of teaching. Teachers with a learning view generally break reading and writing down into component tasks to be taught directly and practiced. Teachers with an acquisition view find ways to make written language comprehensible. They engage students in authentic reading and writing tasks and scaffold instruction following a gradual release of responsibility model.

Current research in linguistics supports an acquisition view, although there is still debate over how much of a language can be acquired and what should be taught. In the following chapters we present relevant aspects of phonology, orthography, morphology, and syntax. Concepts from these areas of linguistics can help inform readers as they decide what their view of language development is and how they can organize instruction to help all their students become proficient users of oral (or signed) and written languages.

APPLICATIONS

1. In this chapter, we distinguish between learning a language and acquiring a language. If you have studied or taught students a second language, evaluate your experience. Was the teaching method used consistent with a learning view or an acquisition view? Write down some reasons for your decision and prepare to discuss these with classmates.

2. Reflect on the writing instruction you have received. Different teachers may have used different approaches. Which view of writing described in this chapter corresponds most closely to each of your experiences? Make some notes on your experiences and bring them to class for discussion.

3. We discussed two views of second language development in this chapter, a learning view and an acquisition view. In the first reproducible that follows we list a number of activities for a classroom with emergent bilingual students. Mark each one as typical of what goes on in a class where the teacher takes a learning view and a class where a teacher takes an acquisition view. Bring your marked form to class to discuss with classmates.

4. We also discussed the two views of literacy that correspond to learning and acquisition views of written language development. In the second reproducible that follows we list a number of classroom activities. Mark each one as typical of what goes on in a class where the teacher takes a learning view and a class where a teacher takes an acquisition view. Bring your marked form to class to discuss with classmates.

Directions:

Label each activity (L) for a learning or (A) for an acquisition view.
Some activities can have both labels.
Be prepared to explain your choices.

The teacher:

_____ teaches grammar points in an orderly sequence.

_____ involves students in role-play of historical events.

_____ provides students who are at different levels of proficiency with options for completing an assignment.

_____ supplements instruction with visuals and realia.

_____ has students practice dialogues.

_____ pronounces minimal pairs (words that sound nearly the same, such as *chair* and *share*) and has students circle the correct answer on a worksheet.

_____ uses gestures to help make input comprehensible.

_____ pairs more and less proficient students during a classroom activity.

_____ has students work in small groups to complete a hands-on science experiment.

_____ corrects students when they make errors in their pronunciation or grammar.

_____ assigns students grammar exercises to complete as homework.

_____ teaches both language and content and writes both language and content objectives.

The students:

_____ repeat a dialogue after the teacher.

_____ work in pairs to complete a Venn diagram comparing and contrasting birds and fish.

_____ point to their hands, their feet, their head as the teacher gives them commands.

_____ complete the basic sentence, "The baby drinks_____," filling in words *milk*, *juice*, and *water* the teacher supplies.

_____ work in pairs to write a summary of a limited-text picture book about whales.

_____ draw the events of a story the teacher has read in sequence.

_____ change the verbs in a paragraph from present tense to past tense.

_____ work together to create a mural of the life and plants in the rain forest.

_____ translate the opening passage of the classic *Don Quixote* into English.

_____ act out a play they have written about the first Thanksgiving.

_____ memorize a list of food words.

Directions:

Label each activity (L) for a learning or (A) for an acquisition view.
Some activities can have both labels.
Be prepared to explain your choices.

The teacher:

____ preteaches vocabulary.

____ does a shared reading with a big book.

____ makes sure that students only read books that fit their level.

____ has students segment words into phonemes.

____ writes words the students dictate for a story and has students help with the spelling of difficult words.

____ asks students to look around the room and find words starting with a certain letter.

____ uses decodable texts.

____ sets aside time for SSR each day.

____ teaches Latin and Greek roots.

____ has students meet in literature circles.

____ conducts phonics drills.

____ chooses predictable texts.

____ teaches students different comprehension strategies.

____ does a picture walk of a new book.

____ uses a variety of worksheets to teach different skills.

The students:

____ look up words in the dictionary to write definitions.

____ make a Venn diagram to compare two stories.

____ practice sounding out words.

____ read in round-robin fashion.

____ correct peers when they make a mistake during reading.

____ identify words on a big book page that start with the same sound.

____ group cards with classmates' names by criteria such as first or last letter.

____ write rhyming poetry and then discuss different spellings for the same sound.

____ ask the teacher how to spell any word they don't know.

____ read a language experience story they have created with the teacher.

____ work in pairs to arrange words from a familiar chant into sentences.

____ divide words into syllables.

____ on a worksheet, draw a line from each word to the picture that starts with the same sound.

____ make alphabet books on different topics.

4 /fɔɹ/

English Phonology

Humans love to communicate. Whether it is face to face, on the phone, by texting, or with sign, people constantly communicate with one another. In fact, with the increasing use of smartphones, it seems that some people never stop talking and tweeting.

- How do people understand and produce language?
- What is phonology, and how do linguists describe the phonology of a language?

In this chapter we focus on oral communication, which most people take for granted. Few people ever stop to think about how they are able to produce and understand language. A commonsense view is that a speaker starts with an idea and encodes it into language. Understanding a message requires the listener to decode the acoustic signal (the sound waves or speech stream) into language to understand the original idea. All this seems to happen effortlessly. Speakers and listeners concentrate on the message, not how they are producing and comprehending ideas. Communication through oral language seems so easy that, for most people, it is almost like breathing. Figure 4.1 represents this commonsense view of how communication takes place.

The Complexities of Communication

Human communication is much more complex than the commonsense view would suggest. Sending and receiving messages involves more than encoding and decoding ideas. Once a person has an idea, he needs to decide which of several ways to communicate it. As Halliday (1994) points out, the context of situation requires a certain register. A register includes the field, so the speaker has to draw upon his knowledge of the topic of conversation and the vocabulary related to that topic. For example, when David takes his car to the shop, he needs to be able to use words

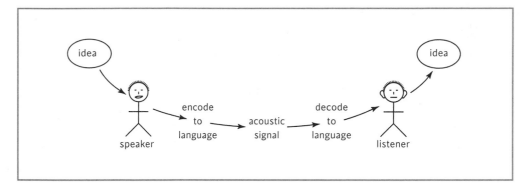

Figure 4.1 *Commonsense view of communication*

such as *cabin filter* or *alignment* to explain what he wants done. These words take on particular meanings in this context.

He also needs to use the proper tenor. He needs to choose words that signal his relationship to the mechanic. If he uses a tone that is too formal, he may be perceived as being condescending and get a cool response from the mechanic. On the other hand, if he is vague and very informal, the mechanic may not understand what needs to be done. Finally, he needs to connect his ideas clearly so that his request is cohesive. This aspect of the register is referred to as the mode.

Speakers signal their meanings by gestures, facial expression, and tone of voice. All of these features help convey the meaning. Even the same words, uttered with a different tone of voice, can signal different meanings. The boyfriend who doesn't notice the difference between "Marry my daughter, will you?" spoken in a threatening tone and the same phrase delivered in a pleading tone is in for a great deal of trouble. The situation and the roles and status of the speaker and listener all affect the meanings of messages.

The listener does much more than simply decode the message. For one thing, listeners predict what they will hear based on the context and then sample the acoustic signal to confirm their predictions. Listening is not a precise process. Otherwise, people would always "hear" exactly what others say. As many long-term couples can attest, listeners sometimes predict based on previous experiences and fail to listen carefully to what their partner is saying. This can lead to serious problems with communication.

The social context helps determine the meaning. Listeners' predictions are often based more on the setting than the acoustic signal. For example, at a store a customer might predict that the clerk will say, "Have a nice day" at the end of the transaction and not listen carefully to the words the clerk actually says. In the same way, teenagers who come home late from a date can predict what their parents will say and may not listen carefully to their parents' words.

One feature of language that aids listeners is that natural language includes a great deal of redundancy. Listeners get more than one clue. In the statement "She studied at her friend's house yesterday" both *she* and *her* indicate that the person referred to is female. In addition, the past tense *-ed* in *studied* and the adverb *yesterday* both indicate that the action was in the past. These redundant features of language help listeners make sense of messages.

Listeners need to make inferences to fill in information not included in the message. Making inferences depends a great deal on background knowledge. When the speaker and listener have shared knowledge, communication is more successful because the listener can fill in the gaps in the communication more easily. David often has to fill in gaps when Yvonne jumps from one topic to another. Because they have been married for many years, they have shared knowledge, so David can usually follow her non sequitur jumps. Often, people learning an additional language have background knowledge that is different from that of native speakers, and this makes it difficult for them to make inferences. For example, if the speaker refers to a kitchen, the listener's knowledge of what is in a typical kitchen may differ from that of the speaker, and this may cause a breakdown in the communication. A kitchen in New York City is very different from a kitchen in rural Cambodia.

Linguistic analyses of communication

Linguists have developed complex models to describe human communication. *Speech Acts Theory* (Bach and Harnish 1979) attempts to account for the different factors involved in communication. For example, successful communication depends on speakers and listeners sharing knowledge of references. If a speaker refers to the Pentagon, he or she will assume that the listener knows that the reference is to a particular building in Washington, D.C. The speaker and listener may also share common feelings about people or places that are mentioned. Some may see the Pentagon as a place that offers the country protection while others see it as a place where war is promoted.

Listeners have to decide on which meaning of a word fits the context of the communication. *Polysemy* is the term linguists use to refer to words with more than one meaning. Emergent bilinguals whose vocabulary is still developing may know only one meaning of a word and might become confused when that meaning does not fit. For example, they would probably know that *fork* refers to an eating utensil and then be confused if someone says, "There's a fork in the road." Native speakers are seldom aware of the amount of ambiguity in language because they automatically choose the meaning that fits the context without considering other possible meanings of a word. If someone is going to the bank, the context determines whether they are going to a building or the edge of a river.

In addition, listeners have to decide if an utterance is literal or nonliteral. In most cases, this is obvious. If someone says, "I have a frog in my throat," she assumes that she will not be taken literally. There are times, though, when nonnative speakers take statements literally and become confused. For example, it is hard for a person just learning English to realize that the words they hear don't help them understand the meaning when people say things like "The teacher had a cow when the student came in late" or "Don't worry, he is just pulling your leg!"

Mary, a high school teacher working with emergent bilinguals, developed a good activity for her students. She knew that they had difficulty with idioms. She had them take an idiom from a list of traditional idioms, draw a picture of the literal meaning, and then write the nonliteral or intended meaning. One student, for example, chose the idiom "He killed two birds with one stone." She drew a picture of two birds in a tree and a boy shooting a stone at them with a slingshot. Then she wrote the nonliteral meaning, "accomplishing two things with one action." Another student drew a girl with blue skin for the idiom "feeling blue." She explained that it really means "feeling sad, down, or depressed." This activity helped Mary's emergent bilinguals to better understand that not everything that native English speakers say should be taken literally.

Parish has written an amusing series of children's books whose main character, Amelia Bedelia, is a nonnative speaker of English. Amelia has difficulty making inferences, and she takes everything literally. Amelia works as a maid for a family. When the husband tells her to "go fly a kite" she does just that. When she reads a recipe that says the bread will rise, she watches the pan carefully to see if it will lift off the counter. She also has trouble with ambiguity. When she is told to plant the *bulbs*, she plants light bulbs. Fortunately, Amelia always redeems herself with her wonderful cooking. What makes this series of books so amusing is that the kinds of communication breakdowns that occur are quite rare. Most listeners know whether to interpret a message literally or nonliterally. However, emergent bilinguals like Amelia sometimes do not realize that certain expressions carry nonliteral meanings.

Listeners have to decide whether a remark has a direct or an indirect meaning. Again, this is a real challenge for someone learning a new language. For example, "Is there any salt on the table?" is not simply a question. It is also an indirect request to pass the salt. If a listener treats this simply as a question and answers, "Yes, the salt is right in front of me," communication will break down. Many comments have indirect meanings. "The garbage is full" or "The potatoes are boiling over" are more than simple reports; they are indirect requests for the listener to do something.

Oral communication is more complex than most people assume. An analysis of the process shows that it involves much more than encoding ideas into language, transmitting the language, and decoding the sounds into ideas. Speakers use gestures, facial expression, tone of voice, and the redundancy in language, among other things, to convey a message. Listeners predict what they will hear and assume that it will fit the context. They sample the acoustic signal to confirm their predictions. Since not all information is included in a message, listeners must also make inferences. Successful communication depends on shared knowledge of references. Further, listeners must decide which meaning of a polysemous word fits the context and whether to interpret the speech literally or nonliterally, directly or indirectly. Even though the process is complex, most humans use language to communicate effectively each day.

Grice's cooperative principle

One reason that conversations generally succeed is that speakers and listeners share a set of assumptions about how to carry on a conversation. H. P. Grice, a philosopher of language, has proposed four maxims that govern communication (1989). These maxims constitute part of the pragmatics of communication. *Pragmatics* is the branch of linguistics that deals with norms of conversation. Grice suggests that there is a cooperative principle that listeners and speakers follow, and he summarizes this principle with these maxims:

1. **Maxim of Quality:** Truth
   Do not say what you believe to be false.
   Do not say that for which you lack adequate evidence.

2. **Maxim of Quantity:** Information
   Make your contribution as informative as is required for the current purposes of the exchange.
   Do not make your contribution more informative than is required.

3. **Maxim of Relation:** Relevance
   Be relevant.

4. **Maxim of Manner:** Clarity
   Avoid obscurity of expression.

Avoid ambiguity.

Be brief (avoid unnecessary prolixity).

Be orderly.

These four maxims constitute the underlying assumptions we make as we converse with others. When someone violates one of these by giving us information that is not accurate, giving too much information, being vague or irrelevant, or not being clear, the conversation is not successful.

Why use sound to communicate?

Humans are social beings who seem driven to communicate. Deaf people develop the ability to communicate with gestures. Hearing people use sounds. Why did sounds, rather than visual signals, develop as the means of communication for hearing individuals? There are several practical reasons: In the first place, if people use sounds to express and receive ideas, their hands are free for other tasks. Thus, they can talk while they work. In addition, sound travels around corners, so a wife in one room can tell her husband in another room that he should take out the garbage. Sound also works much better than gestures in the dark. For humans, then, communication in face-to-face situations using sounds has many practical advantages over other means of exchanging messages.

Humans use sounds to communicate even though using sound means changing the way people breathe and eat. Akmajian and colleagues (1979) point out that "The rhythm of respiration during speech is radically different from the rhythm of respiration during normal breathing" (72). To speak, a person must control the outflow of air. For that reason, rather than breathing in and out in a normal pattern, during speech a person extends the period of exhalation. "One of the greatest distortions of the breathing rate occurs during speech: breath is drawn in rapidly and let out over a much longer period than during normal breathing" (72). People do this without any conscious awareness unless they are trying to talk while exerting themselves during exercise. Humans seem to naturally adjust their breathing to accommodate speech.

Young babies can nurse and breathe at the same time. If adults try to drink and breathe simultaneously, though, they begin to choke. That is because at birth the larynx is higher so that the passage for food and the passage for air are clearly separated. A baby can breathe through the nose while taking in milk through the mouth. Once the larynx drops down, there is the possibility of food or drink going into the lungs rather than the stomach. Why would humans develop in a way that makes choking possible? The reason seems to be that once the larynx drops down, there is more room in the oral cavity for humans to produce sounds. In other words, the development of a greater capacity for speech outweighs the dangers of food or drink going into the lungs.

Even though hearing individuals use sounds to communicate, as the research by Petitto shows, the biologically innate features that facilitate communication among humans is not tied to sounds. Instead, Petitto (2003) has argued that "humans are born with a sensitivity to particular distributional, rhythmical, and temporal patterns unique to aspects of natural language structure" (1). Both sign and speech are instances of natural language that contain these patterns.

The complexity of sound production

Speech production is sufficiently complex that most researchers agree that it is an acquired capacity. During normal communication, humans produce an average of eight *phonemes* (distinctive, meaningful sounds) per second (Akmajian, Demers, and Harnish 1979). Speakers are able to maintain this rate of production over a long period of time without fatigue. Phoneme production involves the brain in sending signals to the lungs, vocal cords, tongue, and lips to contract or relax the muscles.

Even the production of a single phoneme can be complex. For example, in producing a word like *construe* a speaker starts to round the lips to make the sound represented by "ue" even before starting the "str" sequence. Some messages from the brain have to travel further than others to the muscles that control speech. At the same time, some nerve bundles transmit messages more rapidly than others because they are thicker. For that reason, the command to round the lips is sent out earlier than the command to start the "str" sequence so that when it is time to produce the "ue" sound, the lips will be ready. In other words, "the lip rounding in the last vowel in *construe* arrives three phonemes early" (Akmajian, Demers, and Harnish 1979, 74).

The details of this complex operation are not important here. What is important is that the messages the brain sends out to the muscles that control speech are so complicated that they must be acquired. Akmajian and colleagues sum up this point: "These features of speech are complex and automatic physical gestures which cannot be learned, but are among the biologically innate features that facilitate the acquisition of speech by the human species" (1979, 74).

How Linguists Study Phonology

Linguists study phonology in the same way that they study other aspects of language. They take a scientific approach and describe the process of producing meaningful sounds. Linguists do not insist on "correct" pronunciation. The role of the linguist is to describe a language, not to prescribe how people should use it.

The process of describing a language includes a series of four steps.

1. Break the speech stream into discrete units (phonemes).
2. Categorize the units.
3. Group the units.
4. Find dependencies among the units.

In the following sections, we describe each of these steps.

1. Break the speech stream into discrete units

Dividing the speech stream into discrete units is not an easy task. When you listen to someone speaking a language you don't understand, it is a challenge to determine where one word stops and the next one starts. It is even more difficult to decide how many sounds there are in a word. Linguists studying a new language may take months to analyze speech samples to discover the meaningful sounds speakers of that language use to communicate.

To determine whether a sound functions as a phoneme in a language, a linguist tries to find two words that differ by just one sound. For example, in English, *pet* and *bet* are words that signify different meanings, The only difference in sound is the difference between the "p" sound in *pet* and the "b" sound in *bet*, so a linguist might hypothesize that "p" and "b" are two phonemes in English. The linguist would then look for other pairs of words like *tap* and *tab* to confirm the hypothesis that "p" and "b" are phonemes of English. These words are referred to as a *minimal pair* because they differ by just one phoneme. The presence of a minimal pair is evidence that two sounds function as phonemes in a language.

Phonetics is the study of sounds across languages. Many linguists use the *International Phonetic Alphabet* (IPA) to describe sounds and sound systems. This alphabet has symbols to represent all the sounds that have been found in human languages. Phonology is the study of the sounds used by speakers of a particular language. A phoneme is the smallest sound that makes a difference in meaning within a given language. Different languages use different sets of phonemes to communicate ideas. English has about forty phonemes while Spanish has about twenty-three. The exact number of phonemes varies depending on regional variations.

No language has a writing system that uniquely represents each sound in that language. That is, no alphabet has a one-to-one correspondence between sounds and letters. Instead, one letter may represent different sounds, and one sound may be represented by different letters or letter sequences. In English, for example, the same sound is represented by the *c* in *cat* and the *k* in *kite*. On the other hand, the letters *ea* have different sounds in *tea, bread, steak,* and *idea.* Linguists wishing to study the sound system of a language need a more consistent method to record the sounds than an alphabet provides. For that reason, they use phonemic transcription.

In *phonemic transcription,* each phoneme is represented by one and only one written mark. Phonemic transcription makes use of many of the letters of the alphabet, but uses them in a consistent way. For instance, the first sound of *cat* or *kite* is transcribed /k/. Phonemes are indicated by placing the character between slash marks. To show the first phoneme in *pet,* a linguist would write /p/. In the discussion that follows, it is important to be clear about whether we are referring to letters, words, or phonemes. We will use italics to indicate letters and individual words, and slash marks to set off characters that represent phonemes. For example, we might write that the sound represented by *b* in a word like *blue* is transcribed as /b/.

The number of phonemes is not the same as the number of letters. For example, a linguist would transcribe the seven-letter word *stripped* with five phonemes, /strɪpt/. In this word there is only one /p/ sound even though it is spelled with two *p*'s, so linguists simply write /p/ to represent the sound. In addition, the *-ed* spelling only represents one sound, /t/, so linguists use one phoneme for this sound.

A linguist could also show more details in the pronunciation of a sound by using *phonetic transcription.* The first sound in *pet* could be written as [pʰ]. Phonetic transcription is written within square brackets. The small raised *h* represents a puff of air that speakers of English produce as they make the /p/ sound at the beginning of a word. This feature, aspiration, is phonetic, not phonemic, because in English aspiration is never used to signal a change in meaning. There are not two words that have different meanings because one has [p] and the other has [pʰ]. Other languages, such as Korean, use aspiration to show meaning differences between words that are otherwise alike in sound. So in Korean /p/ and /pʰ/ are two phonemes.

The study of the sound qualities of speech sounds is called *acoustic phonetics,* and the study of how speech sounds are produced physically is called *articulatory phonetics.* Even though phonemes have physical properties that can be studied (acoustic waves), a phoneme is a perceptual unit, not a physical entity. Phonemes actually differ in their physical production depending on the other sounds around them. For example, although the /p/ in *pet* is aspirated, the /p/ in *sip* is not. Listeners ignore this physical difference between these two speech sounds and perceive both sounds as the phoneme /p/. The phonemes of a language don't sound the same each time they are produced, but all the variations are perceived as instances of the same sound by speakers of a language. That is why linguists claim that phonemes are perceptual, not physical units.

2. Categorize the units

The second step in describing the sound system of a language is to categorize the units. For phonology, linguists categorize the phonemes. In order to categorize the phonemes, linguists describe phonemes by telling where and how they are produced. Each phoneme has unique articulatory properties. For example, /p/ is produced by stopping the air with the lips. The place of articulation is referred to as *bilabial* (the two lips), and the manner of articulation is called a *stop*, since the air is completely stopped for a moment and then released to make the sound. During the production of this sound, the vocal cords do not vibrate, so this type of sound is called *voiceless* or *unvoiced*.

Each phoneme can be described by its place and manner of articulation and whether or not it is voiced. Thus, /p/ is a voiceless bilabial stop.

The physiology of speech

To understand how phonemes are categorized, it is important to have a clear picture of the process of producing sounds. The speech sounds of English and other languages are created by changes in the vocal tract, the area between the vocal cords and the lips. Figure 4.2 shows the key physical features involved in speech production. As air comes up from the lungs, it

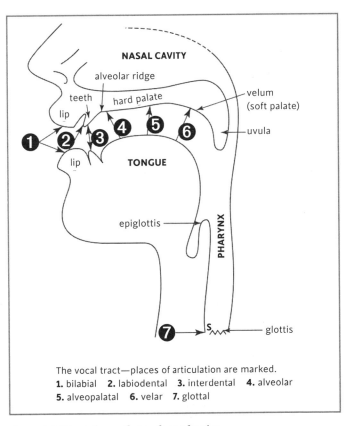

The vocal tract—places of articulation are marked.
1. bilabial   **2.** labiodental   **3.** interdental   **4.** alveolar
5. alveopalatal   **6.** velar   **7.** glottal

Figure 4.2 *Physiology of speech production*

passes through a narrow area, the glottal region, which contains the vocal cords. These are elastic bands of tissue located in the larynx. They can be brought close together so that the air passing through causes them to vibrate. This results in what is referred to as *voicing*. Or they can be held apart so no voicing occurs.

After the air passes through the vocal cords, it continues up through the pharynx into the oral cavity. If the flow of air is not constricted, a vowel sound is produced. Different vowel sounds result from movements of the tongue and lips. These change the shape of the oral cavity so that different sounds are produced. For all vowels, the air flows freely through the oral cavity and the vocal cords vibrate, so all vowels are voiced.

Consonant sounds are formed when the air is constricted as it moves toward the lips. This constriction can involve simply slowing the air down, stopping it completely, or a combination of slowing and stopping. The different consonant sounds also depend on where the air is slowed or stopped. For English consonant sounds, the air may be constricted at the lips, the teeth, the alveolar ridge (the hard ridge behind the upper front teeth), the hard palate, the soft palate or velum, and the glottis. Air can be constricted in the oral cavity and also pass through the nasal cavity if the velum is lowered. In the following sections, we describe the different categories of the vowel and consonant phonemes of English.

English vowels

English has a complex system of vowels consisting of short, long, and *reduced vowels*. The short vowels are also called *lax vowels*, and the long vowels are called *tense vowels*. These terms reflect the relative tension of the muscles in the tongue, cheeks, and lips as the sounds are produced. Reduced vowels occur in unstressed syllables. All vowels in English are voiced. The vibration from the vocal cords provides the energy needed for a vowel sound. Different vowels are formed by changing the shape of the vocal tract as the vibrating air molecules pass from the vocal cords toward the lips.

Vowels vary considerably across dialects, and the exact number of vowel phonemes varies as well. For example, some people pronounce *cot* and *caught* with two different vowel sounds. For others, these words are pronounced the same. Speakers who pronounce *cot* and *caught* differently produce different phonemes, while other people only produce one. In our description of vowel sounds, we have chosen to present the phonemes common to most dialects of American English. Also, while we have used characters that are consistent with those in the International Phonetic Alphabet, that system has some variations for different dialects of English, and we have attempted to follow the representations most commonly used for American English.

Short vowels

There are nine short-vowel sounds. English spelling usually represents each of these short sounds with just one letter. Figure 4.3 shows where the short vowels are produced. The figure represents the areas of the mouth if a person were facing to the left (see Figure 4.2). For example, /ɪ/ is made in the front of the mouth high up. What does that mean, though? Although there is considerable variation among speakers, and although the placement of a vowel depends on the other sounds in the word, in general this vowel is produced by moving the tongue toward the front of the mouth and raising the tip of the tongue up toward the roof of the mouth. In a word like *sit*, this is the movement of the tongue for the vowel. For each vowel phoneme, we include a word in parentheses that contains that vowel sound.

	front	central	back
high	ɪ (pit)		ʊ (put)
	i (peat)		u (boot)
mid	ɛ (pet)	ʌ (putt)	ɔ (bought)
low	æ (pat)		ɑ (pot)

Figure 4.3 *Short vowels of English*

A good way to feel the differences among these vowels is to say the words on the chart in sequence from high front to low back: *pit, peat, pet, pat, putt, put, boot, bought, pot*. In the first four words the tongue moves toward the front of the mouth, and the vowel sound is made by moving the tongue slightly lower for each phoneme. In producing *peat* the tongue glides up and toward the front of the mouth. For *pat* most speakers open their jaw slightly to make this lower vowel sound. The word *putt* is produced with the tongue in the middle of the mouth. For *put* the tongue moves slightly up and back. *Boot* is produced in nearly the same position but with more rounding of the lips, which has the effect of lengthening the vocal tract. *Bought* is produced in the mid back area. The last word, *pot*, is produced with the tongue low and back.

Many native speakers of English have difficulty in feeling these variations in tongue position. They produce these phonemes effortlessly without conscious awareness of the tongue movements. It may help to make these sounds in front of a mirror to try and observe where the tongue is for each sound. English language learners often have difficulty distinguishing between words that differ by just one of these vowel phonemes. However, during normal conversation, they can usually rely on context cues to determine the meaning.

Long vowels

There are five long vowels of English. As each long vowel is produced, the tongue moves from one part of the mouth to another. These vowels are also called *diphthongs* from Greek roots meaning "two sounds" because the sound quality changes as each long vowel is produced. The long vowels are indicated with two characters in the IPA transcription system and are usually spelled with two letters as well. The first IPA character indicates the tongue position at the beginning of the sound, and the second shows the direction that the tongue moves. The tongue glides up and toward the palate for vowels represented with an /ɪ/ and up and toward the velum for those with a /ʊ/ (see Figure 4.2 for the parts of the mouth). Figure 4.4 shows where the long vowels of English are produced. Again, the vowels are placed as though the figure were a mouth with the front of the mouth to the left.

	front	central	back
high			
mid	eɪ (bait)		oʊ, ɔɪ (boat, boy)
low			aɪ, aʊ (bite, bout)

Figure 4.4 *Long vowels of English*

The long-vowel phonemes are present in the words *bait, boat, boy, bite,* and *bout.* The tongue starts toward the front and moves slightly up for *bait.* The tongue starts in the middle back area and moves up toward the front for *boy.* To produce the vowel in *boat* the tongue starts in the middle back area and moves up toward the roof of the mouth in the back. It starts down low in the back for *bite* and then moves up toward the front as the vowel is produced. For *bout,* it also starts low in the back, but then it moves up toward the back.

Reduced vowel and vowels preceding /ɹ/

English has one reduced vowel, the *schwa* /ə/. The character that represents the schwa is an inverted *e* and is written as /ə/. This vowel is produced with a weaker airflow, so the syllable where it appears does not receive stress. Reduced syllables occur in words with two or more syllables. For example, in the first syllable of *about* the vowel sound is unstressed. This is the same sound that occurs in a one-syllable word like *putt.* The difference is that in *putt* the vowel is stressed, but in *about* it is not. The two phonemes /ə/ and /ʌ/ are both mid, central vowels. The only difference is in the stress. The schwa sound occurs frequently in English. It is the sound many English speakers make when they are trying to think of something to say. The mouth is relaxed, and the tongue is in a neutral position.

Generally, it is possible to determine which syllable in a polysyllabic word is unstressed. A good way to do this is to overemphasize one syllable at a time to see which one seems most natural. For example, in *imagination* there are five syllables, i-mag-i-na-tion. When you strongly stress one syllable each time you say the word, you can tell (if you are a native speaker) that the second and fourth syllables (mag) and (na) get the strongest stress and the first syllable gets a secondary stress. The stressed syllables here are also lengthened. The other syllables are reduced. When transcribing the word, then, the reduced syllables would be represented with a schwa. Here is a transcription of *imagination*: /ɪ m æ ʤ ə n ɛɪ ʃ ə n/. Note that only short vowels are reduced, not long vowels.

Vowels take on a different quality when they are followed by *r*. For this reason, children (and adults) often have trouble in spelling words with a vowel followed by *r* (the *r*-controlled vowels). The character used to represent the *r* sound in English is an inverted *r* (/ɹ/). To make this sound, a speaker curls the tongue up toward the middle of the mouth, but the tongue does not touch the palate. As the speaker produces a preceding vowel, she is already beginning to move the tongue into the position for the /ɹ/. This movement is what changes the sound of the vowel. Figure 4.5 shows how vowels preceding /ɹ/ should be transcribed.

The vowel sound in *winner* is represented by a character that we have not discussed before. If we include /ɚ/ as a separate phoneme, then there are sixteen vowel phonemes in American English. The other examples in Figure 4.5 can be seen as variant pronunciations of vowels that occur before /ɹ/.

Educators who understand the complexity of the English vowel system can better appreciate the difficulty children have as they attempt to represent these sounds as they write. Since there are about sixteen sounds, American English spelling uses various combinations of the available letters to represent them. In addition, emergent bilinguals often have difficulty learn-

phoneme	example
ɑɹ	arm (short vowel)
ɔɹ	four (short vowel)
ɚ	winner (short vowel)
ɪɹ	near (long vowel)
ɛɹ	hair (long vowel)
ʊɹ	tour (long vowel)

Figure 4.5 *Vowels before /ɹ/*

ing the vowel sounds of English. Spanish and Japanese, for example, only have five vowel phonemes, and none of them corresponds exactly to an English vowel. An understanding of the vowel phonemes of English can be helpful for educators working with emergent bilinguals. This knowledge constitutes an important part of their pedagogical language knowledge.

English consonant phonemes

Consonant phonemes are produced by restricting or stopping the flow of air as it passes through the vocal tract. Consonants can best be described by telling where and how the air is constricted and by noting whether the sound is voiced or voiceless. Consonants generally appear in matched pairs, one voiced and the other voiceless. Figure 4.6 shows the consonant phonemes of English. The place of articulation is indicated along the top of the chart, and the manner of articulation is shown down the left side.

Notice that for the most part, the characters used to represent the consonant phonemes are the same as the letters used to spell words in English. Only a few of the consonant phoneme characters are different from the letters used in English spelling.

The two interdental fricatives /θ/ and /ð/ are represented in English spelling by the digraph *th*. These symbols are the Greek letter *theta* and the Old English *eth*. They occur in the words *breath* and *breathe*. It may be difficult to hear the difference between the two sounds. The *eth* occurs in articles (*the*), pronouns (*their*), and some other function words while the *theta* appears in nouns (*thing*), verbs (*thank*, *throw*), adjectives (*thin*), and adverbs (*thoughtlessly*).

The two alveopalatal fricatives /ʃ/ and /ʒ/ represent the sounds usually spelled with *sh* and *ti*. In a word like *shirt* the first sound is /ʃ/, and in *flash* it is the last

		bilabial	labiodental	interdental	alveolar	alveopalatal	palatal	velar	glottal
stops	voiceless	p			t			k	
	voiced	b			d			g	
nasals	voiced	m			n			ŋ	
fricatives	voiceless		f	θ	s	ʃ			h
	voiced		v	ð	z	ʒ			
affricates	voiceless					tʃ			
	voiced					ʤ			
approximants	voiced				ɹ, l				
glides (semivowels)	voiced						j	w	

Figure 4.6 *English consonants*

sound. In *nation* the phoneme is spelled with *ti*. The /ʒ/ occurs less frequently. It is the sound of the *si* in *fusion*, the *su* in *casual*, and the *ge* in *beige*. These two alveopalatal fricatives combine with a stop to produce the affricates /tʃ/ and /dʒ/. The voiceless affricate /tʃ/ is the sound that occurs at the beginning and end of *church*, while the voiced affricate /dʒ/ is the sound at the beginning and end of *judge*.

Another phoneme that is represented by a character that is not part of the Roman alphabet is /ŋ/. This is a sound that is usually spelled *ng*, and the character looks like an *n* and a *g* combined. The sound occurs only at the end of syllables, such as in the word *sing*.

The American English sound usually spelled with *r* or *rr* is represented by an inverted *r*, /ɹ/. The /j/ represents the sound usually spelled with a *y* in English as in *yes*. It is a letter from the Roman alphabet, but it does not represent the same sound as the *j* spelling represents. That sound, as mentioned earlier, is represented by /dʒ/.

The nine characters that do not use the usual Roman alphabet letters to represent English sounds are shown in Figure 4.7. All of these except the /ɹ/ are usually spelled with two or three letters.

Several of the spellings of these phonemes are digraphs. Digraphs are two letters used to indicate one sound. Since there is only one sound in each case, linguists represent the sound as a single phoneme. Digraphs differ from blends such as *pr* or *st*. In blends, two letters are used to represent two dif-

Phoneme	Typical spelling	
ʃ	sh	shirt, flash
ʒ	si, su, ge	fusion, casual, beige
θ	th	thin, thank
ð	th	this, then
tʃ	ch, tch	beach, watch
ŋ	ng	ring
dʒ	j, dg	judge
ɹ	r, rr	run, herring
j	y	yes

Figure 4.7 *International Phonetic Alphabet characters*

ferent phonemes. When pronounced, each of these phonemes maintains its sound. For example, a word like *blend* is transcribed as /blɛnd/. The two consonant phonemes at the beginning and at the end are both pronounced and are represented by separate phonemes. In contrast, a word like *choice* contains a digraph, not blends. It is transcribed as /tʃɔɪs/ because the *ch* represents the first phoneme. Digraphs are also used to spell long-vowel sounds (diphthongs) as well. In *choice* the *oi* is a digraph, and it is transcribed as /ɔɪ/. The term *diphthong* refers to a sound, and *digraph* and *blend* refer to spellings.

Stops

Figure 4.8 lists the stop consonants in English. We list both the oral stops and the nasals. In the case of the nasals, the air is stopped in the oral cavity but released through the nose. We will refer to the oral stops as *stops* and the nasal stops as *nasals*.

There are three pairs of oral stops. Oral stop phonemes are formed by completely blocking the air for an instant and then releasing it. The first two stops, /p/ and /b/, are formed by stopping the air by closing the lips. Thus, they are called *bi* (two) *labials* (lips). These are the sounds at the beginning and end of *pop* and *bib*. Bilabials are some of the first sounds babies produce, so that is why parents and grandparents, in many languages, are called by words starting with /p/, /b/, or /m/, as in *papa*, *mama*, or *papou* (in Greek). Note that these names often contain the low, back vowel /ɑ/, which is one of the first vowels children produce.

The only difference between /p/ and /b/ is in voicing. English uses voicing to distinguish these sounds, and English speakers attend to this meaningful clue. In some other languages, such as certain dialects of Arabic, these two bilabial stops are simply two ways of producing one phoneme, so speakers of those languages do not pay attention to the voicing difference since it doesn't signal a change in meaning. Arabic speakers learning English, then, might have trouble hearing the difference between words like *pig* and *big* if they are presented the words in isolation. Of course, context clues would prevent them from getting these two words confused during normal communication.

The next two stops are /t/ and /d/. These phonemes are present at the beginning and end of words like *tot* and *dad*. The sounds are made by placing the blade of the tongue behind the upper front teeth along the alveolar ridge to block the air for a moment. Many of the consonants of English are produced in the alveolar

		bilabial	labiodental	interdental	alveolar	alveopalatal	velar	glottal
stops	voiceless	p			t		k	
	voiced	b			d		g	
nasals	voiced	m			n		ŋ	

Figure 4.8 *Stops*

region. In other languages, like Spanish or Japanese, these sounds are produced by placing the tip of the tongue against the back of the front teeth to form a dental stop. For that reason, the /t/ or /d/ phonemes sound slightly different in Spanish and Japanese than they do in English.

The last pair of oral stops, /k/ and /g/, is formed by raising the blade of the tongue up against the velar region in the back of the mouth to temporarily block the air. These phonemes occur at the beginning and end of words like *kick* and *gig*. The three pairs of stops are set apart in the vocal tract. One is made with the lips at the front of the mouth, one in the middle, and the other at the very back. This physical separation helps listeners distinguish the stops from one another.

English has three nasal consonants: /m/, /n/, and /ŋ/. The first two have the sounds of the letters *m* and *n* in words like *Mom* or *Nan*. The last one has the sound of *ng* in *ring*. This sound only occurs at the end of syllables in English, never at the beginning.

English nasals are voiced. They are produced by stopping the air in the oral cavity and lowering the velum so that the airflow can pass through the nasal cavity. The phoneme /m/ is produced by blocking the air with the lips, the /n/ by stopping the air at the alveolar ridge, and the /ŋ/ by blocking off the velar area. Thus, these three nasals are produced in the same places as the stops /b/, /d/, and /g/. This can be shown by making the sound of /m/, stopping the air from going out of the nose, and then opening the mouth. The result should sound like a /b/. The relationship between stops and nasals is also noticeable when a person has a cold. Then an /n/ comes out sounding like a /d/ because air can't flow smoothly through the nasal cavity, and *band* and *bad* may sound alike.

Fricatives

The fricatives for American English are shown in Figure 4.9.

		bilabial	labiodental	interdental	alveolar	alveopalatal	velar	glottal
fricatives	voiceless		f	θ	s	ʃ		h
	voiced		v	ð	z	ʒ		

Figure 4.9 *Fricatives*

Fricatives are produced by constricting the airflow through the vocal tract. The resulting friction sets the air molecules in motion as they pass through the narrow opening and produce a sound. The fricatives also come in voiceless and voiced pairs except for /h/. There are nine fricatives in English.

The labiodental (lips + teeth) pair /f/ and /v/ are made by pressing the upper teeth on the lower lip. This slows the air and produces a sound heard at the beginning and end of *fluff* and *verve*. The interdental (between the teeth) fricatives /θ/ and /ð/ are made by putting the blade of the tongue between the teeth and pressing up and forcing air across the tongue through the opening. Since people have different spaces between their teeth, the tongue can be used to produce a similar sound for people with quite different tooth gaps. The difference in sound between these two phonemes is more difficult to hear than some of the others, but it is evident in pairs like *thigh* /θ/ and *thy* /ð/. Words like *with* can be pronounced using either sound depending on the speaker's dialect and on the sound that follows. These phonemes can also occur at either the beginning of words or the end as shown in *thin* and *bath* /θ/ and *then* and *bathe* /ð/.

The phonemes /s/ and /z/ are made by putting the blade of the tongue just below the alveolar ridge, as in producing /t/ or /d/, but unlike the stops, lowering the tip of the tongue enough to let some air go through and cause turbulence. These phonemes occur at the beginning of words like *sip* and *zip* and the end of words like *kiss* and *fuzz*. It is easy to hear the difference in voicing in this pair. The vocal cords vibrate during /z/ but not in making an /s/. One way to detect voicing in more difficult cases is to block the ears while making the sound. That makes the vibration of the vocal cords easier to perceive.

The next two sounds /ʃ/ and /ʒ/ are produced by flattening the tongue along the roof of the mouth in the alveopalatal area. The /ʃ/ phoneme occurs at the beginning or end of words, such as *ship* or *dish*, but the /ʒ/ is less common. Speakers of some dialects pronounce this sound at the end of a word borrowed from French like *beige* or *rouge*. Most commonly, /ʒ/ occurs in words like *confusion* where it is represented by *si* in spelling.

The /h/ phoneme is a special case. It is produced by slowing the air as it passes through the glottal area. In a word like *hop*, the /h/ can be felt in the throat, causing some vibration before the onset of the vowel sound. The /h/ sound is voiceless.

Affricates

The two affricates in American English are shown in Figure 4.10.

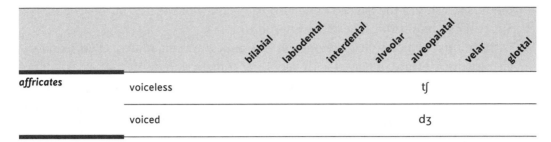

		bilabial	labiodental	interdental	alveolar	alveopalatal	velar	glottal
affricates	voiceless					tʃ		
	voiced					dʒ		

Figure 4.10 *Affricates*

Affricates are formed by briefly stopping the air and then releasing it with some friction. Thus, affricates are a combination of a stop and a fricative. English has two affricates, /tʃ/ and /dʒ/. The /tʃ/ is a combination of /t/ and /ʃ/ while the /dʒ/ combines /d/ with /ʒ/. The /tʃ/ can be heard at the beginning and end of *church*, and the /dʒ/ occurs at the beginning and end of *judge*. English spelling reflects the combined sounds in affricates by spelling some words that end in /tʃ/ with *tch* as in *watch* and /dʒ/ with *dge* as in *badge*. However, English words do not begin with *tch* or *dge*, and this is something that children learning to spell need to figure out.

Approximants and glides

Figure 4.11 lists English approximants and glides.

There are two approximants, /l/ and /ɹ/. The sounds of these phonemes are those that occur at the beginning and end of *lull* and *roar*. To form the /l/, a speaker

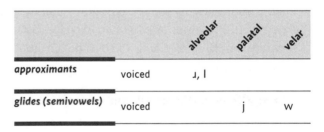

		alveolar	palatal	velar
approximants	voiced	ɹ, l		
glides (semivowels)	voiced		j	w

Figure 4.11 *English consonants*

places the tip of the tongue against the alveolar ridge and lowers one side of the tongue to let the air pass through on that side. Since the air passes on one side, the /l/ is referred to as a lateral approximant. It is possible to tell which side of the tongue a person lowers by making the kind of clicking sound used to signal a horse. Most speakers can make that click best on one side, and that is the side the speaker also lowers to produce an /l/.

The American English /ɹ/ is produced by curling the tongue tip up and back slightly. The tongue does not touch another part of the mouth, but raising and curling the tongue changes the shape of the oral cavity. Many other languages make the *r* sound by flapping or tapping the tongue against the back of the front teeth. Spanish has the flapped *r* and also has a trilled or rolled *r*, but neither of the Spanish *r* sounds is the same as the English /ɹ/.

The final two consonant phonemes, the glides, are sometimes called semivowels because they are produced with very little constriction of the air passage, more like a vowel. These two phonemes are the /j/ sound at the beginning of *yes* and the /w/ that occurs at the start of *wet*. These glides only occur at the beginning of syllables in English or as part of a blend like *beauty* /bjuti/ or *swing* /swɪŋ/. The /j/ is produced by moving the tongue up toward the alveopalatal region, and for the /w/, the tongue moves up and back toward the velar region while rounding the lips.

In all, American English has twenty-four consonant phonemes: nine stops, nine fricatives, two affricates, two approximants, and two glides. The twenty-four consonant phonemes, together with the sixteen vowel phonemes, make forty phonemes for American English. Speakers of English acquire the ability to produce and understand these sounds early in life. Some of the phonemes, the bilabials, and the low back vowel, are acquired early, and others, such as the /ɹ/, come later. However, by the time they reach school, most native English-speaking children have good control over the complex phonological system of English. Teachers of young children sometimes worry that their students don't yet "have their sounds," but this concern usually reflects an inability to do classroom exercises that require students to identify or produce certain sounds as part of an exercise. Often, young children simply don't understand what they are being asked to do. On the other hand, observation of children in natural communicative situations generally reveals that they do "have their sounds."

Phonetic variations: Allophones

Phonemes are sounds that make a difference in meaning. Phonemes, however, are not always pronounced in the same way. They undergo changes in pronunciation depending on their position in words and the other sounds around them. Nevertheless, we perceive all of these variations as the same phoneme.

Allophones of /k/, a case of assimilation

Each phoneme in English or any other language is actually a group of sounds, called *phones*. The phones that make up one phoneme are called its *allophones*. The particular allophone that a speaker produces depends on the preceding or following sound. Phones of a phoneme are written in square brackets.

For example, when English speakers say, "Keep cool," they produce two allophones of /k/, one at the beginning of each word. We invite readers to say, "Keep cool," and to notice exactly where the tongue hits the velum in each word. Most speakers will notice that the point of contact is further forward for *keep* than for *cool*. Thus, the /k/ phoneme is produced at a slightly different place in the mouth for each allophone of this phoneme. Linguists represent the fronted allophone of /k/ in *keep* as [k⁺] and the back allophone in *cool* as [k⁻]. There is also a neutral allophone that is simply written as [k]. Adults are good at ignoring these physical differences because what matters is that this is an occurrence of /k/. The first word is *keep* not *beep* or *seep*.

These allophones of /k/ are the result of a general process in language called *assimilation*. Phonemes assimilate to neighboring sounds. Just as immigrants may change some habits to become more like the people in their new country, phonemes become similar to the phonemes next to them. In this case, the /k/ in *keep* is produced further forward in the mouth because the following vowel sound, /i/, is a high front vowel. The brain sends a message to block the air at the velum to form /k/, but even as the tongue is moving to that position, it is preparing for the next sound in the sequence. The tongue doesn't go all the way back along the velum because it is getting ready to move to the front.

In producing *cool*, the tongue blocks the air to form /k/ at a point further back in the mouth because the following vowel, /u/, is a back high sound. By stopping the air further back along the velum, the tongue is moving closer to the position to make the /u/. Thus, the /k/ is assimilating to the /u/.

Assimilation is a common process in all languages. It is a kind of physical short-cut between two tongue positions, a more efficient way of producing phonemes. Since speakers generate some eight phonemes per second, this kind of economy is necessary and natural. The production of /k/ is conditioned by the anticipation of the following sound, in much the same way that a person might eat a light meal if a heavy meal is to follow later in the day.

The /k/ phoneme also has the allophone [kʰ] since it is aspirated at the beginning of a syllable. This variation applies to all three of the voiceless stops in English, /p/, /t/, and /k/. All phonemes have allophonic variations. Phonemes are not constant physical realities like cement blocks. They are perceptual units that differ from one another by the fact that they signal differences in meaning. The allophones of a phoneme are all perceived as the same sound by speakers of the language despite the physical differences in their production. While phonemes signal a difference in meaning, allophones never indicate a meaning difference.

Allophones of /t/, a complex case

Some phonemes are much more complex than the /k/ phoneme. In English, /t/ has six variations, depending on its position in a word and the other phonemes around it. The following words each contain a different allophone of /t/: *top, pot, kitten, letter, train,* and *stop.* Using phonetic transcription, linguists represent these allophones and describe the conditioning environment (the neighboring sounds that influence the pronunciation) of each as shown in Figure 4.12 (Farmer and Demers 1996, 75).

All six allophones of /t/ involve physical differences. We described /t/ as a voiceless, alveolar stop that is made by blocking the air with the blade of the tongue at the alveolar ridge. The first allophone, [tʰ], is produced when /t/ starts a syllable. As the air is released, an extra puff of air is produced. This is called *aspiration* and is represented by a small raised *h*. At the end of a word, though, the /t/ is not released. In addition, the air is partially blocked in the glottal region before being stopped in the mouth. This process of blocking the air in the throat is called *preglottalization.* This allophone is represented by [ʔt]. The /ʔ/ is the symbol for a glottal stop. The third allophone [ʔ] is not simply preglottalized, it is a glottal stop produced by stopping the air in the glottal region, not in the mouth. One can produce a word like *kitten* without pressing the tongue against the alveolar ridge for the /t/, but the tongue does move there for the /n/ that follows. The next allophone, [D], is called a flap because the tongue taps or flaps against the back of the front teeth or along the alveolar ridge. The symbol is a capital *D*, and the sound is much the same as a /d/. Words like *metal* and *medal,* the first with a flapped [D] and the second with a /d/, sound identical to most native English speakers. This flapped [D] is similar to the Spanish *r* in a word like *pero.* Children learning to spell often represent this allophone of /t/ with a *d* in their writing.

The next allophone, [ť], is actually an affricate. The air is stopped with the tongue pressing against the alveolar ridge and then released into an /ɹ/ sound. What happens is that the tongue flattens along the top of the mouth to block the air. Physically this

articulatory description	phonetic symbol	conditioning environment	example
released, aspirated	[tʰ]	syllable initial (first sound in a syllable)	top
unreleased, preglottalized	[ʔt]	word final after a vowel	pot
glottal stop	[ʔ]	before a syllabic /n/	kitten
flap	[D]	between vowels when the first vowel is stressed	metal
alveopalatal stop	[ť]	syllable initial before /ɹ/	train
released, unaspirated	[t]	when the above conditions are not met	stop

Figure 4.12 *Allophones of /t/*

tongue movement is very similar to the motions used to produce the voiceless alveo-palatal affricate, /tʃ/. Young children can feel that these two phonemes are produced in a similar manner, and they sometimes spell a word like *train* with a *ch* instead of a *t*. The final allophone, [t], occurs whenever none of the conditions for producing the first five variations is present. For example, in *stop* there is no aspiration because air is already being released as /s/ is produced, there is no constriction of air in the glottal region, and the tongue doesn't flap against the front teeth.

The allophones of a phoneme are in *complementary distribution*. What this means is that each allophone of /t/ falls into one, and only one, of the six categories. Together, these categories make up all the possible allophones of /t/. No allophone can fit into two different categories. For example, when the /t/ is at the start of a word, it is aspirated and written as [tʰ]. This is the only category for /t/ at the beginning of a word.

The alternative to complementary distribution is *overlapping distribution*. If categories overlap, an allophone could be in either of two categories. Although allophones of phonemes are in complementary distribution, as we will explain in Chapter 6, spellings of some phonemes are in overlapping distribution. There is more than one possible spelling for the same sound even in the same conditioning environment. For example, the /i/ phoneme can be spelled as *y* in *city* and as *ee* in *payee*.

We have described all these allophones of /t/ in some detail to show how complex phonemes can be. Depending on the other sounds around them, phonemes are produced in different ways. During normal communication, speakers of English ignore all these allophonic variations and focus on the meaning differences that phonemes signal. As young children learn to read, they begin to connect sounds with letters. They ignore the physical variations among allophones of a phoneme as long as their focus is on making sense of written language. However, allophonic variations may pose difficulties when children are asked to perceive and manipulate phonemes during exercises and tests of phonemic awareness because then the focus is on the phonemes themselves, not the meaning differences they signal.

Although adults are good at ignoring allophonic variations as they listen to a language they speak well, they may experience difficulties in perceiving the phonemes in a language they are trying to learn. Language learners often complain that speakers of the new language talk very fast. Actually, even though there are individual differences in rate of speech, speakers of one language don't talk faster than those of another language because speech rate is constrained by human physiology. The reason that language learners think that speakers of a new language talk fast is because the language learner is not so good at ignoring allophonic variations in phonemes. Adults learning a new language may try to pay attention to all the physical differences among the sounds they hear, and, as a result, become over-loaded with information. The effect of attending to all these details is similar to trying to understand someone speaking very rapidly.

3. Group the units

Once linguists categorize the phonemes of a language, the next step in developing a description of the language is to group the units. There are a number of ways to do this. For example, phonemes could be grouped as vowels and consonants. Linguists can further group the vowel phonemes as long, short, or reduced. For example, there are five long vowels. Vowel phonemes can also be categorized as high, back, low, and so forth. One group of vowel phonemes is made up of the long back vowels.

As with the vowel phonemes, linguists can group the consonant phonemes in different ways. For example, /p/, /t/, /k/ are the voiceless stops of English, and /b/, /d/, /g/ are the voiced stops. Creating groups of phonemes that share certain characteristics allows linguists to make general observations about a language and to compare languages. For example, both Spanish and English have the same set of voiceless stops. However, Spanish and English have different nasals.

4. Find dependencies among the units

The final step in describing the phonology of a language is to find dependencies among the different groups of phonemes. These groups play an important role in phonological rules. In linguistics, *rules* refers to generalizations in the description of the language. Native speakers of a language apply the rules as they talk. They are not consciously aware of the rules, but since they have acquired them, they automatically use them. These are not rules written in a grammar book to be learned. Linguists attempt to make rules explicit as they describe a language. They write them as phonological rules that state the dependencies among phonemes. These rules, or general statements, are ways of describing how one phoneme or group of phonemes depends on or is affected by other phonemes in the speech environment.

Phonological rule: Coarticulation of nasals and stops

One phonological rule is the coarticulation in English of stop and nasal phonemes. *Coarticulation* is a common phenomenon in languages. Coarticulation occurs when two phonemes are produced or articulated in the same place in the mouth. For example, /n/ and /d/ are both alveolars. Coarticulation is an example of assimilation, where one sound becomes similar to another sound.

Earlier we explained that English has three nasals: /m/, /n/, and /ŋ/. In addition, English has three pairs of oral stop consonants, /p/ and /b/, /t/ and /d/, and /k/ and /g/. Figure 4.13 shows the place of articulation for the oral stops and the nasals.

As Figure 4.13 shows, English has a biliabial nasal, /m/, and a pair of bilabial stops, /p/ and /b/. English has an alveolar nasal, /n/, and a pair of alveolar stops, /t/ and /d/. And English has a velar nasal, /ŋ/, and two velar stops, /k/ and /g/. Now consider the following words: /læmp/ (*lamp*), / æmbɚ/ (*amber*), /hɪnt/ (*hint*), /bænd/ (*band*), /θæŋk/ (*thank*), and /lɪŋgwɪstəks/ (*linguistics*). In each word, a nasal precedes an oral stop consonant. For example, in /læmp/ the /m/ precedes /p/.

A careful analysis of the other words listed above in which nasals precede stops

		bilabial	alveolar	velar
stops	voiceless	p	t	k
	voiced	b	d	g
nasals	voiced	m	n	ŋ

Figure 4.13 *Oral stops and nasals*

shows that the nasal and the stop are always produced in the same place in the mouth. The /m/ and /p/ in /læmp/ are both bilabials. English restricts the possible combination of nasal and oral stops. There are no words, for example, where /m/ is followed by /t/ or /k/, at least when the two sounds occur in the same syllable. This generalization can be stated as a phonological rule: Whenever a nasal precedes an oral stop within a syllable, the two stops will have the same place of articulation. That is, they are coarticulated.

Coarticulation of nasal and oral stops is an example of assimilation. The two sounds depend on one another. In this case, they are produced in the same place in the mouth. To produce an /m/, for example, a speaker blocks the air with the lips and allows air to pass through the nasal cavity. To make a /p/ or /b/, the speaker blocks the air with the lips and also blocks off the flow of air through the nose. To make the *mp* sound in /læmp/, the speaker stops the air at the lips, allowing air to pass out of the nose and then blocks air from entering the nasal cavity. The mouth is already in position to make a /p/ and that is the sound that is produced when air is first blocked from passing through the nose and then released at the end of the word. It is easy to test this process by making an /m/, stopping the /m/ sound and then opening the mouth. The result is /p/ or /b/.

This rule operates very consistently. The word *pumpkin* follows the rule for coarticulation since /m/ is followed by /p/. However, many English speakers say /pʌŋkɪn/ in casual speech. What is interesting is that this variation also follows the rule because when the second /p/ is deleted, a velar stop /k/ follows the nasal, so the nasal changes from /m/ to the velar nasal /ŋ/. Another word with two possible pronunciations is /ɪnpʊt/. This is a compound word, and the two stops are in different syllables. In the word, an /n/ is followed by a /p/. Even though the nasal and the stop are in two different syllables, most speakers follow the rule for coarticulation and pronounce this word as /ɪmpʌt/ so that the bilabial /m/ precedes the bilabial /p/. The word can also be pronounced /ɪnpʌt/ in careful speech. This shows that the rule for coarticulation may not always cross a syllable boundary.

The tendency to pronounce an oral stop after a nasal accounts for the pronunciation of words like *warmth*, *something*, and *symphony*. Even though no oral stop follows the nasal in these words (in *symphony* the *p* is part of the *ph* digraph and pronounced as /f/), speakers often insert one. All three words are commonly pronounced as though they had a /p/ sound after the /m/. In the case of *symphony*, the presence of the letter *p* makes the /p/ insertion even more likely. Children often spell words like *something* with a *p*. On the other hand, since the nasals and the oral stops are produced at the same point in the mouth, young children learning to spell often omit the nasal. They might write *wind* as *wid*. This spelling is not as inaccurate as it may seem, since the vowel picks up the nasal sound in a word like this. A linguist could represent the word phonetically as [wɪ̃d]. The diacritic over the [ɪ] indicates a nasalized vowel. Studies of children's spelling development often show that children do spell words the way they sound (the way linguistics would represent them) even though this results in a spelling that is not conventional.

The spellings of the sounds of nasals preceding stops are complicated by the fact that there are three nasal phonemes but only two graphemes that usually represent nasals. There is no letter to represent /ŋ/. Usually, this phoneme is spelled *ng* as in *ring*. However, when a velar stop follows a nasal as in /θɪŋk/ the sound is spelled with an *n*. The word is spelled *think*, not *thingk*.

It can be difficult to decide how to pronounce words with *ng* spellings. The *ng* can be in one syllable and pronounced /ŋ/ as in *singer*, or the *ng* can be in different syllables as in *finger*. In this case the *n* represents the /ŋ/ phoneme, and the *g* is pronounced as /g/. A town near where we used to live in California is named Sanger. Until we talked with locals, we didn't know whether the *ng* in the town name was pronounced like the *ng* in *singer* or the *ng* in *anger*. Both pronunciations are possible. The only way to know the conventional pronunciation is to hear someone from the area pronounce the name. Later, in Texas, we lived near Harlingen. Flight attendants not familiar with the area had trouble pronouncing the name of the city. In this case, the *n* is pronounced /n/ and the g is pronounced /dʒ/. There is no assimilation since the *g* does not represent a stop sound. Someone learning English as an additional language would need to hear any two-syllable word spelled with *ng* to decide how to pronounce it.

Morphophonemic rule: Plural

A second example that involves coarticulation is the rule governing the pronunciation of the plural suffix in English. This rule is different from the preceding one because it only applies to certain morphemes, or meaningful parts of words. Rules such as the rule for the plural suffix are called *morphophonemic* rules because they are phonological rules that apply to specific morphemes rather than to all the cases of the co-occurrence of two phonemes. Morphemes are the smallest units of meaning in a word. For example, in a word like *trees*, *tree* is a morpheme, and so is *s*. The *s* carries the meaning of plural. In Chapter 7 we discuss morphemes in more detail. In this chapter, we describe one rule that explains the pronunciation of the plural morpheme, usually spelled *s* or *es*.

Although there are two spellings of the plural morpheme, there are three pronunciations: /s/ as in *cats*, /z/ as in *dogs*, and /əz/ as in *bushes*. Given a new word like *quark*, a person who has acquired English knows that the plural will have the sound of /s/, not /z/ or /əz/. Native speakers would agree with this pronunciation even if they hadn't heard the word before. The reason for this agreement is that in the process of acquiring a language, a person acquires morphophonemic rules, such as the rule for plurals. Knowledge of the rule is subconscious. Linguistic analysis brings this subconscious knowledge to a conscious level.

To discover the rule for the plural morpheme, linguists collect a number of words, and for each, they determine how a native speaker would pronounce the plural morpheme. The words in Figure 4.14 provide a small sample of words with a plural suffix.

mats	ships	shelves	rugs	watches
plays	dramas	beds	foxes	cabs
baths	cells	roses	cars	tacks
buses	lashes	cliffs	mazes	judges

Figure 4.14 *Plurals*

The second step a linguist would take to discover the rule for the plural would be to transcribe the words and group together all the words with each of the three plural pronunciations. Notice that the spellings are not useful for discovering the rule, since there are two spellings and three pronunciations. Figure 4.15 shows how the words would be categorized.

The third step, and the most difficult one, is to determine the environment that conditions each of the plural forms. Assimilation is a very common phonological process. In this process, one sound shares some features with a sound next to it. That is, one sound assimilates to become more like a nearby sound. In this case, since the plural is at the end of the word, no other phoneme follows, so it must be the final phoneme in the base word that determines whether the plural is pronounced as /s/, /z/, or /əz/. The phonemes that precede the /s/ plural are /t/, /θ/, /p/, /f/, /k/, and those that precede /z/ are /eɪ/, /ə/, /l/, /v/, /d/, /g/, /ɪ/, /b/. The linguist would need to decide what the phonemes in each of these groups have in common that makes them different from the phonemes in the other group.

Both groups include consonants, so the plural is not conditioned by whether consonants or vowels precede the suffix. Both groups have stops and fricatives, so it does not appear that the manner of articulation causes the change. Both groups have sounds produced at the same place as well. For example, both /p/ and /b/ are bilabials, so the place of articulation must not be the cause (as it was with nasal assimilation). The only consistent difference between these two groups can be seen by considering the difference between /p/ and /b/ or between /f/ and /v/. In each case, these phonemes are pairs in which one is voiced and one is voiceless. A careful examination of the two groups of phonemes shows that all the

/s/	/z/	/əz/
mæts (mats)	pleɪz (plays)	bʌsəz (buses)
bæθs (baths)	draməz (dramas)	læʃəz (lashes)
ʃɪps (ships)	sɛlz (cells)	faksəz (foxes)
klɪfs (cliffs)	ʃɛlvz (shelves)	meɪzəz (mazes)
tæks (tacks)	bɛdz (beds)	watʃəz (watches)
	rʌgz (rugs)	dʒʌdʒəz (judges)
	kɑɹz (cars)	
	kæbz (cabs)	

Figure 4.15 *Transcription of plurals*

phonemes associated with /s/ are voiceless and all the phonemes associated with /z/ are voiced.

At this point a linguist could say that when the preceding phoneme is voiceless, the plural is /s/ and when the preceding phoneme is voiced, the plural is /z/. This would describe what is going on, but it wouldn't explain why voiceless sounds are followed by /s/ and voiced sounds are followed by /z/. A linguist would need to note that the only difference between the plural suffixes /s/ and /z/ is that /s/ is voiceless and /z/ is voiced. The plural rule, then, is an assimilation rule. The plural assimilates in voicing with the final phoneme in the base word. Both sounds are either voiceless or voiced.

This helps explain the words in the first two columns, but what about the words in the third column? The phonemes preceding /əz/ are /s, ʃ, z, tʃ, dʒ/. The list includes both voiceless and voiced sounds. However, what all these phonemes have in common is that they have a sound quite similar to the sound of /s/ or /z/. This set of sounds is referred to as the *sibilants*. Sibilants are characterized by a kind of hissing sound.

It would be hard to distinguish between the singular and plural of the words in the last column if the plural simply involved the addition of /s/ or /z/. How could someone decide if /bʌss/or /meɪzz/ referred to one bus or one maze or two buses or mazes? Drawing out the sound of the /s/ at the end of *bus* would not signal plural very clearly. For that reason, English adds a schwa sound between the end of the base word and the plural morpheme. This is a process called *epenthesis*, inserting a sound into a word. Since the added sound /ə/ is voiced, then the plural is /z/, which follows the general rule of /z/ representing the plural after a voiced sound.

This linguistic analysis leads to a rule for the pronunciation of the plural morpheme. The rule can be stated as "If the base word ends in a sibilant sound like /s/ or /z/, the plural is /əz/. In all other cases, the plural is /s/ if the base ends in a voiceless sound and /z/ if it ends in a voiced sound." This complicated rule is acquired subconsciously and forms part of a native speakers' knowledge of phonology. Even though most people could not state the rule, they could apply it to any word, like *quark*, that they encounter. In fact, this same rule applies to possessives. In *Pat's* the possessive is /s/, in *José's*, the possessive is /z/, and in *Clarise's* the plural is /əz/. The rule also applies to the third person *s* used to indicate present tense in words like *walks* /s/, *runs* /z/, and *rushes* /əz/. In addition, it applies to contractions of *is* and *has*. This is shown in contractions in sentences such as *Pat's here* /s/, *Sam's here* /z/, and *Tess's here* /əz/ as well as *Pat's gone* /s/, *Sam's* gone /z/, and *Tess's gone* /əz/. The contractions for a word ending in a sibilant like *Tess* are used in oral language but seldom written as a contraction.

Since this is a morphophonemic rule, it applies to specific morphemes, not all the words that end in the sound of /s/ or /z/. There are pairs of words like *place* and *plays* or *piece* and *peas* that show that either pronunciation can occur when the phoneme is not a plural, a possessive, a third person *s*, or a contraction. In each pair, the phoneme that precedes the final phoneme is a voiced sound, a vowel. In *place* and *piece* the final phoneme is /s/ while in *plays* and *peas* the final phoneme is /z/. In English, if the final morpheme is a plural, possessive, third person *s*, or a contraction *s*, it is possible to predict the sound of the final phoneme, but in cases where the final phoneme is not one of these, we do not know whether to pronounce it as /s/ or /z/. This is why the rule is called a morphophonemic rule. It applies only to certain morphemes, not to all the words in the language. On the other hand, the rule for nasal assimilation is a general phonological rule of English that applies to all words, not to certain morphemes.

Linguists use their knowledge of the categories of phonemes to describe dependencies among phonemes. They state these dependencies as rules. Morphophonemic rules such as the plural rule form part of a person's knowledge of phonology. When the person learns to read, he or she develops knowledge of the orthography and also begins to associate the sounds of the plural with the spellings. As in the case with nasals preceding stops, the sound–letter correspondences for the plural are complex. The *s* spelling is associated with two different sounds, /s/ and /z/. Children sometimes spell words like *plays* with a *z* because that is the sound they hear. However, as they read, they realize that the sound /z/ can be spelled in different ways.

Phonotactics

Linguists can also describe dependencies among phonemes in a more general way rather than as a rule that applies to specific phonemes. For example, they can describe how phonemes can be combined to form words in a language. The linguistic term for possible phoneme combinations is *phonotactics*. For example, in English, /ŋ/ only appears at the end of a syllable, never at the beginning. A native English speaker who tries to pronounce the common Vietnamese name *Nguyen* typically experiences difficulty. Even though English speakers have no trouble pronouncing words that end in /ŋ/, they find it difficult to pronounce words starting with /ŋ/. This helps confirm that phonemes are perceptual, not physical units, since English speakers have no trouble with the physical production of the sound /ŋ/ unless it begins a word.

This knowledge of sound combinations, or *phonotactics*, allows an English speaker to decide that *glark* is a possible English word, but *tlark* and *dlark* are not.

Every language puts constraints on how the phonemes can be combined. In English a number of different consonant blends are possible at the beginnings of words, but some combinations never occur. For example, if the first consonant phoneme in an English word is a stop, the second can only be an approximant or a glide, the two types of consonants that are most like vowels. Figure 4.16 shows how this pattern works.

Another example of a phonotactic rule is that English allows up to three consonant phonemes at the beginning of syllables. However, there are constraints on the kinds of phonemes that can be combined. Figure 4.17 lists the possibilities. What is interesting, from a linguistic perspective, is that the kinds of phonemes that can be combined fall into certain classes. In order to form a three-consonant cluster, the first phoneme must be /s/. The second phoneme must be a voiceless stop, and the third phoneme must be an approximant or a glide, the kinds of consonants that are most like vowels.

Not all the possible combinations occur, but the only words in English that start with three consonant phonemes start with one of the combinations listed in Figure 4.17.

stop	approximant or glide	example	
p	l	/pleɪ/	play
	ɹ	/pɹeɪ/	pray
	j	/pju/	pew
b	l	/blu/	blue
	ɹ	/bɹu/	brew
	j	/bjuti/	beauty
t	ɹ	/tɹu/	true
	w	/twɪn/	twin
d	ɹ	/dɹu/	drew
	w	/dwɑɹf/	dwarf
k	l	/klu/	clue
	ɹ	/kɹu/	crew
	j	/cue/	cue
	w	/kwɪk/	quick
g	l	/glu/	glue
	ɹ	/gɹu/	grew

Figure 4.16 *Initial blends combining stops, approximants, and glides*

voiceless stop	approximant or glide	example	
s	p	l	/splæʃ/	splash
s	p	ɹ	/spreɪ/	spray
s	p	j	/spju/	spew
s	t	ɹ	/strit/	street
s	k	l	/skləɹousɪs/	sclerosis
s	k	ɹ	/skɹim/	scream
s	k	j	/skju/	skew
s	k	w	/skwɪnt/	squint

Figure 4.17 *Initial combinations of three consonant phonemes*

Young children who grow up in an English-speaking environment acquire knowledge of English phonotactics. This is subconscious knowledge. They use this information as they speak, but they can't explain how they know that certain combinations are possible and others are not. Part of acquiring a language is acquiring the phonemes, but people also acquire the knowledge of how to combine the phonemes into words.

Conclusion

In this chapter we considered two questions:

- How do people understand and produce language?
- What is phonology, and how do linguists describe the phonology of a language?

A commonsense view of communication is that speakers encode ideas into language and transmit the language through acoustic signals. Listeners decode the signals and receive the idea that speakers send. However, this view of communication is extremely limited. Oral communication is quite complex. Speakers choose language that is appropriate for the context of situation. They convey their meaning using facial expressions, gestures, and tone of voice. Listeners predict what speakers may say, and they make inferences to fill in missing information. To comprehend a message, listeners must share knowledge of reference with speakers, they must determine the correct meaning of ambiguous words and phrases, and they must decide if the speaker is using language that is literal or nonliteral, direct or indirect.

Oral communication involves the production and comprehension of speech sounds. The scientific study of speech sounds is phonology. Linguists describe the phonology of a language by following four steps. First, they break the speech stream into meaningful parts, or phonemes. Next, they categorize these phonemes. Consonant phonemes in English can be described by their place and manner of articulation as well as by their voicing. Vowel phonemes are described by their length and the position of the tongue in the vocal tract. The third step is to group phonemes into natural classes, such as long vowels or stop consonants. Finally, linguists look for dependencies among phonemes. These can be stated as rules. Many phonological rules involve the process of assimilation. Some rules apply generally in English and others apply only to certain morphemes.

A knowledge of phonology is an important part of any teacher's pedagogical language knowledge. When teachers understand phonology, they can better choose methods and techniques for teaching a second language and for teaching reading.

APPLICATIONS

1. Look back at Figure 4.1, the commonsense model of communication. Make a list of different facts about communication that this model fails to capture. Then create a model that includes these missing features.

2. Read one or more of Parish's Amelia Bedelia books and list the expressions she fails to understand. Make a table like the one below that lists the expression, Amelia's interpretation (the literal meaning), and the conventional nonliteral meaning.

expression	literal meaning	nonliteral meaning
dust the furniture	put dust on the furniture	remove dust from the furniture

3. As people produce sounds, they go through a series of physical actions. For example, to produce /p/ a person would briefly stop the air with the lips and then open the lips to release the air. At the same time, they would hold their vocal cords apart so they would not vibrate. Describe how the following phonemes are produced using the model description of /p/: /d/, /m/, /l/, /w/, /eɪ/, and /u/.

4. For each phoneme in English, find a minimal pair of words, and transcribe the words. Following the model below, complete a chart by adding all the other consonant and vowel phonemes. You do not need to include the schwa or the /ɚ/. For these phonemes, the difference is with stress, so it is harder to find pairs of words. Your chart should include thirty-eight phonemes and a pair of transcribed words for each. You should also write the word in conventional spelling following the transcribed word. The words may have the phonemes at the beginning, middle, or end of a syllable.

/p/	pɪl (*pill*)	tɪl (*till*)
/b/	bæt (*bat*)	sæt (*sat*)

5. Transcribe the following words:

see	chance	dread
crazy	shout	bath
just	yes	ring
bridge	five	toy
mast	then	taste

6. We described a phonological rule that accounts for the different pronunciations of the plural morpheme. The past-tense morpheme also has three possible pronunciations: /t/, /d/, and /əd/. Follow the same steps we described for the plural to create a rule that accounts for the three pronunciations of the past tense. The steps include: (1) Make a list of words in past tense. Include words that have each of the past-tense pronunciations. (2) Transcribe the words. (3) Group the transcribed words that have the same pronunciation of the past-tense morpheme under three columns: /t/, /d/, and /əd/. (4) State a rule that accounts for the different pronunciations of the past tense. To form the rule try to find what all the words where the plural is /t/ have in common. Then do the same for the other two pronunciations. Finally, try to explain why this rule is an example of assimilation.

5 /faɪv/

Implications from Phonology for Teaching a Second Language and Teaching Reading

- What insights from phonology can help teachers choose a method for teaching a second language?
- What insights from phonology can help teachers choose a method for teaching reading?

Phonology plays a role in both second language and written language development. Most researchers agree that babies acquire their first language. There may be some debate over whether language is innate or whether humans have a special cognitive capacity for language, but there is agreement that humans acquire their first language without instruction. When it comes to learning a second language or learning to read, though, there is less agreement. As we discussed earlier, some researchers argue that a second language or written language can be acquired in the same way that a first language is acquired. Others claim that a second language or written language must be learned. Still others might say that any oral language can be acquired, but that written language must be learned.

In this chapter, we consider how insights from the linguistic area of phonology can help inform these debates. We examine the role of phonology in methods of teaching a second language and methods of teaching reading. Evidence from linguistics can help educators evaluate different methods and the theories underlying those methods.

Second Language Teaching and Phonology

Students learning English as a second language must develop the ability to comprehend and produce the sounds of English. That is, they must develop control over

English phonology. Methods of second language teaching have approached phonology in different ways. In methods based on a theory that language is learned, attention is paid to how sounds are produced, and students learn to pronounce the sounds of the new language. In methods based on a theory that language is acquired, less attention is given to teaching pronunciation since the belief is that the phonology of a language will be acquired in the process of developing proficiency in the second language.

Phonology in Methods with a Learning View

In Chapter 3 we discussed two views of second language development: a learning view and an acquisition view. We then examined different orientations toward language teaching and methods of teaching consistent with those orientations. Figure 5.1 summarizes the orientations and methods associated with a learning view as well as the role of phonology for each method.

In the grammar translation method students study parts of the language, the grammar and the vocabulary, and use that knowledge to translate texts from the foreign language to the native language or from the native language into the foreign language. The goal of instruction is to enable students to read and write the language. Originally, grammar translation was used to translate great works of literature from Latin and ancient Greek, languages no longer spoken. Little attention was paid to speaking and listening, so phonology, the study of speech sounds, does not play a role in instruction.

The direct method involves students in activities using the target language to communicate. Speaking is an important part of this method. The focus, though, is on using language to communicate, and limited attention is given to developing correct pronunciation.

Orientation	Method	Role of Phonology
Grammar based	Grammar translation	Essentially no role since speaking is not included
Communicative	Direct method	Speaking is included with an emphasis on comprehensible communication
Empiricist	Audio-lingual	Attention to correct pronunciation through drills, role-play, etc.
	Notional Functional	Emphasis is on communication and pronunciation is acquired
	Suggestopedia	Create a relaxed atmosphere and role-play to acquire correct pronunciation

Figure 5.1 *Learning orientations, methods, and role of phonology*

The empiricist orientation holds that language is speech, and language is learned as a set of habits. Methods that followed this orientation include the Audio-lingual Method (ALM), the Notional Functional approach, and Suggestopedia. All these methods emphasize communication, but the Audio-lingual Method focuses on correct pronunciation out of context while Suggestopedia and the Notional Functional approach are based on the assumption that correct pronunciation is acquired in the context of meaningful communication.

Contrastive analysis

The linguistic base for ALM is *contrastive analysis*. Structural linguists contrasted the native language with the second language. Their analyses were very thorough. For example, to contrast the phonological systems of two languages, a linguist first describes each language. Then he or she contrasts the two systems. For phonology, this includes a phoneme-by-phoneme comparison. For each phoneme, the linguist asks:

a. Does the native language have a phonetically similar phoneme?
b. Are the variants of the phonemes (allophones) similar in both languages?
c. Are the phonemes and their variants similarly distributed? (For example, in English /ŋ/ is syllable final, but in Vietnamese it can be syllable initial.)

As these questions show, the comparison is very detailed. Results of contrastive analyses have been used to develop teaching materials. For example, to develop materials to teach Spanish to English speakers, linguists compared English and Spanish phonology, morphology, and syntax. Lado (1957) even contrasted the two cultures. The assumption was that if a certain sound or vocabulary item were the same in the two languages, that part of the language would be easy to learn. On the other hand, in areas where the two languages differed, learning would be more difficult. Over time, linguists developed a hierarchy of difficulty. The most difficult case was a situation in which one item in the native language was represented by two or more items in the second language. For example, English has one /ɹ/ phoneme and Spanish has two different *r*'s, so the prediction would be that an English speaker would have difficulty distinguishing and pronouncing the two Spanish /r/ sounds.

Linguists identified these problem areas and then developed exercises to give students practice with the difficult forms. However, many of the predictions based on the linguistic contrasts between languages were not borne out as students attempted to learn the language. Students had trouble learning some items that were predicted to be easy, and they easily learned some items that were predicted to be difficult. For instance, once English speakers learned to produce the rolled Spanish /r/ sound, they had no trouble distinguishing and producing the two /r/ sounds.

Methods based on a theory that second languages are learned, such as ALM, often include drills and tests that require students to distinguish between minimal pairs. These minimal pairs are based on the contrastive analysis of two languages. Since phonemes are perceptual units, speakers of some languages may regard two sounds as the same if they are allophones of one phoneme in their language, even though they are separate phonemes in English. For example, in English /d/ and /ð/ are two phonemes. English has minimal pairs such as /dɛn/ (*den*) and /ðɛn/ (*then*) and /brɪd/(*breed*) and /brɪð/ (*breathe*). Spanish has these same two sounds, but they are allophones of one phoneme. There are no minimal pairs of words in Spanish that differ by these two sounds. In other words, the sounds do not signal a difference in meaning in Spanish.

In words such as *dedo* (*finger*) or *dado* (*die*), the first sound is more like the English /d/ and the second sound is like the English /ð/. In Spanish, [ð] the voiced interdental fricative is an allophone of /d/. These two sounds occur in different environments. The stop occurs at the beginning of a syllable or following a consonant phoneme, and the fricative follows a vowel. This is one instance of a general rule in Spanish that voiced stops (/b/, /d/, /g/) become voiced fricatives following a vowel.

A Spanish speaker learning English has acquired the subconscious knowledge that in Spanish the difference between the sounds [d/] and [ð] do not make a meaning difference since in Spanish they are allophones, and so the physical differences between the sounds can be ignored. However, in English, the difference can't be ignored because /d/ and /ð/ are separate phonemes. Spanish speakers acquiring English will come to understand this difference between the two languages, again at a subconscious level, in the process of trying to make sense of the new language. This is not a problem as long as the focus is on making meaning. Spanish speakers may still spell some English words like *that* with a *d* instead of a *th* while they are acquiring English spelling conventions. Spanish spelling reflects the fact that in Spanish both sounds are spelled with a *d*.

In an ALM class, Spanish speakers learning English would be given practice with the two phonemes so that they could learn to distinguish them more easily. However, exercises or tests that focus on the sounds themselves may cause problems for Spanish speakers. Exercises involving /d/ and /ð/ could be confusing. Spanish speakers may still perceive these two sounds as variations of one phoneme. If asked to substitute *then* for *den* the Spanish speaker might not perceive these as different words. In addition, since Spanish doesn't contain words that start with /ð/ students might pronounce these two words the same way.

To take one other example, English has two phonemes, /tʃ/ and /ʃ/, and Spanish has only one of these phonemes, /tʃ/ (although some dialects of Spanish may also include [ʃ]). Linguists using contrastive analysis would predict that Spanish speakers learning English would have difficulty producing /ʃ/, since Spanish lacks that phoneme. However, Spanish speakers learning English don't have difficulty pronouncing /ʃ/. In fact, Spanish speakers often pronounce words like *chair* as /ʃɛɹ/. Perhaps, once they realize that English has the /ʃ/ sound, they decide that this sound replaces the /tʃ/ sound and overgeneralize its use.

Medina (1999) has written a poignant poem, "T-Shirt," that plays on these two sounds. Jorge calls his instructor "Teacher" but she interprets his pronunciation as "T-Shirt" and says, "Besides, when you say it, it sounds like 't-shirt.' I don't want to turn into a t-shirt" (25). Jorge uses the /ʃ/ sound where a native English speaker would use /tʃ/. Jorge would probably have trouble with exercises and tests based on the contrastive analysis of Spanish and English. English spelling is not too helpful, either, since some English words, those borrowed from French like *machine* and *Chevrolet*, retain the *ch* spelling to represent the /ʃ/ phoneme.

Even though linguists performed careful analyses of the two languages, the results were not helpful in planning instruction. The attempt to analyze language, divide it into parts, and present the parts in the context of exercises and drills simply did not work very well. Students have a hard time learning the pronunciation of a second or foreign language when teachers rely on drills and exercises based on contrastive analysis.

Tongue Twisters

Even though having students identify minimal pairs in words like *pat* and *bat* has not proven to be useful in helping students develop nativelike pronunciation of a language, students do benefit from engagement in language games including songs, poems, and chants. Students also enjoy tongue twisters. In his book *A Twister of Twists, a Tangler of Tongues*, Schwartz (1972) has collected tongue twisters from many different regions of the United States as well as from different languages. Students who speak these languages enjoy trying to say the tongue twisters rapidly. They often know additional tongue twisters that they remember. In addition, several Internet websites that deal with linguistics feature tongue twisters.

Schwartz begins his book by presenting a very difficult example in English: "One of the hardest tongue twisters in the English language is 'Peggy Babcock.'

Try to say it five times as fast as you can. If you are like most people I know, your tongue won't cooperate" (9).

Most people can't even say this name twice in a row. Just what makes tongue twisters like this one so difficult? Part of the difficulty comes from the physical movement of the tongue, but part also comes from the mixed patterns the brain has to deal with. A phonological analysis of *Peggy Babcock* reveals both difficulties.

The name would be transcribed as /pɛgibæbkɑk/. To produce these sounds, the tongue must move rapidly from front to back. Both /p/ and /b/ are bilabials, produced as far forward in the mouth as possible. The other two consonant phonemes /g/ and /k/ are produced at the back of the mouth. The sequence of consonant phonemes is /p/, /g/, /b/, /b/, /k/, and /k/. In other words, the tongue goes front, back, front, front, back, back. The brain is sending messages to the tongue, lips, and other parts of the mouth to control these movements.

At the same time, the brain is sending messages to the vocal cords. They vibrate to produce the voiced consonants /b/ and /g/ and they are held apart to make the voiceless phonemes /p/ and /k/. Here is the pattern of voicing: voiceless, voiced, voiced, voiced, voiceless, voiceless. Now consider where most people run into trouble. For many speakers it is the second time through when the first name comes out as *Pebby* instead of *Peggy*. Why might this occur?

Two different patterns (at least) are at work here, the front/ back movement of the tongue and the on/off pattern of the voicing. Figure 5.2 shows the relationship between these two patterns.

As shown by the last two rows, in which the front/back and voiceless/voicing are represented by pluses and minuses, the two patterns start out the same, but then change with the first /b/. The brain is very good at picking up patterns. People can repeat rhymes rapidly. But here the two patterns seem to conflict and speech is short-circuited. Speakers who say *Pebby* the second time through produce the right voicing (the /b/ is voiced), but in the wrong position (the /b/ is front instead of

phoneme	p	g	b	b	k	k
position	front	back	front	front	back	back
voicing	voiceless	voiced	voiced	voiced	voiceless	voiceless
front = − back = +	−	+	−	−	+	+
voiceless = − voiced = +	−	+	+	+	−	−

Figure 5.2 *Peggy Babcock*

the /g/, which is back). If the front/back and voiceless/voiced alternations matched one another, this name would not be a tongue twister. Other tongue twisters, like "Rubber baby buggy bumpers," also play on these same alterations between front and back, voiceless and voiced.

Some tongue twisters, such as "She says she shall sew a sheet," require rapid movement between two points in the mouth that are close together, /s/ and /ʃ/. Several tongue twisters use this contrast. Again, this alteration seems to cause problems primarily because the pattern is complex. Speakers do not have trouble shifting between /s/ and /ʃ/ as long as the two sounds alternate following a regular pattern. However, here the pattern is irregular. In addition, *says* contains a voiced phoneme /z/ that is produced at the same place as /s/. The result, for most people, is a twist of the tongue.

Tongue twisters, along with songs, chants, poems, and other kinds of wordplay can help emergent bilinguals develop the phonology of a new language. In addition, teachers with linguistic knowledge can help students analyze and come to understand why some phrases are so difficult to pronounce.

Phonology in Methods with an Acquisition View

Methods of language teaching, based on a learning view, have been replaced by methods that are based on an acquisition view in many classrooms. Figure 5.3 summarizes these methods and the role of phonology in each method

Methods associated with an acquisition view assume that learners use language input to develop subconscious rules for a new language, including phonological

Orientation	Method	Role of Phonology
rationalist	Silent Way	Teacher says things only once. Students attempt to duplicate what teacher says.
	Community Language Learning	Teacher translates what to say and student repeats.
	Problem Posing	Focuses more on oral and written communication and less on correct pronunciation
	Total Physical Response	Emphasis on listening and responding physically
	Natural Approach	Students go through a series of stages, and speech emerges naturally.
	CALLA SIOP	Focus is on content learning through language rather than on pronunciation

Figure 5.3 *Acquisition orientations and methods*

rules. These methods include less explicit teaching of pronunciation because the focus is on using language to communicate and to learn academic content. This does not mean that pronunciation is ignored. Rather, pronunciation is a focus when errors prevent students from communicating effectively.

In the Silent Way the teacher only says things once and students attempt to produce the language they have heard. There is little practice with pronunciation. In Community Language Learning students speak in their first language, the teacher translates, and the students repeat what the teacher says to communicate in their new language. Problem Posing is focused on using language to solve social problems, and attention is paid to both written communication and oral communication. However, the emphasis is on communication, not pronunciation. Total Physical Response in the early stages only requires students to respond with physical actions, such as raising their hands. At later stages, students do produce language using techniques such as storytelling but the emphasis is not on correct pronunciation.

The Natural Approach

The *Natural Approach*, developed by Krashen and Terrell (1983), reflects Krashen's theory of second language acquisition. The teacher uses a variety of techniques to make the language input comprehensible. Students focus on constructing meaning as they use the language. There is no grammatical sequence built into the curriculum or materials. According to the Natural Order hypothesis, any student learning a language will develop parts of the language (the phonology, morphology, and syntax) in a natural order as long as they receive messages they understand. In the case of phonology, the hypothesis is that second language learners, like babies acquiring their first language, will pick up correct pronunciations of the sounds of the language as they hear and use the language in natural communication.

Like children acquiring a first language, people acquiring a second language go through a series of stages. Based on classroom observations of students learning a second or foreign language, Krashen and Terrell identified several stages. The first stage, which Krashen called the *Silent Period* or *Preproduction*, is a time when the learner begins to comprehend the speech of others. During this silent period, students communicate using gestures and other nonverbal means. In *Early Production*, students use a few basic words and short phrases in the new language. Students produce longer phrases and sentences during *Speech Emergence*. In *Intermediate Fluency* students begin to use more complex sentences. The theory proposes that language learners go through these stages as long as they receive comprehensible input.

There is no attempt to identify parts of the language and present them in sequence. Studies of child language development have identified the order of phoneme acquisition. For example, /m/ is acquired before /ɹ/. However, the exact sequence of the acquisition of phonemes is not known. Even if we did know the sequence, it would be extremely difficult to design lessons for each phoneme, and there is no evidence that this approach would benefit students. According to Krashen, what is important is to involve students with meaningful language so that it can be acquired, not to present the parts of the language to be learned. In current methods of content-based language learning, such as CALLA and SIOP, pronunciation is not taught explicitly. The assumption is that oral language is acquired as students engage in using a new language to study academic content.

Importance of teacher knowledge of language transfer

Although current methods of second language teaching give less emphasis to pronunciation than some early methods did, this does not mean that phonology is completely ignored. The emphasis now is more on the importance of teacher knowledge than on direct teaching. It is important for teachers to understand aspects of the learners' first language. That knowledge can help teachers predict the way students may pronounce English words.

Even though detailed contrastive analyses of languages did not correctly predict the kinds of problems students might have in producing a new language, people learning a new language do transfer some aspects of their native language into the new language. Knowing about the native language of students enables teachers to predict the way a student may pronounce English words. This allows teachers to better understand that some pronunciations are normal.

On the other hand, there are some cases in which pronunciation can impede communication. Recently, we listened to a Filipino man who described a house as "decrepit." Despite his impressive vocabulary, his pronunciation made it hard to figure out what he was saying. He stressed the first syllable in *decrepit* and changed the pronunciation of the following vowels. When students' pronunciation makes comprehension difficult, teachers can include language objectives that focus on pronunciation.

A useful resource for teachers is *Language Transfer Issues* (Freeman et al. 2011). This resource guide lists common transfer issues for native speakers of ten of the most common second languages spoken by emergent bilinguals in U.S. schools: Spanish, Vietnamese, Hmong, Haitian Creole, Cantonese, Korean, Khmer, Russian, Arabic, and Tagalog.

This resource includes grammar transfer issues, such as plurals and articles; phonics (sound–symbol) transfer issues, such as consonants and short vowels; and word study transfer issues, such as prefixes and suffixes. For each consonant and vowel phoneme, the guide lists whether or not a speaker of each of the languages might have difficulty with the English phoneme. For example, Spanish speakers are predicted to have problems with /dʒ/ since that phoneme does not occur in Spanish. The guide can help teachers develop the pedagogical language knowledge (Bunch 2013) they need to work effectively with emergent bilinguals. The emphasis here is on teacher knowledge, not on direct teaching of a phoneme like /dʒ/ through drills or exercises.

Reading and Phonology

Each of the two views of written language development we described in Chapter 3 places a different value on the role of sounds. Sounds play a central role in the learning view of reading and a much smaller role in an acquisition view of reading. As with second language teaching, the importance of phonology differs based on whether methods are based on a learning view or an acquisition view.

Phonology in Reading Methods with a Learning View

Approaches to teaching reading based on a learning view places heavy emphasis on the role of sounds and the associations between sounds and letters. The process of teaching beginning reading includes helping students develop phonological and phonemic awareness, then learning the letters and the sounds they represent, and finally learning the relationships between the sounds and the letters or combinations of letters.

A teaching sequence related to phonology, from a learning perspective, would include teaching:

1. phonological awareness
2. phonemic awareness
3. names and sounds of letters
4. phonics rules

Phonological and phonemic awareness

Researchers often distinguish between phonological awareness and phonemic awareness. *Phonological awareness* is the ability to distinguish larger units of speech, such as words and syllables. *Phonemic awareness* is a type of phonological awareness.

It is the ability to identify the phonemes in a word and manipulate them in various ways, such as adding a phoneme, deleting a phoneme, or substituting one phoneme for another. Thus, a child with phonemic awareness could change *at* to *sat* by adding an /s/, or change *sat* to *cat* by substituting /k/ for /s/.

Adams (1990) identified five levels of phonological and phonemic awareness. These include the ability:

1. to hear rhymes and alliteration in nursery rhymes
2. to do oddity tasks (picking out words that start with a different phoneme from others in a series, for example)
3. to blend or split syllables
4. to perform phonemic segmentation (count the number of phonemes in a word like *cat*)
5. to perform phoneme manipulation tasks (adding, deleting, substituting a phoneme).

All these tasks involve students in manipulating sounds of language. Some of the tasks can be described in simple terms that most young children would understand, such as telling which words sound the same or rhyme. However, other tasks, such as adding or deleting a phoneme, involve more abstract thinking. When asked what word results when we delete the /k/ from *cat*, most adults visualize the letters of the word to determine the answer. Young children who do not read face a different challenge than adults. The solution involves deleting a sound from a word. There is nothing concrete about this, and it is not the way people normally use words and sounds since there is no meaningful communication.

A very important article by Stanovich (1986) titled "Matthew Effects in Reading" reviewed a number of research studies. Stanovich used the biblical concept found in the book of Matthew: the rich get richer and the little the poor have will be taken away from them. Stanovich noted that good readers read more, and the benefits of reading, such as increased vocabulary, make these good readers better. On the other hand, poor readers read less over time, and because they read less, they fall further behind their classmates.

In his review of the research, Stanovich identified phonemic awareness as the key factor that differentiated good from poor readers. Children with phonemic awareness became good readers, and those who lacked phonemic awareness struggled with reading. The studies did not clearly show whether phonemic awareness was needed for someone to learn to read, or whether it was developed as a result of reading. Good readers have phonemic awareness, but this correlation does not show which factor is the cause and which is the effect. Stanovich used the term *reciprocal causation* to account for a bidirectional relationship. According to Stanovich, phonemic awareness appears to help children learn to read, and reading helps build phonemic awareness.

Phonological and phonemic awareness are the first skills in a hierarchy that students must learn to identify words. Phonemic awareness may develop in some children as the result of early literacy experiences. However, other children come to school without phonemic awareness, so the best solution from a learning perspective is to teach phonemic awareness directly and systematically. Phonological and phonemic awareness are seen as necessary steps toward being able to apply phonics rules to identify words.

A linguistic perspective on phonics

Phonics is central to methods of teaching reading based on a learning perspective. However, studies in psycholinguistics and reading that have investigated phonics have raised questions as to the importance of phonics. Clearly, readers do use knowledge of sound–letter correspondences as they read. Methods of teaching reading from both a learning view and an acquisition view include activities to help students make the connections between sounds and letters.

While children do need to understand that the letters in words represent sounds in the language, there is a question as to how effective phonics instruction is. Linguistic studies of phonics have raised doubts about teaching phonics. Two quite different studies are reviewed here. The first study was designed to determine the number of phonics rules that would be needed to account for the sound–letter correspondences in a set of words. A second study looked at how often commonly taught phonics rules apply to a set of words. In addition, studies in eye movement show that readers make only limited use of visual information during reading. These studies provide evidence that can help teachers evaluate claims for the value of teaching phonics.

The Southwest Regional Laboratory study

One of the problems in trying to determine the sequence of rules to teach is that there are too many rules. In an early study Berdiansky and her colleagues (1969) analyzed 6,092 one- and two-syllable words taken from school reading materials designed for six- to nine-year-olds. These words represented a good sample of what children this age are expected to read.

The analysis of these 6,092 words was rather complex. The researchers transcribed each word and established the correspondence between the letters and the sounds by drawing an arrow from each phoneme to the letter or letters that represented the sound of the phoneme. Figure 5.4 shows how several words would be analyzed.

Since it is not possible to associate each phoneme with a single letter, the researchers drew an arrow from each phoneme to the letter or letters that represented the sound of the phoneme. Once the researchers had completed this task for all the 6,092 words, they created a chart. For each phoneme on the chart, they listed all the letters or letter combinations used to spell that sound. For example, /p/ could be spelled *p* or *pp* and /eɪ/ could be spelled with *a*, *ea*, aCe (where *C* represents any consonant). *Made* is an example in Figure 5.4.

Once the results for all 6,092 words were analyzed in this way, the researchers had to decide what constituted a phonics rule. They decided that if a sound was spelled a certain way at least ten times in the data, they would call it a rule, and if there were fewer than ten instances of the sound–letter(s) correspondence, they would call it an exception. So, for example, since the phoneme /p/ was spelled with the letter *p* more than ten times, one of the rules was /p/ = *p*.

By using this thorough procedure, the researchers were able to determine the number of rules and exceptions that would be needed to account for the sound–letter correspondences in these one- and two-syllable words in materials designed for six- to nine-year-olds. They found that there were 211 correspondences, 83 for the consonants and another 128 for the vowels. Of these correspondences, 166 qualified as rules because they occurred at least ten times, and the other 45 were listed as exceptions.

What this means is that to decode these words relying entirely on phonics the six- to nine-year-old readers would need to know 211 correspondences. As they read, they would have to decide, in each case, whether to use one of the 166 rules or one of the 45 exceptions. This linguistic analysis shows that there are too many phonics rules and too many exceptions for phonics alone to enable children to decode words even if a teacher was able to teach that many rules and exceptions.

Figure 5.4 *Sound–letter correspondences*

The Clymer study

Those who take a learning perspective and emphasize the use of phonics to identify words often acknowledge that there are many sound–letter correspondences, but they often claim that just a few basic rules can account for the correspondences in most words. A review of most basal reading programs shows that phonics rules that are presented are not in the linguistic form of "pronounce *p* as /p/." Instead, they are more general statements, such as "When a vowel is in the middle of a one-syllable word, the vowel is short," or "When words end with silent *e* the preceding vowel is long." These more general rules are thought to account for most phonics correspondences, especially in short words.

An important question is "How often do these commonly taught phonics rules work?" This is the question Clymer (1963) investigated. Clymer was teaching in an elementary school, and as he presented different phonics generalizations from a list he had been given, one of his students, Kenneth, kept finding exceptions to the generalization. Clymer's experience with Kenneth led him to undertake a research project.

Clymer began by reviewing four widely used sets of basal readers. He found a total of 121 phonics generalizations in these readers. He noted that different series included different sets of rules and introduced them in different sequences. He commented that, "Of the 50 different vowel generalizations, only 11 were common to all four series" (253). In addition, even when the same rule appeared, it came in a different sequence and at a different grade level. Clymer's review showed that across reading series, there is no consistency in which rules are taught or when they are taught.

Clymer chose forty-five generalizations to examine. He wrote, "The selection of these was somewhat arbitrary. The main criterion was to ask, 'Is the generalization stated specifically enough so that it can be said to aid or hinder in the pronunciation of a particular word?'" (254). Once he had chosen the generalizations, Clymer selected a set of words to test them against. He made a composite list of all the words introduced in the four basic reading series and added words from the Gates Reading Vocabulary list. This gave him about 2,600 words. He checked the pronunciation of each word, giving it a phonetic spelling based on *Merriam-Webster's New Collegiate Dictionary*. Then he tested each generalization against all the words in his list.

The results of Clymer's study showed that many commonly taught rules only work some of the time, although there is considerable variation. For example, the rule "Words having double *e* usually have the long /e/ sound" works 98 percent of the time. In Clymer's sample, there were eighty-five words like *seem* that followed the rule, and the only exceptions were two instances of the word *been*. On the other hand, the rule "When there are two vowels side by side, the long sound of the first one is heard and the second is usually silent" works only 45 percent of the time. This rule, popularly expressed as "When two vowels go walking, the first one does the talking," could apply to many words. Clymer found 309 words like *bead* that followed the rule, but 377 others like *chief* that did not.

Clymer also found that the vowel in the middle of a one-syllable word is short only 62 percent of the time. The silent *e* rule works only 60 percent of the time. Clymer's study is important because it was based on words young readers frequently encounter. Using words from the four basal reading programs and the Gates Reading Vocabulary list, Clymer showed that many rules simply do not work often enough to be useful to readers trying to use phonics to identify words.

Evidence from eye movement research

Evidence from eye movement research (Paulson and Freeman 2003) raises additional questions about the importance of phonics. Researchers have studied how readers' eyes move as they scan a text. This research, carried out over the last one hundred years, has become more sophisticated as new technology has developed. In early studies, readers had to wear a harness or actually bite down on a bar as they read so that their head wouldn't move. Current technology does not hinder head movement, so the reading is quite natural. The text is projected on a computer screen so that the eye movements can be tracked with great accuracy.

Although readers have the sensation that their eyes move smoothly across the page as they read, the eye actually moves in a series of jumps called *saccades*. Each time the eye stops or fixates, information is sent to the brain. When the eye is moving, no information is recorded. However, the brain fills in the gaps between fixations to produce the perception that the movement is continuous. The brain operates in the same way during reading as it does when people watch a movie. The series of frames that flash by are perceived as one continuous action, not as a series of still pictures. In fact, the brain works this way all the time. As people look around a room, the eye makes a series of fixations, but people sense a continuous motion, not a series of snapshots.

Eye tracking equipment can record exactly where on the page the eye fixates during reading. At each fixation, an oval area that covers five of six letters is in clear focus. This is called the *foveal area*. A larger area of thirty to forty spaces around the fixation point is in peripheral vision. This area is called the *parafoveal*. For example, Figure 5.5 shows a line of text with the fixation, the foveal area, and the parafoveal area marked.

What eye movement research shows is that readers do not fixate words one letter at a time moving from left to right. In fact, readers do not fixate each word in a text. As Paulson and Freeman (2003) report, research over the last hundred years has been very consistent in reporting that readers fixate between 60 and 80 percent of the words in a text. This is true of both proficient and struggling readers. It is true of readers reading in their first language or in a second language. This finding has been remarkably consistent.

Figure 5.6 shows the eye movements from one page of a bilingual fourth-grade reader. The gray dots represent the fixations, and the numbers show the order of the fixations. Excluding the chapter title, the reader fixates forty-three times on a passage of sixty-three words. Her fixation rate is 68 percent. Notice that the reader does not fixate each letter or even each word. She is sampling the text to gather enough information to construct meaning. This reader was able to retell the story accurately even though she did not fixate all the words.

Since readers do not fixate all the words or all the letters in a word, they can not be using the kinds of phonics rules generally taught in schools to decode each word. To apply phonics rules, a reader would need to fixate all the letters of each word.

Phonology in Reading Methods with an Acquisition View

Phonology also plays an important role in methods of teaching reading based on an acquisition view. From an acquisition perspective, students acquire the ability to use graphophonics as one of three cue systems that enable them to construct meaning from texts. *Graphophonic knowledge* includes knowledge of phonology, orthography, and the relationships between phonology and orthography. As teachers read to and with them, beginning readers acquire phonological and phonemic awareness. In this process, teachers use different strategies to help students build phonological and phonemic awareness.

A good resource for teachers of beginning readers is Opitz's book *Rhymes and Reasons: Literature and Language Play for Phonological Awareness* (2000). This book contains a good explanation of the difference between phonological and phonemic awareness. The book also lists a number of books that can be used to teach students phonological and phonemic awareness with suggestions for ways to use each book.

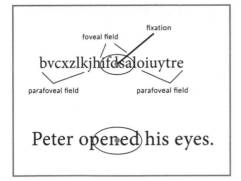

Figure 5.5 (above) *Fixations, foveal field, and parafoveal field*

Figure 5.6 (right) *Eye movement record with fixations numbered* (from Paulson and Freeman 2003)

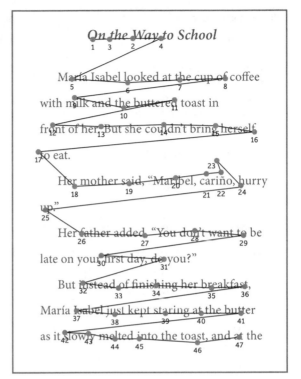

This valuable resource can help teachers teach phonological and phonemic awareness in the context of good children's literature.

By interacting with interesting texts, students gradually acquire graphophonic knowledge and use graphophonic cues along with syntactic and semantic cues to construct meaning from texts.

Phonics and graphophonics

The difference between the use of phonological information made by teachers with a learning view and those who take an acquisition view can be understood by examining the difference between phonics and graphophonics. Those who hold a learning view of reading assume that phonics is the most important skill for students to develop. In contrast, those who take an acquisition view reason that readers acquire knowledge of graphophonics as they read. Graphophonics is often confused with phonics. However, there are some important differences between the two. These are summarized in Figure 5.7.

Phonics (learning view)	Graphophonics (acquisition view)
• **Conscious:** learned as the result of direct, systematic, explicit teaching	• **Subconscious:** acquired in the process of reading and being read to
• The primary source of information used in decoding words	• One of three sources of information used in constructing meaning
• A prerequisite for reading that develops through practice with decodable texts	• A result of reading that develops through engagement with texts that have characteristics that support reading
• Can be tested independently of meaningful reading	• Can only be assessed in the context of meaningful reading

Figure 5.7 *Phonics and graphophonics*

Conscious or subconscious?

The first difference between phonics and graphophonics is that phonics knowledge is conscious, but graphophonic knowledge is subconscious. Phonics rules are learned and become conscious knowledge. Students can recite phonics rules, such as "When two vowels go walking, the first one does the talking." Graphophonics, in contrast, is subconscious knowledge that is acquired as people read. It is this knowledge that allows readers to pronounce the final *s* in *pleks,* with the sound of /s/ and the final *s* in *plems* with a /z/ sound even though they would never have seen these invented words before. Readers can use graphophonic knowledge to pronounce new words, but they can't state the rule for the pronunciation.

Most important cue or one of three cues

A second difference between phonics and graphophonics is that from the learning perspective, phonics is seen as the most reliable way of turning written marks on a page into the sounds of the oral language, but from an acquisition perspective, graphophonics is just one of three linguistic cueing systems. Teachers who hold a learning view believe that students can apply phonics rules to decode most words, or, at least most short words. However, although American English spelling is systematic, as we will discuss in Chapter 6, no spelling system has a one-to-one correspondence between the letters and the sounds in a language. Spelling is different from phonemic transcription because it serves both readers and writers by giving both sound and visual cues to the meanings of words. As a result, knowledge of phonics does not always allow students to decode words successfully.

We were reminded that phonics is not always helpful. Our daughter visited Thailand, where she bought us T-shirts. On the back is written the name of a city in Thailand she visited. The Roman alphabet rendering of the city name is Phuket. The natives pronounce the word /pukɛt/, but that's not how shoppers read it at our local grocery store!

Teachers who take an acquisition view of reading see graphophonics as one of three cueing systems that readers use along with their background knowledge to make sense of texts. Studies of reader miscues, in fact, show that struggling readers often rely too much on letters and sounds, while more proficient readers make greater use of syntactic and semantic cues as they read.

Kucer and Tuten (2003) conducted a study of the reading of twenty-four graduate students. Their results indicate that these proficient readers do make use of syntactic and semantic context and rely minimally on graphophonic cues. They reported that "Approximately 87 percent of all initial miscues made sense within the previous context of the story, 94 percent maintained the previous syntactic structure of the sentence in which they were found, and 88 percent were acceptable with the previous meaning of the sentence in which they were located" (288). These high percentages show that proficient readers make use of both the syntactic and semantic cues from the text as they read. When they make miscues, the miscues usually make sense in the sentence and the story, and proficient readers correct most miscues that don't make sense.

Kucer and Tuten considered all miscues, including omissions and insertions. They found that only 35 percent of all the miscues these proficient readers made had high graphic similarity to the text, and an additional 11 percent had some similarity. That meant that over 50 percent of the time, these readers made miscues that didn't look or sound like the words in the text even though they had a good understanding of the text. This suggests strongly that these readers were not using graphophonic cues in many cases. Instead, they were constructing meaning by relying primarily on syntactic and semantic context. They made only minimal use of graphophonemic information.

The results for the twenty-four proficient readers stand in sharp contrast with their analysis of the twenty-two struggling readers in this same study. Despite claims that struggling readers rely too heavily on context, these struggling readers made little use of context and relied heavily on graphophonic information. The proficient readers, on the other hand, made minimal use of graphophonic information and relied heavily on the syntactic and semantic context. As Kucer and Tuten put it, "these adult readers cause us to question early reading programs that rely heavily on the teaching of graphic and sound (phonic) strategies, especially in isolation" (290).

A prerequisite for reading or a result of reading

A third difference between phonics and graphophonics is that phonics knowledge is considered a prerequisite for reading, and graphophonic knowledge is developed as the result of reading and being read to. Teachers who take a learning view believe that students who know their phonics rules can use them to attack words. Until students can sound words out, they cannot be expected to read full texts.

Teachers who hold an acquisition view believe that graphophonics is acquired in the process of reading. In fact, the only way that this subconscious knowledge can be developed is through reading and being read to. Knowledge of graphophonics is a result of, not a prerequisite for, reading. These teachers follow a gradual release of responsibility approach to the teaching of reading. For beginning readers, this includes read-alouds, shared reading, guided reading, and independent reading. This approach is generally referred to as *balanced reading* or *guided reading* (Fountas and Pinnell 2012–2013).

Choosing books to support reading development

Teachers who approach reading from an acquisition view also know the importance of choosing quality materials for students to read. Students benefit when teachers use books with characteristics that support reading. The checklist in Figure 5.8 is helpful in deciding whether a book has these characteristics.

Alphabet books

In addition to using books that have characteristics that support reading, teachers who hold an acquisition view ensure that beginning readers learn the names of letters and begin to associate letters and sounds. One way they do this is by using alphabet books.

Many alphabet books for young readers focus on initial sounds. *Annie, Bea, and Chi Chi Dolores* (Maurer 1996) , contains names of activities associated with school activities, such as "J jumping rope," "K kicking a ball," and "L lining up." Another book for beginning readers, *ABC and You* (Fernandes 1996), has student names and characteristics on each page from Amazing Amanda to Zippity Zack. After the teacher reads this book, students can work together to create a class alphabet book with the names of all the students in the class. Students might discuss what characteristic to connect with each of their classmates. They would also have to decide what to do if several students' names start with the same first letter and if some letters are not represented by a student name. This kind of problem-solving activity promotes students' learning as they work collaboratively.

Characteristics of Text That Support Reading

1. Are the materials authentic? Authentic materials are written to inform or entertain, not to teach a grammar point or a letter–sound correspondence.

2. Are the materials predictable? Prediction is based on the use of repetitive patterns, cumulative patterns, rhyme, alliteration, and rhythm. Books are also predictable if students have background knowledge about the concepts presented.

3. Is there a good text-picture match? A good match provides nonlinguistic visual cues. Is the placement of the pictures predictable?

4. Are the materials interesting and/or imaginative? Interesting, imaginative texts engage students.

5. Do the situations and characters in the book represent the experiences and backgrounds of the students in the class? Culturally relevant texts engage students.

Additional Considerations for Older Students with Limited English Proficiency

1. Is the text limited?

2. Are the pictures, photographs, or other art appropriate for older students?

3. For content texts, are there clear labels, diagrams, graphs, maps, or other support visuals?

4. Is the content age-level appropriate?

Figure 5.8 *Checklist: Characteristics of text that support reading*

It Begins with an A (Calmenson 1993) is an unusual alphabet book that presents students with a series of riddles to solve. Each rhyming page gives clues and asks, "What is it?" For example, the *C* page reads, "This takes your picture. It starts with a *C*. Get ready, get set. Now smile for me! What is it?" Students enjoy solving the riddles, and groups of students could work together to create a similar book of their own with a riddle for each letter of the alphabet. Writing rhyming pages also helps students become more aware of different spellings for a given sound.

An alphabet book that encourages older children to play with sounds and which can help them develop phonemic awareness is *The Disappearing Alphabet Book* (Wilbur 1997). This playful book asks what would happen if letters of the alphabet were to disappear. For example, the *P* page reads, "How strange that the banana's slippery peel, / Without its *P* would be a slippery EEL!" This book helps students realize that sometimes when they delete a letter from one word they create another word. Again, students could collaborate to make a book modeled on this one.

Teachers can use alphabet books as part of a theme study. There are alphabet books on many different topics. For example, one teacher, Veronica, read *The Icky Bug Alphabet Book* (Pallotta 1986) as part of a unit on bugs. As a follow-up activity, her first graders collected and brought in real insects. Veronica wrote the names of the insects on strips of paper and talked with her students about bugs whose names started with the same sounds and letters. Then, the students drew pictures of their bugs on the strips and hung them under the corresponding letter of the alphabet. To make an alphabet book, Veronica helped the students organize the labeled pictures into a class Icky Bug Alphabet Book. In the process, they discovered that not all the letters of the alphabet were included, so they had to decide what insects could be put on these pages. As they worked together, Veronica's young students became more conscious of initial letter sounds and spellings.

Teachers who take an acquisition view use alphabet books to help young students develop an understanding of the relationships between letters and sounds. These alphabet books are authentic, predictable texts that help students develop the alphabetic principle.

Assessed independently or assessed in context?

A final distinction between phonics and graphophonics is that phonics can be assessed independently of meaningful reading, but graphophonics can only be assessed during reading. Researchers and teachers can test students' knowledge of phonics by asking them to pronounce nonsense words or words the children have not likely seen before. It is easy to construct worksheets and quizzes to practice phonics skills and test phonics knowledge since it is conscious, learned knowledge. However, graphophonics can only be assessed in the context of reading. Using miscue analysis, researchers can evaluate readers' use of graphophonics as part of a more complete analysis of how they use linguistic cues from all three cueing systems to construct meaning.

An explanation for the acquisition of graphophonics

One explanation for the development of graphophonic knowledge comes from the work of Moustafa (1997). She asks how children develop their knowledge of letter–sound correspondences. Her explanation rests on the linguistic analysis of syllables into onsets and rimes. English words like /strim/ (*stream*) and /pleɪt/ (*plate*) contain syllables made up of two parts. The initial consonant phonemes comprise the onset of the syllable. Thus, in these two words, the onsets are /str/ and /pl/. The rime is the part from the vowel to the end of the syllable. For these words the rimes are /im/ and /eɪt/.

In poetry, the rime is the part of the word that rhymes. Consider this poem by Chute (in Prelutsky 1986, 53).

My Teddy Bear
A teddy bear is a faithful friend.
You can pick him up at either end.
His fur is color of breakfast toast,
And he's always there when you need him most.

The rimes of the rhyming words in this poem would be transcribed the same even though they are spelled differently. The first couplet (*friend / end*) has the rime /ɛnd/ and the second couplet (*toast / most*) has /oʊst/ as the rime. In rhyming poetry like this, the onsets differ, but the rime is the same.

Although syllables can be divided into an onset and a rime, some syllables, like in the word *end* in the poem, have no onset. In this word, no consonants precede the vowel, so this word has only a rime. In English, every syllable has a vowel sound, so every syllable must have a rime. Onsets and rimes refer to the sounds in words, not the spellings. In longer words with several syllables, each syllable can be divided into its onset and rime.

Moustafa summarizes a great deal of research to show how children develop graphophonic knowledge. She reports that Treiman (1985) conducted experiments that showed that children are able to divide words into onsets and rimes. She played word games with eight-year-old children and with adults. She found that her subjects were able to split syllables into onsets and rimes, and that they had trouble splitting syllables in any other way. The ability to split syllables up in this way seems natural and does not require instruction.

Knowledge of onsets and rimes seems to be part of the subconscious phonological knowledge speakers of English acquire. They use this knowledge to figure out new words by finding analogies with known words. Moustafa reports on a study by Wylie and Durrell (1970) of first-grade children. They gave them sets of letters that represent rimes in English, such as *-ack, -eck, -ick, -ock,* and asked them to circle the one that says /æk/. Later, they asked children to circle the letter that says /æ/, for example. Children did much better at identifying the rimes than the individual phonemes. Wylie and Durrell's research suggests that children can identify rimes more easily than phonemes.

In addition, Moustafa reports on experiments by Goswami (1986) in which she gave children pairs of words like *hark* and *harm* or *hark* and *lark*. These words have similar sequences of letters, *har* in the first pair and *ark* in the second. She found that children who knew only one word in the pair (based on a pretest) could figure out the other word by analogy. In both words, the letters *har* represent three phonemes. What is interesting is that children did much better with words like *hark* and *lark*, two words with the same rime, than with words like *hark* and *harm*, which have different rimes. In *hark* and *harm* the *h* represents the onset, and the *ar* represents part of the rime. Moustafa interprets Goswami's research as showing that children use their knowledge of onsets and rimes, not their knowledge of phonemes, to recode new words by analogy.

Moustafa's work suggests that graphophonic knowledge develops as children learn new words by analogy with known words by relying on their natural ability to divide syllables into onsets and rimes. The key, then, is for children to build up a large number of known words. The more words they know, the more words they can use to make analogies. A number of studies have shown that children develop vocabulary more rapidly when they read than when they are taught vocabulary directly (Nagy, Anderson, and Herman 1985).

In sum then, phonology plays an important role in reading in English since English is an alphabetic language. Even though there is not a one-to-one correspondence between letters and sounds in English, the letters provide cues that readers can use to help construct meaning from texts. Methods of teaching reading based on the view that reading must be learned put great emphasis on phonics instruction in beginning reading. Methods based on an acquisition view of reading suggest a balanced, guided reading approach using a gradual release of responsibility. Through being read to and reading, children acquire graphophonic knowledge. In this approach, graphophonics is seen as one of three cueing systems that readers use. Teachers expose students to the sounds and letters through meaningful reading and authentic literacy activities. Evidence from linguistics and a clear understanding of the differences between phonics and graphophonics can help educators make informed decisions about the best way to teach reading.

Children's spellings

Children also develop graphophonic knowledge when they are engaged in meaningful writing. As children begin to write, they invent spellings for the words in their messages, and these spellings provide good evidence of their developing graphophonic knowledge. An early study by Read (1971) provides evidence from children's spelling of their knowledge of phonology. Their acquired knowledge is revealed in different ways in their spelling. For example, they use names of the letters to spell vowels. The sound of /ɪ/ is spelled with the letter *e* in words students spell as *egle* (*eagle*) and *fel* (*feel*), and the sound of /aɪ/ is spelled with the letter *i* in *lik* (*like*) and *mi* (*my*).

Children's spellings reflect phonetic details in the language. For example, children often omit nasals that precede consonants and write a word like *and* as *ad* leaving out the *n*. When writing, young children feel where the sound is being produced in their mouths and use just one letter to represent the two sounds (/n/ and /d/) that are produced in the same place in the mouth. Similarly, they use the letter *d* to represent the sound of /t/ in a word like *letter*. This spelling more closely corresponds to the way speakers pronounce /t/ in this position.

Read's study showed that children's spellings reflected their knowledge of many details of English phonology and phonetics. Over time, their invented spellings change to become more conventional. Studies of children's spellings show that they move through a developmental sequence, moving from invented to conventional spellings of most words (Freeman and Freeman 2006).

Children acquire phonology in the process of comprehending oral language. They use this acquired knowledge as they learn to read. Then, when they begin to write, their spelling reflects this knowledge. Their awareness of how sounds relate to spellings, which developed as they were read to and with, is brought to a conscious level as they attempt to represent their own ideas using invented spellings at first and then moving toward conventional spellings.

Conclusion

In this chapter we addressed two questions:

- What insights from phonology can help teachers choose a method for teaching a second language?
- What insights from phonology can help teachers choose a method for teaching reading?

Teachers with a good understanding of phonology as part of their pedagogical language knowledge are in a good position to evaluate methods of teaching a second language and methods of teaching reading. For both second language teaching and teaching reading, approaches based on a learning view emphasize explicit teaching of phonology. In second language teaching, this is shown by attention to teaching correct pronunciation. In reading, phonological and phonemic awareness are seen as important precursors to developing a knowledge of phonics.

Teachers who take an acquisition view involve students in meaningful activities during which the students need to use language to communicate ideas that are important to them. When students have difficulty in pronouncing words, teachers may provide focused lessons on certain sounds that cause confusion. In general, though, the focus is on meaningful communication rather than on the development of nativelike pronunciation.

In teaching reading, teachers who take an acquisition view plan activities to help students make connections between sounds and letters. They may do this through the use of songs, chants, poems, and alphabet books. During read-alouds and shared reading, teachers help students understand the connections between sounds and letters. They also involve students in writing. Students apply their knowledge of phonology as they begin to write. Teachers who take an acquisition view assume that graphophonic knowledge develops best when students are focused on constructing meaning as they read and write.

Teachers with an understanding of phonology can evaluate methods of teaching a second language and teaching reading. Although teachers would only directly teach phonology as part of a class in linguistics, knowing about phonology should be part of every teacher's pedagogical language knowledge.

APPLICATIONS

1. If you are a second language learner of English or if you have been a student in a foreign language class, reflect on how you were taught to pronounce words in a second language. Did the teacher use a method that was consistent with a learning view or with an acquisition view of second language teaching? How effective was the instruction? Be prepared to share your reflection with others.

2. In this chapter, we briefly describe the role of phonology in different methods of second language teaching. Choose one of the methods and conduct additional research on the role of phonology in that method. Be prepared to share your results.

3. Charles Read's early studies of spelling development show how children's knowledge of phonological awareness is revealed in their writing. Read his 1971 study of children's spelling development. Then collect some writing samples of emergent writers and analyze how their spelling reveals their growing awareness of how letters represent sounds. The Read study can be found at: http://homepages.wmich.edu/~hillenbr/204/Read%20&%20 Treiman_Childrens_Invented_Spelling_final.pdf.

4. Try replicating the study Berdiansky and colleagues conducted (on a smaller scale). Choose fifty different words taken from a textbook for beginning readers. Transcribe the words and then draw a line from each phoneme to

the letter or letters that represent that sound as shown in Figure 5.4. Then chart your results. For each different phoneme, list all the possible spellings. Be prepared to share your findings with other students.

5. Linguists have carried out extensive studies comparing languages. Observe English language learners you work with. Is there some feature of their speech that seems to reflect their first language? For example, Spanish speakers might pronounce words like *Spanish* with an /ɛ/ sound at the beginning, before the /s/. Some Asian students may simplify final consonant clusters and pronounce words like *walked* without the sound of the *ed*. Identify one or two features, and then find some information about the students' first language. Is there something in the first language that helps account for the way the students pronounce English? In evaluating these students, how does the school treat these features of the English learners' speech?

6. We explained why the name *Peggy Babcock* is a tongue twister. Try analyzing "She says she shall sew a sheet." Fill in the chart below by transcribing the sentence. Circle the phonemes /s/, /z/, and /ʃ/. Use these data to explain why this is a tongue twister.

sentence	She	says	she	shall	sew	a	sheet
transcription							

6 /sɪks/

English Orthography

Spelling not only has always held an undisputed place as a special branch of instruction in schools, but has been given great consideration as one of the most important and essential subjects of the whole curriculum. . . . The badly spelled letter is apt to be regarded as an unmistakable sign of illiteracy, and even when internal evidences of culture exclude such a charge, the orthographic blunders are deemed at least significant of a partially defective education or of a neglect of essentials that is almost morally reprehensible.

—Oliver Cornman, *Spelling in the Elementary School* (1902)

- How did the English writing system develop?
- Should the spelling system be reformed?
- How can teachers help students take a scientific approach to spelling?

These comments with which Cornman began his book *Spelling in the Elementary School* reflect the opinion of many people now, more than a hundred years later. "Orthographic blunders" are still treated as "almost morally reprehensible" by some, particularly if the misspelled word appears in a job application or a formal letter. Most elementary schools devote time each day to spelling instruction even with the invention of computer word-processing programs that come with a spell check and autocorrect features.

In his book, Cornman reports on research showing that dropping all spelling instruction for four years in a major school system had no effect on students' ability to spell, whether measured in isolation or in students' compositions. Cornman also reports on an earlier study by Rice (1897) that showed "no correlation between the amount of time devoted to spelling and spelling achievement as measured on tests involving words in sentences and compositions" (Krashen 2009, 4). Krashen reports on additional studies showing that many differences that might appear in spelling accuracy between students who receive formal instruction in spelling and those who don't disappear by grades 4 or 5.

Learning and Acquisition Views of Spelling Development

There have been two approaches to helping students, both native English speakers and emergent bilinguals, develop the ability to spell words conventionally. Teachers who take a learning view assume that spelling should be taught in a consistent and systematic way. Teachers who take an acquisition approach assume that as students write for real purposes, they will gradually use more conventional forms of spelling.

The learning view, which predominates in American schools, is probably familiar to most readers. Teachers assign lists of words for students to study. They practice using these words in different ways. Teachers may ask students to write each word several times or use each word in a sentence. Teachers may also require students to include the weekly words in their compositions. Usually there is a test at the end of the week, or there may be a spelling bee. These activities usually are included in English language arts all the way through grade 12.

Teachers who take an acquisition view do involve students in activities that help them focus on words. They may discuss different spellings. They may also involve students in linguistic investigations to help students discover common spelling patterns. In all cases, though, spelling is contextualized as part of writing instruction. Since students write for real purposes, such as composing a letter to the principal requesting a field trip or writing a letter to the editor of the newspaper concerning an environmental issue, they are motivated to use conventional forms to communicate more clearly.

In the early stages of learning to write, students will often invent spellings. Teachers with an acquisition view understand normal spelling development and support students as they move through different stages. The typical developmental patterns have been well documented (see Freeman and Freeman 2006, 2009). For example, students learning to write in English begin with the consonants in words. In English, there is more consistency in the correspondences between consonant phonemes and letters representing those phonemes than there are between vowel phonemes and the letters representing them. Over time, young writers of English begin to add in vowels. In contrast, students learning to write in Spanish often begin with vowels. There are five vowel phonemes in Spanish, so the correspondence between the phonemes and letters representing them are quite consistent. Later, Spanish writers add consonants.

As students develop literacy, they acquire certain knowledge that is not taught. Earlier, we discussed the concept of phonotactics, subconscious knowledge of the possible sound combinations in a language. As children learn to read and write, they also acquire a subconscious knowledge of possible spellings in a language. Readers, for example, know that *bleck* is a possible English spelling, but *lbekc* is not. This knowledge of possible combinations of letters is called *graphotactic knowledge*.

It is this acquired knowledge of graphotactics that makes it possible for readers to unscramble words in puzzles or jumbles that often appear in daily newspapers or books of word games. For example, consider the following series of letters that make up a word: g-a-r-i-n. Most readers can figure out the solution to this jumble fairly quickly as *grain*. In the process of solving the jumble, readers might try ending the word with *-ing*. They might try starting with *in*. However, while readers would attempt some combinations, they would be unlikely to consider others, such as starting with *ng* or even *ai* since that would leave too many consonants to end the word. The five letters of *garin* have 120 possible permutations, but no jumble solver ever goes through all 120. Instead, readers rely on their subconscious graphotactic knowledge to solve the puzzle quickly.

Six-letter combinations are more difficult, but most readers can solve them as well. Consider the following letters: u-a-t-e-c-p. What word do these letters form? Adding just one letter to the string of letters raises the number of possible combinations from 120 to 720, so six-letter words present six times as many possibilities. However, most readers can solve them. This set of letters presents a greater challenge because it is a compound, and in compounds, some unusual combinations of letters occur. That's what makes this jumble more difficult. But, as many of you may have figured out, the word is *teacup*.

Teachers who take an acquisition view of spelling involve students in word games to help them increase their awareness of graphotactics, the typical spelling patterns of English. In addition, teachers can show students interesting books about words, such as Agee's *Sit on a Potato Pan, Otis!* (1999). This is his third book of palindromes. Palindromes are phrases that read the same backward and forward. The first palindrome was reputed to have been "Madam, I'm Adam." Agee includes complicated and clever palindromes accompanied by cartoons. In one, a child holds up a protest sign in the kitchen as her father cooks a meal. The sign reads, "Revile liver!"

Palindromes are rare because the combinations of letters that can spell words left to right seldom spell them right to left. English graphotactics governs possible combinations of letters. Only a few words can be read backward and forward. However, Agee is very creative. An unusually long palindrome included in his book is "A man, a plan, a cat, a bar, a cap, a mall, a ball, a map, a car, a bat, a canal: Panama." Looking at palindromes, talking about them, and trying to write palindromes helps students think about words and how they are spelled.

The ability to recognize combinations of letters as possible English words develops as the result of reading. Even though extensive reading and writing improves spelling ability (Krashen 2004), some students who are avid readers and write frequently still misspell some words (Hughes and Searle 1997). Many poor spellers think that good spellers just memorize all the words. However, rather than having students try to memorize correct spellings, teachers who take an acquisition view attend to spelling and provide strategies and resources for their students.

The orthographic system

Whether teachers take a learning or an acquisition view, they need to be aware that people (other teachers, administrators, parents, community members) are often very concerned about how well students can spell words. One reason that spelling gets so much attention in schools is that English spelling is complex. Most people agree that English spelling is not very logical. Why does English have silent letters like the *l* in *walk*? Why does English allow words like *great* and *grate* in which one sound, /eɪ/, is spelled in different ways? Why does English have words like *through* and *though* in which one set of letters, *ough*, represents different sounds?

Many writers have called for spelling reform. Mark Twain, for example, wrote a clever essay proposing a number of changes to make American English spelling more regular. Plans for changes in the way words are spelled are often circulated on the Internet. These proposals point out the inconsistencies in the system. Most of the suggestions are more humorous than serious. Nevertheless, there is a widespread belief that English spelling is inconsistent and unpredictable.

Although people usually focus on the spelling system, spelling is part of the *orthography* of a language. Orthography is a more general term used to refer to all aspects of writing, including the spelling, the punctuation, the spacing, and special features, such as boldface or italics. With the widespread use of computers, writers have many choices of fonts or special ways to emphasize their text. Punctuation and special marks attempt to capture the intonation features of oral language. In this chapter, our focus is only on the way letters are used to spell words, not on the other aspects of English orthography.

Orthography is not usually included in a book on linguistics; however, since this book has a focus on classroom applications of an understanding of language, it is important to address the issue of the writing system of English. We begin this chapter by tracing the history of writing from early systems to alphabetic writing. We describe the development of American English spelling and explain the logic behind the current system. We conclude the chapter by describing different ways teachers can involve students in linguistic investigations of spellings. Both native English speakers and emergent bilinguals need to develop knowledge of English spelling to read and write effectively. When teachers understand how the writing system works, they can better assist all their students as they develop the ability to use conventional forms of written language.

The Development of Writing Systems

Oral and signed systems of communication are effective for face-to-face contexts. These were the first communication systems created. Over time, different groups of people developed systems of written communication. The earliest systems enabled people to keep records, usually for trade. Writing is an aid to memory, and merchants needed to keep track of what was bought and sold. Different kinds of writing systems evolved from there.

In China the current characters can be traced back to a period between 1200–1050 BC, although writing had developed even earlier. The current system of written Chinese is complex. Characters generally represent syllables and may stand alone as words or function as parts of longer, polysyllabic words. The characters are composed of parts that may represent physical objects, such as the sun; abstract nouns, such as love; or sounds. The system is referred to in different ways but often as *logosyllabic*, a term that refers to the syllabic structure of the writing system and the fact that characters or parts of characters may represent objects (retrieved from http://en.wikipedia.org/wiki/Written_Chinese on 9/29/2013).

Other writing systems also use characters to represent syllables. For example, both Japanese and Cherokee have *syllabaries* rather than alphabets. Using characters to represent syllables increases the number of characters that are needed, but it can better represent the relationship between spellings and sounds in some languages. The Cherokee syllabary was developed in the early 1800s by Sequoyah. Sequoyah, a native Cherokee himself, is known as the only person in recorded history who created a writing system as a member of a nonliterate people. He recognized that the Cherokee people needed a written language for political and economic purposes. At first, he tried to develop a system with one character for each word. After working on this project for a year, he abandoned it, realizing that it would not be practical to have such a complex writing system. No one could remember all the characters.

His next effort was more successful. He created a syllabary consisting of 86 characters. Although this was still a complex system, people could and did learn it. As a result, many of the Cherokee people became literate. Sequoyah's accomplishment is notable. The system was widely adopted, and the Cherokee people began to publish a newspaper using this writing system (retrieved from http://en.wikipedia.org /wiki/Sequoyah on 9/29/2013).

Japanese has a complex writing system that includes *kanji*, made up of adopted Chinese characters, and two syllabaries. *Hiragana* is used with *kanji* for native Japanese words and for grammatical elements, such as particles. *Katakana* is used for foreign words and loanwords, including scientific names. Despite the complexity of the system, which mixes these three methods of representing words in Japanese, it does not appear that people have more difficulty in learning (or acquiring the ability) to read and write in Japanese than in other languages.

Alphabetic Writing Systems

Many of the world's writing systems, including English, are alphabetic. In these systems there is an attempt to have one letter to represent each sound. Even though no language uses a writing system that has a complete one-to-one correspondence between letters and sounds, all alphabetic systems follow the general principle that each letter in a word represents one of its sounds.

For example, the Thai script has forty-four consonants and fifteen vowel symbols that combine into twenty-eight different forms as well as four tone marks. The consonants are written horizontally with vowel marks above or below the consonants. This kind of system is referred to as an *abugida* rather than an alphabet since the consonant and vowel sounds are written as a unit instead of having a separate character for each vowel. According to tradition, this script was created in 1283 by King RamKhamhaeng the Great (retrieved from http://en.wikipedia.org/wiki/Thai _alphabet on 9/30/2013).

Another writing system was created during the Joeson Dynasty by Sejong the Great around 1443 in Korea and is now the official writing system in both North and South Korea. The Korean *Hangul* script is an alphabet with twenty-four consonant and vowel letters. These letters are grouped into blocks to represent syllables. Each syllabic block has two to five letters including at least one consonant and one vowel. In this way, the Korean alphabet is written to represent syllables. The blocks may be arranged either horizontally or vertically (retrieved from http://en .wikipedia.org/wiki/Hangul on 9/30/2013).

Early writing systems

According to Samoyault (1998), a literary critic and author of books on writing systems, "Though people all over the world have been writing for more than 5,000 years, the first true alphabets weren't developed until the period between 1700 and 1500 BC in areas bordering the eastern shores of the Mediterranean" (1). The earliest writing consisted of pictures or symbols representing ideas. These writing systems are referred to as *pictographic* or *ideographic*. Early writing was usually connected to religion or magic. Generally, only priests or their scribes could write or could interpret the written marks. In fact, the early Egyptian writing, called *hieroglyphics*, means "priest writing."

Cuneiform

The earliest known writing system is cuneiform, invented by the Sumerians living in Mesopotamia around 3300 BC. This early system used marks to record the number of different kinds of items that the Sumerians traded. The word *cuneiform* means "wedge-shaped." These early writers used sticks or reeds to make marks on clay. When they pressed a stick into the clay, the resulting mark was a triangular wedge shape.

The Sumerian cuneiform writing system could be read by people who spoke different languages because the pictures and more abstract symbols represented numbers and items that were traded. Speakers of different languages interpreted the marks in their own language. This was a useful system for trade across different language groups. Pictographic or ideographic writing has the advantage of communicating ideas directly to people who speak different languages or different dialects of a language. Since there is no correspondence between the written marks and sounds, speakers of different languages can all interpret the message. Samoyault explains that "From the Sumerians, cuneiform writing spread to Akkadians, Babylonians, and Assyrians, and eventually became the writing system of the entire Middle East" (5). The disadvantage of pictographic writing is that a writer has to learn a great number of different symbols, one for each idea.

Hieroglyphics

The writing system that developed in Egypt around 3200 BC, about the same time as cuneiform developed, was known as hieroglyphics. It differed from the cuneiform writing of Mesopotamia in that it included both pictures and marks that stood for sounds. Since the Egyptian system included some written marks representing sounds, it represents a mixed system intermediate between pictographic or ideographic writing and alphabetic writing.

These early writing systems used pictures or more abstract drawings to express ideas. These systems were fairly easy to read as long as the symbols were not too abstract. The writing communicated ideas directly. However, these were a difficult system for writers, since they had to learn a picture or symbol for each thing or idea.

Pictographic and ideographic writing was replaced by alphabetic writing. An alphabetic system is more indirect. It uses letters to represent the sounds of words that, in turn, represent things or ideas. Alphabetic systems are easier than earlier systems for writers because writers only have to learn a small number of letters, and then they can combine these letters in different ways to produce any word they want to write. The limitation of alphabetic writing is that it can only be understood by a reader who speaks that language.

Early alphabets

The Egyptian writing system combined symbols that represented things with symbols that represented sounds. The first system in which all the marks represented sounds was developed in Syria around 1500 BC in the port city of Ugarit. The people in this important port city needed a simple system for communicating widely. This Ugaritic alphabet still used wedge-shaped cuneiform symbols at first to represent the sounds because clay was readily available. However, this was cumbersome for writers.

About four hundred years later, another group of traders, the Phoenicians, introduced papyrus, a smooth, paperlike substance made from the papyrus plant, for writing. Because they used papyrus rather than clay tablets, they were able to produce lines instead of the triangle shapes that resulted from pressing sticks into clay. This linear writing made it easier to write different letters. The Phoenicians introduced an alphabet with only twenty-two letters. This writing system used letters to represent consonant sounds, but it did not include vowels.

Some writing systems, such as Arabic and Hebrew, originally consisted of consonants. Currently, in these writing systems vowels are represented by placing diacritics, various small marks, over the consonants or by separate characters. In English, while letters representing vowel phonemes differentiate many words, like *sit*, *set*, and *sat*, the letters representing vowels are not as important as those representing consonants. Most English speakers have trouble reading a sentence in which the consonants are deleted, such as _ _ i_   i_ _ _ oo _ a _ ou_ _i _ _ ui _ _ i _ _, even when blanks are inserted to show the missing letters. On the other hand, most readers can decipher the same sentence with the vowels deleted: Th _ s _s _ b_ _k _b _ _ t l _ ng_ _ st _ cs.

Greek and Latin alphabets

The Greeks developed an alphabet that included both consonants and vowels. They used the Phoenician system as a base. Some of the letters of the Phoenician alphabet represented sounds that were not part of Greek, so the Greeks used those letters to represent vowel sounds. Then they added more letters to represent sounds in Greek not present in the Phoenician language. The result was the first true alphabet. Now each sound was represented by a letter. The English word, *alphabet*, comes from the first two letters of the Greek writing system, *alpha* and *beta*. The Greek alphabet contained twenty-four letters.

The Romans based their alphabet on the Greek. They added letters such as *v*, *x*, and *y* to represent sounds in Latin that did not occur in Greek. The Roman alphabet is the most widely used alphabet in the world. The alphabet used for writing English is based on the Roman alphabet.

The Cyrillic alphabet is an additional variation of the Greek alphabet. It was developed by St. Cyril and his brother, who converted the Slavs to Christianity. They included characters to represent Slavic sounds not found in Greek. This alphabet is used today in Russia, the Ukraine, Serbia, and Bulgaria. The development of the Cyrillic alphabet, like that of the Roman alphabet, was based on the need to find ways to represent sounds in languages that were different from Greek.

Emergent bilinguals whose first language is written in a non-Roman alphabet need to learn the Roman system as used by English speakers. Some alphabets, such as Thai or Chinese, are completely different from English. Others, such as Cyrillic, are based on the Greek alphabet and share some characters with the Roman alphabet. However, a Russian learning English has to learn that *p* represents the sound of /p/, not the sound of /r/ as it does in Russian. Even English learners who use the Roman script in their first language have to learn different sound values for the letters in English. For example, *h* is silent in Spanish but sometimes pronounced in English, and *j*, which has a sound closer to the sound represented by the English letter *h* in Spanish, is pronounced as /dʒ/ in English. An Italian speaker learning English would need to learn that *chi* is pronounced /tʃi/, not /ki/, and *ci* is /si/ or /sɪ/, not /tʃi/.

The Development of English Spelling

Modern English spelling developed over time. In the following sections, we trace changes in spelling and pronunciation through three historical periods: Old English, Middle English, and modern English, as well as changes effected by Noah Webster in America. After conventional spellings were established, the pronunciation of words, particularly the vowels, continued to change. An examination of these changes helps us understand our present spelling system. An excellent source for additional information about the development of all facets of the English language is Baugh and Cable's *A History of the English Language* (2012).

Old English

The Old English period dates from about 450 to 1100. During this time, the Roman alphabet was introduced to the Anglo-Saxons by Irish missionaries in the fifth century to write Old English (Tompkins and Yaden 1986). This alphabet was much like the modern English alphabet, but Old English did not use the letters *j*, *k*, *v*, or *w* and only used *q* and *z* rarely. In addition, Old English used other letters to represent sounds in the language. These included /æ/ (called an *ash*), ð (the barred *d*) for both voiced and voiceless *th*, a kind of *z* (the yogh), written as ʒ, that represented the /g/ sound, and two other symbols, a second character for *th* and one for *w*.

During the Old English period, some sounds were spelled differently than they are in modern English. For example, the /ʃ/ sound was spelled *sc* so *ship* was spelled *scip*. Both /k/ and /tʃ/ were spelled with the letter *c*. Thus the word *folk* was spelled *folc* and *child* was spelled *cild*. In addition, the vowel sound /ɪ/ was spelled with either *i* or *y*. This accounts for variations in modern English like *gypsy* and *gipsy*. However, in modern English, *y* is seldom used to represent the sound of /ɪ/ although there are some words like *gym* that use *y* to spell the sound. The letters *u* and *v* were interchangeable, and scribes put two *u*'s together to form the *w* (Tompkins and Yaden 1986).

Also during this period, the sound of /k/ was pronounced in words like *knee* (written as *cneo*), and the letter *f* represented both the /f/ and /v/ sounds, the voiceless and voiced labiodental fricatives. These two sounds were allophones of /f/. The phoneme was pronounced /f/ at the beginning or end of a word and /v/ in the middle. Modern English uses *f* and *v* to represent these two sounds, which are now two phonemes. The historical development of *f* and *v* spellings helps account for the alteration in the plurals of words ending in *f* like *thief* and *thieves* and *wife* and *wives*. The current spelling represents the sounds made during the Old English period.

Middle English

The Norman conquest of England in 1066 brought great changes to the language and signaled the beginning of the Middle English period, which dates from about 1100 to 1500. Many words were added from French and Latin. In addition, Norman scribes introduced a number of changes in the spelling of English words. For example, they replaced *cw* with *qu* so Old English *cwen* became Middle English *queen*. Many words spelled with *u* in Old English were spelled with *o* in Middle English, especially when the *u* was followed by a letter with a similar shape, such as *m, n,* or *u.* Thus Old English *cuman* was written *come* in Middle English (Tompkins and Yaden 1986). The Norman scribes also substituted *ou* for *u* to make English spelling more like French spelling. The Old English word *hus* was written as *hous* in Middle English.

In Old English the letter *h* represented two sounds. In Middle English these two sounds were replaced by one guttural sound spelled with *gh.* Modern English keeps this spelling, in words like *cough* or *laugh*, although the letters *gh* are now pronounced as /f/. The letter *v* was used in many French loanwords. However, *u* and *v* were interchangeable during this time to represent either the vowel sound or the consonant sound. Shakespeare spelled *universal* as *vniuersall* for example. It wasn't until late in the eighteenth century that the current practice of using *u* to represent the vowel sound and *v* to represent the consonant sound was established.

Other changes during the Middle English period included replacing the Old English yogh (ȝ) with the French letter *g*, changing *hw* spellings, which represented the actual sequence of sounds, to *wh* (the transcription of a word like *where* begins with /hw/ because the sound of /h/ occurs before the sound of /w/), beginning to use *v* for the sound previously written with *f* (*driven*), and using *k* and *ch* for the two sounds spelled with *c* in Old English (*folk* for *folc* and *child* for *cild*).

Modern English

English spelling has continued to change during the modern English period, which extends from about 1500 to the present time. However, a number of forces combined to stabilize spelling. William Caxton established the first printing press in England in 1476, but Caxton and other early printers were businessmen and were not concerned with consistent spellings. In fact, they brought Dutch typesetters to work in England, and these Dutch workers are thought to have introduced some spellings like the *h* in *ghost*. Over time, though, the publishing industry employed people who had formerly worked as scribes and who had learned spelling conventions. At the same time, several prominent spelling reformers called for consistency in spelling. As more books were produced with consistent spellings, these spellings became the norm.

Although spellings were becoming fixed for the most part during the early part of the modern English period, changes in spellings continued to be introduced. Many Greek and Latin words entered English during this period. Some English words derived from Latin had been changed to conform to French spelling patterns.

During this early modern period the spelling of some of these words were changed back to more closely resemble their Greek and Latin roots. For example, a *b* was added to *debt* and *doubt* to mirror the Latin spellings *debitum* and *dubitare*. The words had been spelled without the *b* in Old French and Middle English. In addition, a *c* was added to *scissors* because scholars recognized that the word had come from the Latin word *sciendere*, meaning "to cut." Similarly, an *l* was added to *faute* (*fault*) to reflect the Latin root *fallere*. Other spellings were changed so that the word would be spelled similarly to another Old English word. For example, an *l* was added to *could* to make it analogous with *should* and *would*, which were spelled with an *l* in Old English. The *l* was not pronounced by the end of the sixteenth century in any of the words, but writers wanted all three modal auxiliaries to be spelled alike.

Conventional spellings of many words came to be established by the end of the eighteenth century. Books such as Samuel Johnson's *Dictionary of the English Language*, published in 1755 with more than 40,000 entries and thousands of quotations, helped to fix many spellings. However, changes in pronunciation during this same time resulted in variation between sounds and spellings in current English. The major change, which occurred in the 1500s, is referred to as the Great Vowel Shift. The long vowels were pronounced at a higher point in the mouth. In Middle English the vowel in a word like *feet* was pronounced more like the vowel sound in *fate*. By 1500, *feet* had developed its current pronunciation. In addition, high vowels became diphthongs and moved to a lower position. A word like *town* was once pronounced more like *tune*.

The series of changes in pronunciation came after the spelling was fixed. As a result, some of our current spellings do not match well with pronunciations. For example, spellings of pairs of related words like *divine* and *divinity* and *extreme* and *extremity* reflect a period before the Great Vowel Shift when the second syllable of each of these words was pronounced with the same vowel sound as the first syllable. Thus, in *divine* the current pronunciation of the second vowel sound is /aɪ/, but earlier it was pronounced /ɪ/, the same sound as the *i* in the first syllable.

Linguists can reconstruct the early pronunciations of words like *divine* by examining rhyming texts. For example, at one time the words *good* and *food* rhymed. A mealtime blessing shows this:

God is great, God is good,
Let us thank Him for our food

This was originally a rhyming couplet and these words were pronounced alike. However, the vowel shift affected the two words differently, and now they do not rhyme. The reconstruction of early languages, including the pronunciation, is the focus of historical linguistics. This work is complex, but historical linguists have worked backward from present languages to recreate earlier languages.

The Great Vowel Shift was gradual, and by the time it was completed, many spellings of vowel sounds no longer corresponded to their pronunciations. Other changes in vowels included final, unstressed vowels, especially *e* becoming silent. During Middle English, the *e* in a word like *come* was pronounced as a schwa, but in modern English these *e*'s are not pronounced at all. Unstressed vowels in the middle of words were reduced to a schwa, and vowels followed by *d*, *th*, and *f* were shortened. This explains spellings of words like *bread*, *breath*, and *deaf* (Tompkins and Yaden 1986). However, not all words now spelled with *ea* followed by *d*, *th*, or *f* were shortened as shown by words like *mead*, *heath*, and *leaf*.

In addition to changes in the pronunciation of vowels, consonant sounds were simplified. Combinations that were formerly pronounced as blends were reduced to single sounds. The letters *gh*, which at one time were pronounced as two sounds, came to be pronounced as /f/ at the end of words like *laugh*. The initial consonants in the blends *kn*, *gn*, and *wr* were no longer pronounced. In addition, the *b* was no longer pronounced in words like *bomb*, the *n* became silent in *mn* combinations like *hymn*, and the *l* was not pronounced in *lk* combinations like *talk*. Even though the pronunciation changed, the spelling stayed the same. All these changes in pronunciation added to the differences between sounds and spellings.

American English spelling

Noah Webster was a patriot who wanted to create a uniquely American English language, different from the language of England. He also wanted to reform spelling by simplifying it. Webster was very influential, and several of the reforms he advocated were put into effect. The changes came as the result of the wide use of his *American Spelling Book*. This was the first spelling textbook published in America. It set the standard for American spellings. Eventually, Webster's spelling book sold more than seventy million copies.

Most Americans can recognize British spellings. American spelling, thanks to Webster, differs in several ways. Words spelled with *our* in England are spelled *or* in America (*favour*, *favor*). British words ending with *re* are spelled using *er* in American English (*center*, *centre*). However, American spelling accepts *readers theatre*. Some establishments (*Pointe Centre*) maintain *re* spellings to add what the owners hope will be regarded as a touch of class.

Other changes include the substitution of *se* for *ce* (*defence*, *defense*), the shift from *x* to *ct* (in words like *connexion*, *connection*), the change from *ise* to *ize* (*recognise*, *recognize*), and the dropping of *k* (in words like *musick, music*). Some of Webster's ideas did not take hold. He wanted to simplify some spellings, like changing *bread* to *bred* and *give* to *giv*. He also wanted the spellings to reflect American English pronunciation in words like *wimmen*. Even though not all of his reforms were accepted, Webster had a profound influence on American English spelling.

Making Sense of the American English Spelling System

This brief historical overview helps explain why American English spelling does not correspond to the pronunciation of some words. The main reason that spellings do not always match sounds is that after conventional spellings were established, pronunciation continued to change. Most current proposals for spelling reform are humorous, not serious. It would be nearly impossible to change the way words are spelled. Who would go back and fix all the books and other print materials? Even if there was a strong move to change spelling, whose dialect would prevail? The changes might seem logical at first glance, but they would be nearly impossible to put into effect.

What many reformers don't realize is that the current system is a good compromise. Writing systems are designed to serve two different groups of people, writers and readers. Changes that would make writing easier make reading more difficult, and changes that would make reading easier make writing harder. The different spellings of homophones like *bread* and *bred* make it easier for readers to recognize that the words have different meanings, but writers need to remember two spellings for the /ɛ/ sound. Most reforms are aimed at simplifying the task of writing words by making spellings more closely correspond to sounds. That is, the reforms favor writers. But most people read a great deal more than they write, so spelling reforms would not really be beneficial.

To understand spelling, it is necessary to realize that it is a complex system much like the American educational system. School systems attempt to balance the needs of several different groups—students, teachers, administrators, parents, community members, and politicians, to name a few. Any proposal to change the system comes under scrutiny by each of these groups. A change that might be good for teachers might not be considered beneficial for students. Anyone who wants to reform schools needs to take into account the concerns and needs of all the different groups involved. Most reforms fail because only certain groups benefit, usually at the expense of other groups. Reformers who want to change spelling so that each word is spelled the way it sounds fail to recognize that other forces besides sound shape spelling (Cummings 1988).

The strongest demand on the spelling system is the phonetic demand to spell a given sound consistently. Every time a phoneme occurs, it should be spelled the same way. A second demand comes from analogy. Words that come from the same root and share the same meaning should be spelled the same way. This is the semantic demand. Finally, there is the demand that words should reflect their historical backgrounds. This is the etymological demand, a force that keeps spellings constant across time and across languages. Because of this demand, some spellings reflect the way words were pronounced in earlier periods and others reflect the spelling of the language from which a word was borrowed. Figure 6.1 summarizes the demands on the spelling system.

Current alphabetic writing systems such as English do spell most words like they sound. The phonetic demand is the strongest demand on the spelling system. However, there are exceptions. The semantic demand results in cases where the spellings convey meanings, not just sounds. Some words that sound the same are spelled differently to signal that they represent different meanings. *Homophones* are words that sound the same but may be spelled differently, like *great* and *grate*. The variation in spelling shows that the words mean different things. The variations in spellings of homophones signal important meanings to a reader that would be lost if every word that sounds the same were spelled the same way.

There are still homographic homonyms, words that are spelled the same, like *bat* and *bear*, that have two or more different meanings. Do the letters *b-a-t* refer to the animal or the stick used in baseball? Do the letters *b-e-a-r* mean an animal or the action of carrying a heavy burden or giving birth? In these cases, readers need to use context to figure out the meaning.

English has many homophones that are spelled differently. Consider this sentence from Smith (1985): "Eye sea too feat inn hour rheum" (56). If this sentence is read aloud, a listener can make sense of it, even though it is a somewhat strange sentence. However, the sentence is quite difficult to read. American English spelling, which uses different spellings for each of these homophones, gives readers visual cues to the meaning.

Force	Demand	Example
phonetic	spell words the way they sound	sit /sɪt/
semantic (analogy)	spell words alike that share the same meaning	hymn hymnal
etymological	spell words to reflect their origins	one (Old English) kangaroo (Australian)

Figure 6.1 *Forces that shape English spelling*

Some writers have used homophones as the basis for books for young readers. Gwynne, for example, has written books like *The King Who Rained* (1988b) and *A Chocolate Moose for Dinner* (1988a), which are very entertaining. The cover illustrations portray the literal meaning of the title of each book. These books can be used for discussions of literal and nonliteral meanings. English language learners often have difficulty understanding jokes based on homophones, and these books can be the basis for discussion of homophones and homonyms in English. In addition, Terban has written *Eight Ate: A Feast of Homonym Riddles* (1982). The answer to the riddle on each page contains a homophone. For example, one page asks, "What is a smelly chicken?" The answer, of course, is "A foul fowl" (9). Young readers enjoy making up their own homophone riddles based on Terban's model.

In addition to homophones, English has pairs of related words like *medicine* and *medical* in which the same letter *c* is used to represent two different sounds, /s/ and /k/. Some reformers have suggested eliminating the letter *c* and using *s* and *k* to represent the two sounds. This would result in the spellings *medisin* and *medikal*. This change would result in a more consistent representation of sounds (easier to write) but would lose the visual connection between these related words (harder for readers to construct meaning). Other reformers have suggested eliminating silent letters like the *g* in *sign*. Readers would then lose the connection between the related words *sign* and *signal*. Besides, if the *g* were dropped from *sign* the resulting word would be *sin* and that could cause real confusion. Many words with silent letters are related to other words in which the letter is pronounced, such as *bomb* and *bombard*.

By using the same letters to spell words that are semantically related, writers signal the meaning link to readers. Both *crumb* and *crumble* are written with a *b* to signal the connection between the words. Even though the *b* is not pronounced in *crumb* it is pronounced in *crumble*. Similarly, in a word like *cupboard* the *p* is not pronounced, but including the *p* in the spelling helps signal the meaning. A *cupboard* is literally a board to put cups on.

The third force that puts a demand on the spelling system is the etymological demand. This demand requires that spellings signal the origins of the words. As a result of this demand, some spellings reflect earlier stages of English. Some common words such as *are* and *some* retain their original spellings even though the pronunciation has changed over time. Loanwords that have come from other languages have also kept the spellings of their origins. In a word like *machine* the French spelling of *ch* for the /ʃ/ sound is kept even though the digraph *ch* usually is pronounced /tʃ/ in English words. *Psychology*, which retains the *p*, comes from Latin. Most spellings that strike readers as unusual are the result of retaining spellings from Middle

English or keeping the spellings of borrowed words from other languages without changing them to conform to English patterns. For example, in English the sound of /k/ is not usually spelled with *kh*, as in *khaki*, borrowed from Urdu.

A study of word histories can help students make sense of many spellings. An excellent book for upper elementary through high school age students is *The Journey of English* (Brook 1998). This beautifully illustrated book traces the history of the English language. Included in the book are interesting facts about English words. For example, the unusual spelling of *Wednesday* becomes clearer when students learn that the day was named after the Norse god Woden. Woden's day became the modern Wednesday. The /ʃu/ sound is spelled *su* in a few English words. One of these is *sugar*, whose origins can be traced back to Sanskrit. This book provides an accurate and reader-friendly history of the English language.

Students can study etymologies of words by using dictionaries such as the Oxford English Dictionary or by using Internet sources such as *The Online Etymology Dictionary* (www.etymonline.com). However, they should check more than one source since different sources may give different information. Teachers can also help students read dictionary entries to understand how a word may have come through several languages to reach English. In the case of *sugar*, for example, the word's history shows that it was borrowed into English from Old French, it came into Old French from Medieval Latin, into Medieval Latin from Arabic, into Arabic from Persian, and into Persian from Sanskrit. So the word comes originally from Sanskrit, and it passed through several other languages on its way to English.

The history of alphabetic writing, the history of English spelling, and the history of individual words are all interesting topics for an English language arts class or an ESL class. When teachers talk with students about spelling and help them understand how the orthographic system works, students become better spellers. Teachers can also involve students in using a scientific approach to investigating aspects of the spelling system.

Spelling Investigations

When teachers investigate spellings with their students, everyone gains valuable insights. Mike, for example, involved his fifth graders in several spelling studies. In one, he had students work in pairs to look through books and write down all the words that contained the /eɪ/ sound. Once they had a list of words, they divided the words into different spellings. The words each pair of students found were combined into a class list, and students added to the list over several days. Figure 6.2 lists some of the words with /eɪ/ students might find. The words are divided by their spelling patterns.

For words with a silent *e* the pattern is written as *aCe*. The *C* represents any consonant letter.

After students had developed a list of words and had divided them into the different

aCe	ai	ea	a	ay
rate	aid	steak	major	day
plane	rail	great	agent	mayor
face	train	break	basic	away
create	aim		acorn	stay

Figure 6.2 *Spellings of* /eɪ/

possible patterns, Mike asked them whether they could make any generalizations about when each spelling occurred. Students noticed that the spellings in the first two columns were the most common spellings. The *ea* spellings of the /eɪ/ sound are very limited. With Mike's guidance, they also concluded that the *a* and *ay* spellings came when the /eɪ/ sound was the last sound in a syllable and that the *ay*, but not the *a*, was used for the /eɪ/ sound at the end of a word. As a result of involving his students in spelling investigations such as these, Mike helped them to take a scientific, problem-solving approach to spelling. Students began to notice different spellings and to look for patterns rather than trying to memorize correct spellings.

The approach Mike used with his students to investigate spellings is the same approach linguists use to study oral language. Linguists try to find what are called *conditioning environments* for the phonological phenomena they are studying, such as the different allophones of /t/. This process becomes difficult for spelling analyses because spellings occur in overlapping, not complementary, distributions. That is, two or more spellings of a sound may occur in the same environment. If each spelling occurred in a different environment, it would be possible to make a generalization that works consistently. For example if the sound of /eɪ/ was always spelled *ai* at the beginning of a word, students could learn that generalization. However, most spellings are not in complementary distribution. Instead, the conditioning environments overlap. The sound of /eɪ/ can also be spelled *a* or *aCe* at the beginning of words, such as *able* and *ate*.

Since there are pairs like *pain* and *pane*, it appears that various spellings are possible in the same environment, in this case between /p/ and /n/. Knowing that the sound of /eɪ/ comes between two consonants like /p/ and /n/ does not allow a student to predict the right spelling of a word.

Although the first three spellings on Figure 6.2 are in overlapping distribution with one another, they appear to be in complementary distribution with the last two spellings. In other words, if a consonant follows in the same syllable, the sound /eɪ/ is spelled as *aCe*, *ai*, or *ea*, but it is never spelled with *a* or *ay*.

Students might find more examples of /eɪ/ spellings with time. For example, the family of *aste* words (*baste, chaste, haste, paste, taste*) doesn't follow the usual pattern because there are two consonants between the *a* and the *e*. Apparently, the *e* still signals that the vowel is long. And *tasty* and *hasty* don't have the *e*, but the vowel is still pronounced with the /eɪ/ sound by analogy with *haste* and *taste*. Some students might also find borrowed words with other spellings of /eɪ/, such as the French *et* that occurs in *filet* or *croquet* or the Old English word *ache*, which has an interesting and complicated history.

As students and teachers investigate spelling patterns like this one, they often find more examples and exceptions over time. What is important is that the process of collecting words, categorizing the words, and trying to make generalizations helps students approach spelling as a problem-solving activity, and many students spell more words conventionally after participating in these investigations.

Investigating consonants: The spellings of /k/

Vowel patterns in English are quite complex. Especially for the long vowels, there are usually several possible spellings. Consonants show less variation. For example, the /b/ phoneme is usually spelled with a *b* or *bb*. Nevertheless, some consonant spellings are also complex and would provide interesting possibilities for investigation. One such consonant is /k/. This phoneme has several possible spellings.

A teacher might begin a unit of study on the spellings of /k/ by asking the class to brainstorm all the ways /k/ can be spelled. Then students could work in small groups and look through different texts to try to find additional examples of /k/ spellings to add to the class list. Figure 6.3 lists several possible /k/ spellings.

The most common spellings of /k/ are *c*, *k*, and *ck*. Students can easily find many examples of these spellings. The letter *x* is unusual because it represents two consonant phonemes /ks/. Words like *fox* would be transcribed /faks/. The spellings with *q* come from French. Words with *q* spellings entered English during the Norman period when French scribes replaced the English *cw* with *qu*. The spelling of *qu* for

Spelling	Example	Spelling	Example
c	cat	ch	chemistry
k	kite	kh	khaki
ck	tack	cc	accord
x	fox	cq	acquire
q	queen	kk	bookkeeper
que	unique		

Figure 6.3 *Spellings of /k/*

/kw/ is one of the most consistent spellings in English. The *que* spelling comes at the end of words borrowed from French, such as *pique*.

The teacher could have students look up words with some of the less common spellings to find out about their histories using reference books or Internet sites. Students would find, for example, that words in which *ch* represents /k/ come from Greek. They could compile a list of these Greek borrowings. Some students might know that the Greek letter *chi*, which appears in different sorority and fraternity names, is pronounced /kaɪ/and written with an *X* in the Greek alphabet. When words with the sound represented by the Greek *X* were brought into the Roman alphabet the sound was spelled with *ch*. Modern English words with Greek roots retain this spelling. Many of these words such as *chloride* and *character* appear in the vocabulary of science and drama. As mentioned earlier, the *kh* spelling of *khaki* reflects its foreign origin as well. This word comes from Urdu and is one of several words borrowed into English from Indian languages.

In words like *account* and *acquaint* the prefix ends with a /k/ sound and the root begins with a /k/. This results in /k/ being spelled *cc* or *cq*. Students might say that there are two /k/ sounds in these words. Each word has two syllables, and in dictionaries the words are divided between the prefix and the root (ac-count, ac-quaint). However, the syllable divisions in writing do not reflect the phonological reality. Linguists transcribe these words as /əkaʊnt/ and /əkweɪnt/ because speakers only pronounce one /k/ sound. The spellings with *cc* and *cq* for /k/ reflect the morphology of the word, not the phonology. These spellings help readers see that these words have two meaningful parts or morphemes.

In the case of *bookkeeper*, a compound word, the first morpheme ends in *k* and the second begins with *k*. Even though only one /k/ sound is pronounced, the spelling keeps the two *k*'s to show the morphology of the word. *Bookkeeper* is an interesting word because it is the only English word with three double-letter spellings in a row.

Initial /k/ spellings

Once students have examined the less common spellings, they could make generalizations about when to use each of the most common spellings: *c*, *k*, and *ck*. The *ck* spelling occurs only at the end of a word. The *c* and *k* spellings can occur anywhere although only a few words end in *c*. A good activity to begin to investigate the letter–sound correspondences with /k/ would be for students to list several words with a syllable-initial /k/ sound that are spelled with either *c* or *k* and then try to find a pattern. Figure 6.4 lists some possible words.

words starting with *c*	words starting with *k*
cap	keep
cost	kite
cut	unkempt
climb	rekindle
crib	
record	
decade	

Figure 6.4 *Words with syllable-initial /k/*

If students collect several words in which the syllable-initial /k/ sound is spelled with *c* and several with *k*, they discover a regular pattern. The *c* spelling is always followed by one of the vowels *a*, *o*, and *u*, or a consonant. The *k* spelling is always followed by *e* or *i*. There are very few exceptions to this pattern, all of them involving *k*. For example, words like *kangaroo*, *koala*, and *kudu* begin with *k* followed by *a*, *o*, and *u*. In *krait*, *k* is followed by *r*, but a little investigation shows that these are all borrowed words.

Why is this pattern so consistent? Students usually recognize that in words like *cent* and *city* the *c* has an /s/ sound. In other words, when readers see the combination *ce* or *ci*, they pronounce the *c* as /s/. The only way to produce the /k/ sound when the following vowel is *e* or *i* is to use a *k*. Students could make the generalization:

> The syllable-initial /k/ sound is spelled with *c* when a consonant or *a*, *o*, or *u* follows, and it is spelled with a *k* when an *e* or an *i* follows.

As students find exceptions to this rule, they can investigate the history of those words.

Final /k/ spellings

The spelling pattern for /k/ at the end of a syllable or word is slightly more complex. The sound has three common spellings, *ck*, *k*, and *c*. Figure 6.5 lists words with each of these spellings.

Only a few words spell the /k/ sound at the end of a word with a *c*. Most of these have the suffix *-ic*, although a few words in English end with *ac*. The spellings *ck* and *k* are much more common. If students collect a number of these words, they can begin to see a pattern. If the last sound before the /k/ is a consonant, the *k* spelling is always used to avoid having three consonants in a row. English words never end in *rck* or *lck* for example.

words ending in *ck*	words ending in *k*	words ending in *c*
pack	peek	panic
check	break	maniac
stick	soak	
rock	park	
duck	milk	
	think	

Figure 6.5 *Words ending with /k/*

Students have to look more closely to decide about spellings in which the /k/ sound is preceded by a vowel. The examples in Figure 6.5 suggest that the /k/ sound is spelled with a *ck* when the preceding vowel sound is short and with *k* when the vowel sound is long. Thus /pæk/ (*pack*) is spelled with *ck* and /breɪk/ (*break*) is spelled with a *k*. Note that /i/ is usually referred to as a long vowel in schools and follows the rule for using *k* after long vowels in a word like /pik/ (*peak*), but it is not a diphthong. In producing a diphthong, a speaker moves the tongue up toward the front of the mouth or up toward the back. Diphthongs are transcribed with two characters because there are two vowel sounds.

This generalization works for all the long- and short-vowel sounds except for /ʊ/, a short vowel that is spelled *oo* in a word like *book*. The *ook* spelling is an exception to the short-vowel/long-vowel generalization. However, the *oo* spelling of many words was pronounced as a long sound, /u/, during an earlier period. Some words with these *oo* spellings, such as *too*, retain the /u/ pronunciation, but many others, such as *good*, are pronounced with a short /ʊ/ sound. Before the Great Vowel Shift discussed earlier, the spelling pattern was consistent, but the shift in pronunciation introduced this exception. In addition, some borrowed words such as *trek* are exceptions to the rule.

Since long vowels in English are generally spelled with two letters and short vowels are usually spelled with one letter, another way to describe the pattern of /k/ spellings at the end of a word would be to say that *ck* is used when the vowel sound is spelled with one letter, and *k* is used when the vowel sound is spelled with two letters. To understand this way of stating the generalization, students would need to count silent *e* as one of the two vowels. The sound of /k/ is spelled with *k* in words like *make*, *spoke*, and *fluke* where a silent *e* follows the *k*. As long as students count the silent *e* as one of the two vowels, the two-vowel letter generalization works very well.

Two possible ways to state the generalization about final /k/ spellings are these:

Spell the final /k/ sound of a word or syllable with *ck* if the preceding vowel is short, and spell the sound with *k* if a consonant precedes *k* or if the vowel is long. The exception to this rule is the short vowel /ʊ/, in words like *book*.

Or

Spell the final /k/ sound of a word or syllable with *ck* if only one vowel precedes and with *k* if two vowels or a consonant precedes. Count a final silent *e* as one of the two vowels.

The spellings of /k/ are complex. However, some patterns are quite consistent. It is not so important that students learn every possible /k/ spelling. What is important is for students to begin to take a scientific approach to investigating English spellings. By collecting words, sorting them into categories, and then trying to find patterns that they can state as generalizations, students bring to conscious awareness aspects of the English spelling system. They start to see spelling as systematic, not just a collection of letters to be memorized. Students who approach spelling as a logical system do much better at spelling than those who try to memorize each word. In addition, students who take a scientific approach begin to develop some of the ways of thinking that all scientists follow when studying interesting phenomena. This approach is much more intriguing than the usual practice of studying a list of words for the Friday spelling quiz.

Investigating spellings across related languages

An investigation that would benefit emergent bilinguals, especially those in dual language bilingual programs, would be to analyze the two languages to find common spelling patterns. This would work well for a language like Spanish or French that is closely related to English, but it would not work for Chinese. However, since over 70 percent of the emergent bilinguals speak Spanish, and the majority of the dual language bilingual programs are Spanish/English, this investigation could be used in many classes.

By investigating similarities and differences in spelling patterns between two languages, students could improve their spelling in each language. In the first place, there are many words in English that are spelled exactly the same in Spanish and have the same meaning. The pronunciation is, of course, different, but the spelling is the same. Some examples include *flexible, cable, funeral, honor, animal, triple,* and *incurable*.

In addition, some suffixes have similar spellings, and the differences are consistent. For instance, the ending *-tion* in English is added to verbs to create nouns, such as *evaporation* and *construction*. The suffix that creates nouns from verbs in Spanish is *-ción* as in *asociación, contaminación,* and *deportación*.

Another pattern that is often found in translating from Spanish to English is that *-mento* is often *-ment* in English as in *documento* for *document, momento* for *moment,* and *departamento* for *department*. A final example that might help Spanish speakers spelling in English comes from Spanish words that end in *-cia* that change their ending to *-acy* in English. So *aristocracia* is *aristocracy* and *democracia* is *democracy*. An excellent spelling investigation for Spanish-speaking students would be to look at these common suffixes in Spanish and English or others that have consistent spellings that transfer from one language to the other.

A different kind of pattern that might help Spanish speakers is to look for suffixes that signal parts of speech in each language. In English *-ly* is added to adjectives such as *quick* and *slow* to create adverbs *quickly* and *slowly*. This is a consistent pattern. In Spanish, the suffix that is added to adjectives to create adverbs is *-mente*. Thus *rápidamente* is the adverb meaning *rapidly*.

Another parallel between English and Spanish has to do with the spelling of the /k/ sound discussed earlier. In English the rule is to use *c* before *a, o, u,* and consonants, and to use *k* before *e* and *i*. The rule in Spanish is the same except that in Spanish *qu* is used rather than *k*. This can be seen in words such as *casa, comer, cuenta,* and *creo* where the *c* is used, and *queso* and *quinceañera* that has the *qu* spelling. The rule works very consistently in Spanish.

Investigating Spelling Rules: Silent *e* and Consonant Doubling

In addition to looking at the spellings of particular consonant and vowel phonemes, students can benefit from investigating spelling rules. Often, spelling rules are taught directly. Teachers provide the rule and give students practice using it. Students may learn a rule and yet have trouble applying it. For example, a teacher might present the rule for changing *y* to *i* and students may be able to recite or write the rule or complete a worksheet with words that follow the rule. However, these same students might still spell a word like *monkeys* as *monkies*.

To help students with spelling rules, teachers can have them use the scientific approach described earlier. The students collect words, categorize them, and then attempt to formulate a hypothesis to account for their data. This hypothesis becomes their working rule, which can be modified whenever new data are discovered that are counterexamples.

Two rules that are frequently taught are what Cummings (1988) calls *procedural rules*. These are rules that involve changes in spelling when adding a suffix to a root word. Two useful procedural rules are the rule for dropping a silent *e* when adding a suffix and the rule for doubling a final consonant when adding a suffix. Both of these rules are very helpful because students can't hear a silent *e* or a double consonant, so they need some way to decide when to drop an *e* or double a consonant.

The silent e rule

Complex English words consist of a root or base word and prefixes and/or suffixes. Procedural rules govern the way words are spelled when prefixes or suffixes are added to a root. The silent *e* rule governs whether a final silent *e* is retained or dropped. For example, in the word *make* + *ing* the *e* is deleted (*making*), but in the word *make* + *shift* the *e* is retained (*makeshift*). Teachers could simply give students a rule for dropping the *e*, such as "Drop the *e* if the suffix starts with a vowel, and keep the *e* if the suffix starts with a consonant." However, even students who learn the rule may have difficulty applying it as they write because they have simply memorized a formula; they haven't constructed an internal rule. A number of steps are involved in helping students develop a rule for the silent *e*.

The first step is to help students visualize complex words as being made up of a base or root and a prefix or suffix. It is hard for students to understand a rule about dropping an *e* if they don't picture the base word as having an *e* to start with. That is, students have to realize that *making* had a base word with an *e* that was dropped to form the complex word. Unless students grasp the basic concept of complex words, the *e* rule will not make sense to them. A teacher might begin, then, by presenting a series of words like *making* and having students work in pairs or small groups to figure out the parts these words consist of. Thus, the students would break a word like *making* into *make* + *ing*. Teachers could either give students a list of words to work on or ask students to examine a page from a textbook and list complex words and then identify their component parts.

Once students understand that some words are complex, the teacher can move to the second step. During this step, students collect words ending in a silent *e*. It is important to give some examples to be sure that students don't include words like *be* in which the *e* is pronounced. Figure 6.6 lists a few words that end in silent *e*. If students work in pairs to compile lists of words, they can combine their results to make a more extensive class list.

The next step is to ask students to try to figure out why these words have a silent *e*. Most students would conclude from looking at the list that a silent *e* usually signals that the preceding vowel has a long sound. This is the case of the words listed in the first column in Figure 6.6. The "Silent *e* makes the vowel long" rule is commonly taught, even though Clymer (1963), in the study discussed earlier, found that the rule only works about 60 percent of the time.

Although the main function of silent *e* is to mark long vowels, the silent *e* plays other roles as well. As students collect words with silent *e*, they can discover these other roles. Like scientists,

lake	edge	love
recede	chance	toe
bike	clothe	avalanche
rope	tease	one
tube	glue	definite

Figure 6.6 *Words ending in silent* e

they revise their original hypothesis, that silent *e* marks long vowels, in light of counterexamples.

Some students might discover a second role for the silent *e*. In words like *chance* and *edge*, the *e* serves to signal the pronunciation of a preceding *c* or *g*. When *c* or *g* ends a word, it is pronounced as /k/ or /g/, but when an *e* follows, the pronunciation changes to /s/ or /dʒ/. Many of the apparent exceptions to the "marks long vowel" rule can be accounted for by adding something like "and gives *c* and *g* a soft sound." With this addition, there are fewer exceptions to the silent-e rule, but there are still some holdouts.

This might be a good time for teachers to discuss words that end in *le* like *nibble*. These *le* words shouldn't be considered exceptions to the rule. The *e* in these words does represent a vowel sound that is pronounced. The transcription for *nibble* is /nɪbəl/. Webster wanted to change all *le* spellings in American English to *el* so that the spelling would reflect the order of the sounds. Although Webster succeeded in changing *re* in words like *centre* to *er*, he failed with *le*. Of course, English also has words like *nickel* that put the *e* at the point in the word where it is pronounced.

There are other exceptions to "the silent *e* makes the vowel long" rule. There are a few pairs of words in English like *cloth* and *clothe* and *bath* and *bathe* in which the *e* not only signals a long-vowel sound but also indicates the pronunciation of the *th* digraph. When an *e* follows, the *th* receives the voiced sound, so it is pronounced /ð/ not /θ/. As a result, *cloth* is pronounced /klɑθ/ and *clothe* is pronounced /kloʊð/. This use of *e* affects only a small number of words in this way, but it does this consistently.

Even excluding *th*, *le*, and the words with *g* and *c*, students will find other words that end in a silent *e* and don't seem to follow the expanded rule. For example, many English words end in *ve* such as *love* or *give*. The *e* doesn't mark a long vowel in these words. Instead, the *e* serves a different function. Earlier, we discussed graphotactics, possible English spelling combinations. One feature of English is that words don't end in *v*. No one decreed that "English words shall not end in *v*." But this is a feature of modern English. In a word like *give*, the *e* serves to prevent the word from ending in *v*. The same is true for words that end in *u* like *glue*. Words that do end in *u* such as *kudu* are borrowed words that retained their original spelling. In addition, English spelling either adds an *e* after *z* as in *gauze* or doubles the *z* as in *buzz* so English words don't end in a single *z*.

A final silent *e* also keeps certain words from ending in single *s*. Usually, a final *s* signals that the word is plural (*boys*), possessive (*boy's*), or present tense (She *runs*). Readers expect that in words ending in *s*, the *s* signals one of these functions. The added *e* helps avoid confusion. Readers know that *teas* is the plural or *tea*, but *tease* is not a plural. English words can also double the final *s* to avoid having the word end in a single *s*, as in *toss*.

In English, some words are called *content words* and some are *function words*. The content words, which carry the primary meanings, include the nouns, verbs, adjectives, and some adverbs. They are the words people use in texting. The function words are conjunctions, prepositions, and other words that connect and show relationships among the content words. In general, function words are short and content words are long. Another feature of English graphotactics is that content words contain at least three letters. In some cases, as with *toe* and *see* an *e* has been added to a short content word so that it has at least three letters. The *e* also signals the long-vowel sound, so, as with the *th*, the *e* plays a double role. It lengthens the content word and makes the preceding vowel long.

Students may find other words ending with silent *e*. Many are borrowed, like *avalanche*, in which the French spelling is retained. Others, like *one* and *come*, reflect the Middle English spellings. During this period these final *e*'s were pronounced. The pronunciation has changed, but the spelling has stayed the same. Finally, English has certain suffixes, including *-ile*, *-ine*, *-ate*, and *-ite* in which the vowel is not stressed. In a word like *engine* the *i* has a reduced sound, /ə/, and the *e* is simply part of the suffix. It does not signal a long vowel. In some cases, words ending in these suffixes have two possible pronunciations. For example, if *approximate* is an adjective ("This is the approximate cost") the vowel is short, but if it is a verb ("Can you approximate the answer?"), the vowel is long. In most cases, though, words ending in these suffixes contain a silent *e* that does not follow the "marks long vowel" rule.

Students are not apt to think of all these uses of silent *e* but if they can find words that are exceptions to the rule that *e* marks a long vowel, they can look at the word history or any other fact that might explain why the exception exists. In some cases, a teacher can supply this information. Figure 6.7 lists the uses of silent *e* at the ends of words. This list is based on Cummings (1988).

Once students understand some of the reasons for silent *e*'s, they can make sense out of the rule for dropping the *e*. The primary function of a silent *e* is to signal that a preceding vowel is long. This is one instance of a general pattern of English graphotactics. In a series of letters VCV (Vowel, Consonant, Vowel) in which the first vowel is stressed, that vowel is pronounced with a long sound. In a word like *make*, the *e* provides the needed vowel to complete the VCV string of letters. What happens when a word like *make* becomes part of a longer, complex word? In *making* the *e* is dropped, but in *makeshift* it is retained. This can be explained by considering the VCV pattern. In *making* the letter *i* serves the same function as the *e*. It provides the vowel needed for the VCV pattern and signals that the *a* has a long sound. On the other hand, in *makeshift* the suffix starts with a consonant, so the

Reason for final, silent *e*	Example
Marks preceding long vowel	make
Marks soft *g* or *c*	edge, chance
Marks voiced *th* and lengthens vowel	clothe
Avoids single final *v, u, z, s*	give, glue, gauze, tease
Avoids 2-letter content words	toe
Appears in borrowed words	avalanche
Appears in Old English words	one, come
Appears in words with certain suffixes	engine, definite

Figure 6.7 *Functions of final, silent* e

e is retained to keep the VCV pattern to signal the long-vowel sound. If the *e* were dropped, the word would be pronounced /mækʃɪft/, with a short-vowel sound, /æ/. Since the suffix starts with a consonant, then the *e* is still needed to signal that the *a* has a long-vowel sound. At this point, students could state a rule for silent *e* as follows:

Drop the silent *e* if the suffix starts with a vowel. Keep the *e* if the suffix starts with a consonant.

If students understand why the *e* was part of the root or base word, they can better comprehend the rule for dropping the *e*. They can also understand the addition they need to make to the rule. Silent *e* also keeps *c* and *g* soft. Words keep the *e* after *c* or *g* if the suffix starts with a consonant (*enhancement*) but also when the suffix starts with *a, o,* or *u* (*peaceable, courageous*) because when *c* or *g* is followed by one of these letters, the sound is /k/ or /g/ as in *cake, go,* and *cut*. On the other hand, if the following letter is *i* or *y* the *c* or g keeps the soft sound (*racy, raging*). The revised rule can be stated:

Drop a final, silent *e* if the suffix starts with a vowel. Keep the *e* if the suffix starts with a consonant. If the letter before the *e* is *c* or *g* also keep the *e* if the suffix starts with *a, o,* or *u*.

This rule works quite consistently. The only exceptions are words ending in *e* such as *agreeing*, or *oe* as in *shoeing*. In these cases the *e* is retained even though the suffix starts with a vowel. A word like *shoeing* with the *e* maintains a visual connection to the base word *shoe* that would be lost with a spelling like *shoing*. The *e* is dropped before a suffix starting with a consonant in *argument, awful, truly,* and *duly*.

Most students don't recognize *awful* as a complex word with *awe* as its base, but it is an exception. *Truly* is often misspelled, probably because it is an exception to the rule. Finally, in words ending in *dge* the *e* is dropped before *ment* as in *judgment*. The combination *dg* seems to signal that the *g* has a /dʒ/ sound, so the *e* is not really needed.

All this sounds quite complicated. It might seem easier to simply give students the rule for dropping a final silent *e* and then pointing out the few exceptions. However, involving students in determining why the *e* was there in the first place helps them make sense of the rule. It also raises awareness of how words are spelled. As they try to figure out the reasons for silent *e*, students are looking closely at words, talking about them, and writing them, and all these activities contribute to their ability to spell words conventionally. Perhaps more importantly, students can begin to see that language can be studied from a scientific perspective. This is what linguists do.

The consonant doubling rule

A second spelling rule that students can investigate governs doubling final consonants before adding a suffix. For example, for the word *run* the *n* is doubled to spell *running*, but with *load* the final *d* is not doubled for *loading*. Again, teachers might plan some activities to ensure that students understand that a word like *running* is a complex word formed by adding a suffix to a base word (*run + ing*). Once students have that concept, they can begin their investigation.

A good way to start to study the doubling rule would be to give students a list of words such as those shown in Figure 6.8 and have students work in pairs or small groups to try to discover a rule for doubling a final consonant before adding a suffix. In this case, a teacher might simply want to say that final consonants are never doubled before a suffix that starts with a consonant. Students almost never misspell a word like *sad + ly* as *saddly*. However, if the suffix starts with a vowel, some words double the final consonant and others do not.

Different patterns of vowels and consonants in a word signal whether a vowel has a long or a short sound. The vowels have a short sound when the

Words that double final consonants	Words that don't double final consonants
biggest	soaked
topped	keeping
cutting	aiming
batter	parked
occurred (occur + ed)	walked

Figure 6.8 *Words for the doubling rule*

pattern is CVC as in *big* and CVCC as in *walk*. Vowels have a long sound when the pattern is VVC as in *soak* or VCV as in *make*. These short and long patterns are the basis for the doubling rule. The rule for doubling the final consonant keeps the preceding short vowel short and the preceding long vowel long.

Words like *big* in the first column of Figure 6.8 have a CVC pattern, so the vowel sound is short. We double the final consonant so that the short-vowel sound of the *i* is retained. If the word were spelled *biger* it would have a VCV pattern and the *i* would be pronounced with a long sound as in *tiger*. If the vowel sound in the base word is long, as it is in *soak*, there is no need to double the final consonant. In words like *park* and *walk* the pattern is CVCC so there is no need to double the final consonant to keep the short sound. The doubling is only used to keep a short-vowel sound short.

The doubling rule could be stated as

> Double a final consonant in a one-syllable word or a word that is stressed on the last syllable before adding a suffix starting with a vowel to preserve a short-vowel sound.

There are only a few exceptions to this rule. *Quitting* is an apparent exception. In this word the final *t* of the base word *quit* is preceded by two letters, *u* and *i*, that normally represent vowel sounds. This would produce a pattern of VVC. However, when *u* follows *q*, the *u* represents a consonant sound, /w/. This word would be transcribed as /kwɪt/. The spelling rule has to do with the sound of the vowel, not the spelling. Letters like *u* can represent either a vowel or a consonant sound. Since the vowel /ɪ/ has a short sound in the base word, *quit*, the final consonant is doubled to preserve that sound.

What about *conferred* and *conference*? In *conferred* the stress is on the *fer* so the *r* is doubled to keep the short-vowel sound. This word follows the usual rule of doubling the final consonant before a suffix that begins with a vowel. In the base word, *confer*, the second syllable is stressed. However, when the suffix *-ence* is added, the stress shifts to the first syllable, and the second syllable has a reduced vowel /ə/. The word is transcribed as /kɑnfɚəns/ with a stress on the first vowel. The second vowel is reduced, not long, so there is no need to double the final *r*. The rule calls for doubling the final consonant in a one-syllable word or a word that is stressed on the last syllable.

Another exception is words that end in *x*. *Fox*, for example, has a short-vowel sound, but the *x* is not doubled when adding a suffix like *-es* for *foxes*. The letter *x* is transcribed as /ks/ or /gz/. Since *x* already has two consonant sounds, the vowel that precedes *x* stays short, even when the suffix begins with a vowel. For that reason, *x* is never doubled.

There are a few other exceptions to this rule. The final consonant is not doubled in *combatant* and *guitarist* even though the stress stays on the final vowel and the suffix starts with a vowel. The final consonant is doubled in *personnel* and *questionnaire*. Both of these words were borrowed from French and retain the original spelling. Despite exceptions like these, the doubling rule is a useful one because it applies in so many situations.

One difference between American and British English spellings is based on doubling final consonants. Americans spell *traveled* and *focused* without doubling the final consonant since the stress is on the first syllable in each word. British English has *travelled* and *focussed*. Americans who frequently read British novels might have trouble remembering the American spelling.

As these examples of investigations into spelling patterns and rules show, teachers can involve students in scientific inquiry into the spelling system. When students take a problem-solving approach to spelling, they begin to see the logic of the system. They are more apt to spell words conventionally when they have examined patterns and rules. In addition, they come to understand how linguists approach language study using the scientific method.

Conclusion

We began this chapter by asking:

- How did the English writing system develop?
- Should the spelling system be reformed?
- How can teachers help students take a scientific approach to spelling?

People have used writing for centuries. The earliest systems were pictographic or ideographic. Written marks represented objects and ideas directly. Such systems were difficult for writers because each word was represented by a different mark, and writers had to remember many different characters. Later writing systems used marks to represent the sounds of words in oral language. The earliest systems only had letters for the consonant sounds. The introduction of letters for both consonants and vowels first occurred in Greek writing. The alphabet we use to write this book developed over many years and is based on the Roman alphabet.

Many people have called for spelling reforms. They would like every word to be spelled the way it sounds. They consider the current spelling system illogical or even crazy. However, writing systems serve both readers and writers. Changing the system so that words are all spelled the way they sound would make writing easier but reading more difficult. Constantly changing spellings to reflect current pronunciation would be an impossible task. In addition, it would be difficult to determine whose pronunciation to follow. The current system is a good compromise. It is indeed a system, reflecting the demand to spell words as they sound, the demand to spell words alike that are related in meaning, and the demand to spell borrowed words and words from earlier periods of English to reflect their origins.

A study of the history of writing and of individual words is interesting. In addition, students can investigate the spelling system and make generalizations to account for the way different sounds are spelled. They can also study certain rules, such as deleting final silent *e* or doubling a final consonant. When students investigate spellings, not only do they become better spellers, they also learn the skills of science and begin to approach the study of language the way linguists do.

APPLICATIONS

1. This chapter outlines the history of writing development. Carry out research on a particular type of writing, such as Egyptian hieroglyphics, and prepare a more detailed report on a particular writing system. Students might work in groups on different writing systems and create a class report.

2. Word histories (etymologies) are interesting. Using Internet sites or a dictionary such as the *Oxford English Dictionary*, look up the following animal names to determine their origins and their original meanings. For example, *aardvark* is an Afrikaans word meaning "earth pig." Try the following animal names:

alligator	crocodile	leopard	porpoise	penguin
beetle	duck	lobster	rhinoceros	porcupine
caterpillar	elephant	moose	spider	walrus
cobra	hippopotamus	octopus	squirrel	

3. Cummings states that three forces shape the spelling system: phonetic, semantic, and etymological. Find words that clearly reflect the effects of each of these three forces by completing the following chart. Use original examples, not those in the chapter. The words that show the phonetic demand should have a 1:1 correspondence between the letters and the transcription characters. Those that show the semantic demand should be pairs of words that share a common spelling even though one or more letters in one word are not pronounced, like *bomb* and *bombard*, or when the same letter represents a different sound in each word, like *medicine* and *medical*. Words

that show the etymological demand should contain unusual spellings that do not follow typical American English patterns.

phonetic demand	semantic demand	etymological demand
pin	bomb/ bombard	avalanche
sat	medicine/medical	kangaroo

4. Many calls for spelling reforms are clever and humorous. For example, Jessica Davidson starts her poem "I Never Will Learn to Read English Aloud" with the lines:

> I never will learn to read English aloud.
> There's mowed, towed, and rowed, and then there's allowed.
> And once I had finally learned to say move,
> I met love, shove, and dove, and what did it prove?
> It proves I'll never discover the coves
> Where the treasure was found, nor the stoves nor the groves.

Davidson's poem contains homophones (*aloud*, *allowed*) and homographs, words with the same spelling but different pronunciations and meanings. Working in pairs or small groups, write a poem like Davidson's.

5. Homophone riddles like those in Terban's book discussed in this chapter can help students become aware that words that sound the same may be spelled differently. Work in groups to write homophone riddles of your own and then try these out with your students or your classmates.

6. Carry out an investigation of the different spellings of a phoneme similar to the investigations described in this chapter for /eɪ/ and /k/. Most long vowels have alternate spellings. A consonant phoneme with many spellings is /ʃ/. Following the model in this chapter, collect words for a long vowel other than /eɪ/ or the consonant phoneme /ʃ/. Categorize the words, and develop generalizations about the spelling patterns.

7. In English the /tʃ/ sound at the end of a word can be spelled *ch* or *tch* as in *beach* and *ditch*. Similarly, the /dʒ/ sound can be spelled *ge* or *dge* as in *cage* and *badge*. Make a list of words with these alternate spellings to try to determine a rule for when to use each one. Is there any consistent pattern, or does the variation seem to be random?

8. When the letter *c* is followed by *a*, *o*, or *u* it has a /k/ sound and when it is followed by *e*, *i*, or *y* it has an /s/ sound. What about the letter *g* at the beginning of a word? When does it have a /g/ sound and when does it have a /dʒ/ sound? The pattern here isn't as consistent as the pattern for *c*. Make a list of words and then come up with a generalization. Consider words like *gin* and *girl*. Look up words that appear to be exceptions to try to discover why they don't follow the usual pattern.

7 /sɛvən/

English Morphology

What Is a Word?

- How do linguists analyze words?
- How do new words enter a language?

Morphology is the study of meaningful parts of words. However, linguists find it difficult to define the term *word*. This may seem strange to anyone who can read. In most modern written languages, each word is set off from other words by spaces. Even in written language, though, it is not always clear whether an item should be considered one word or two. For example, is a contraction like *isn't* a single word? Is a compound like *merry-go-round* one word or three?

When it comes to oral language, decisions about what constitutes a word become even more difficult. When linguists examine the physical speech stream, they do not find breaks between what people normally consider separate words. Consider the sentence, "I should have gone." A spectrographic display of this sentence would show no breaks between the words. In addition, in casual speech, this sentence is pronounced /aɪʃʊdvgɑn/. The word that is written *have* is reduced to /v/ and attached to /ʃʊd/ to form one unit. We might ask, "Is *have* really a separate word?"

Like phonemes, words are psychological units, not physical units. When people speak, they cause sound waves to travel through the air. The interpretation of speech involves perceiving these sound waves as individual words. Humans do this effortlessly in a language they have acquired, but as anyone who has listened to a foreign language realizes, it can be very difficult to pick out individual words in a new language.

The concept of word seems to be more associated with written language than spoken language. Early writers did not put spaces between what we call *words*. Similarly, young children don't put spaces between words even though they must perceive language as being made up of individual units in order to understand it. Through exposure to written language, children begin to adopt the conventions of writing, which include putting spaces between words. These spaces make reading easier. Writingwithnospacesishardtoread. Nevertheless, it is important to recognize that the separation of written words on a page is more a convenience for readers than a reflection of a physical reality. That is one reason linguists find it difficult to define *word*.

Developing a Theory of Morphology

Another reason that linguists find it difficult to define *word* is that words can be broken down into small meaningful parts called *morphemes*. Morphology is the study of the morphemic structure of words. Linguists use the same process to describe the morphology of a language that they use to describe its phonology or syntax.

Break the speech stream into discrete units

The first step in describing the morphology of a language is to divide the speech stream into discrete units. For morphology, the discrete units are morphemes, the smallest meaningful parts of words. In a word like *tree* there is just one morpheme. This word can't be divided into smaller meaningful parts. However, the word *trees* has two morphemes, *tree* and *s*. Each part of the word carries some meaning. *Tree* refers to a kind of tall plant, and *s* carries the meaning of plural. Two other examples of words that consist of more than one morpheme are *injections* and *replacements*. *Injections* can be divided into four morphemes: in + ject + ion + s and *replacements* can also be divided into four meaningful parts: re + place + ment + s.

Categorize the units

The second step in describing the morphology of English or any other language is to categorize the units. Words like *trees* are made up of two kinds of morphemes: free morphemes and bound morphemes. *Free morphemes* are units that could stand alone as words by themselves. *Tree* is a free morpheme. *Bound morphemes* are units that must be attached or bound to a free morpheme. They cannot be written as separate words. The *s* in *trees* is a bound morpheme.

Bound morphemes in English are either prefixes or suffixes. The general term *affix* refers to a prefix or a suffix. Some languages also have *infixes*, bound morphemes that are inserted into the middle of a word rather than being bound to the beginning or the end.

An example of a language that has infixes is Bahasa Indonesia, the language of Indonesia. In Indonesian there are at least five kinds of infixes. They are *-el-*, *-em-*, *-er-*, *-ah-*, and *-in-*. Examples:

- The word *gembung* means "bloated," while *ge**l**embung* means "bubble."
- The word *cerlang* means "luminous," while *ce**m**erlang* means "brilliant."
- The word *gigi* means "tooth," while *ge**r**igi* means "serration."
- The word *dulu* means "first" or "advance" or "olden," while *d**ah**ulu* means "formerly."
- The word *kerja* means "work," while *k**in**erja* means "performance." (retrieved from http://en.wikipedia.org/wiki/Infix, 4/24/2104)

Affixes can be either inflectional or derivational. In English, the inflectional morphemes are all suffixes. The *s* in *trees* is an inflectional morpheme. *Inflectional morphemes* add certain kinds of meaning to a word without changing the part of speech. For example, an inflectional morpheme doesn't change a word from a noun to a verb or a verb to an adjective. In addition, inflectional morphemes don't change the meaning of the whole word. Adding *s* to *tree* to form *trees* doesn't change the meaning of the whole word. English has only eight inflectional affixes. These include the plural *-s* and *-es* and the possessive *'s* added to nouns, the *-s*, *-ed*, *-ing*, and *-en* added to verbs to show tense such as present continuous or past, and the *-er* and *-est* added to adjectives and adverbs to show comparison.

Derivational affixes do change meaning of the whole word and can be either prefixes or suffixes. When a derivational affix is added to a base word, a new word is derived. Derivational affixes may change the part of speech of the base word. For example, adding *-er* to the verb *work* produces the noun *worker*. However, not all derivational affixes change the part of speech. Adding the prefix *un-* to the verb *tie* produces another verb, *untie*. In this case, the affix *un-* changes the meaning of the whole word but not the part of speech. In English, prefixes do not change the part of speech.

If we consider the earlier examples of *injections* and *replacements*, these complex words contain both prefixes and suffixes and both inflectional and derivational affixes. *Injections* has the derivational prefix *in-*, the Latin root *ject*, the derivational suffix *-ion*, and the inflectional suffix *s*. *Replacements* has the derivational prefix *re-*, the base *place*, the derivational suffix *-ment*, and the inflectional suffix *s*. A difference between these two words is that *injections* has a Latin root *ject*, while *replacements* has a recognizable English base, *place*.

Figure 7.1 summarizes this information about English morphology.

Derivational prefixes carry a meaning that is easier to define than the meanings of derivational suffixes. For example, *re-* means *back* or *again* and *pre-* means *before*. Prefixes help readers understand the meaning of a word as long as they know

morphemes of replacements		
free (place)	**bound**	
	prefixes	suffixes
	derivational (*re-*)	derivational (*-ment*)
		inflectional (*-s*)

Figure 7.1 *English morphemes*

the meaning of the base or root. If someone is *unhappy*, the person is "not happy." Suffixes, on the other hand, tell more about the part of speech than the meaning of the word. It is hard to define a suffix like *-ion* or *-ly*. The *-ion* signals that the word is a noun. For example, *injection* is a noun. On the other hand, *-ly* can indicate that the word is an adverb such as *quickly* or an adjective like *friendly*. Prefixes and suffixes serve somewhat different functions and carry different kinds of meaning.

Although roots, such as *ject*, are not affixes, they are not free morphemes either. *Ject* cannot stand alone as a word the way *tree* can. In a word like *inject* there is a Latin root (*ject*) and a prefix (*in-*) but the root is not a recognizable English word. Roots need to be attached to a prefix or suffix to form a word. Many English words have Latin or Greek roots, and knowledge of these roots can help students determine the meaning of words.

Grouping the units

The next step in describing a language is grouping the units. English words can be grouped based on the types of morphemes in the words. Words with just one free morpheme, like *tree*, are simple words. Words with a free morpheme and one or more bound morphemes like *trees* are complex words. Words that consist of two free morphemes like *teacup* are compound words. Finally, words with two free morphemes and one or more bound morpheme are considered compound-complex words. Figure 7.2 shows the types of words in English.

simple	complex	compound	compound-complex
1 free morpheme	1 free morpheme and 1 or more bound morphemes	2 free morphemes	2 free morphemes and 1 or more bound morphemes
tree	trees	hotshot	teacups
rhinoceros	unwanted	bookkeeper	unforeseeable

Figure 7.2 *English words*

English is not a highly inflected language. Many words are simple, especially those that derive from Anglo-Saxon. Words derived from Latin and Greek are more often complex. English has a great many compound words. These can be combinations of various parts of speech. Compound words can add inflections, such as the plural *s* to form compound-complex words, but derivational affixes are seldom added to compound words.

Traditional approaches to classifying words

Words can be grouped based on their morphological structure into simple words, complex words, and so on. They can also be grouped based on criteria that includes semantic and syntactic criteria as well as their morphology. This grouping system divides words into different parts of speech, such as nouns and verbs. There are both traditional approaches to identifying parts of speech and scientific approaches based on research in linguistics.

Most adults remember identifying parts of speech in school. They learned that a noun is the name of a person, place, or thing and then found all the nouns on a worksheet. They learned the difference between main verbs and helping verbs. Usually, language arts texts list eight parts of speech: nouns, pronouns, verbs, adjectives, adverbs, prepositions, conjunctions, and interjections.

The traditional definitions of the parts of speech reflect an earlier period in history. At one time, school was conducted in Latin. When English became the language of instruction, many teachers suddenly had nothing to teach. The children already knew English, so they didn't need to be taught the language of school.

Even though children knew English, they didn't know English grammar. Schools for young children were called grammar schools because that was where grammar was taught. Teachers of English grammar were not linguists; they were former Latin teachers. As a result, they attempted to apply Latin categories to the English language. Many grammar rules reflect the influence of Latin. For example, the rule that English sentences should not end with a preposition is based on Latin, which did not allow prepositions at the end of sentences.

In addition, Latin categories were applied to the classification of English words. Even though English has many words with Latin roots, English is a Germanic language, and trying to make English words fit Latin categories is not easy. The definitions for parts of speech found in grammar books are not good examples of scientific classification. For example, nouns are defined by what they are, names of people, places, or things. Adjectives are usually defined by what they do: modify a noun. Conjunctions join parts of sentences. Each part of speech is defined in a somewhat different way, and, as a result, students have trouble figuring out how to classify words.

Despite the scientific evidence that the study of grammar does not improve reading and writing skills (Weaver 2008), schools still follow the Latin tradition and teach and test grammar. Students are expected to know whether a word is a noun or a verb. Still, memorizing definitions of parts of speech doesn't seem to help students. Fortunately, some creative children's authors have written books that can help children acquire many of the terms of traditional grammar. They have produced colorful, interesting books that contain many of the labels children are expected to master.

Heller has written a series of books, one for each of the traditional parts of speech. She began by writing a more specialized book, *A Cache of Jewels and Other Collective Nouns* (1987). Like the books that followed, this one includes beautiful illustrations and catchy, rhyming language. Heller includes many collective nouns such as "an army of ants" and "a bevy of beauties." Young readers often remember long passages because of the rhyme. For example, the book begins, "A word that means a collection of things, like a cache of jewels for the crowns of kings . . . or a batch of bread all warm and brown, is always called a collective noun." Heller ends this first book on parts of speech with these lines:

> But nouns aren't all collective,
> and if I'm to be effective,
> I'll tell about the other nouns
> and adjectives and verbs.
> All of them are parts of speech.
> What fun!
> I'll write a book for each.

True to her word, Heller has gone on to write a book about each part of speech. For example, *Many Luscious Lollipops* (1989) is a book about adjectives, and *Kites Sail High* (1988) is a book about verbs. Each book includes terms students are expected to know. For instance, the book about adjectives includes articles, demonstratives, and proper adjectives. The book about verbs has pages on tense, mood, and auxiliary verbs. Her book about adverbs, *Up, Up and Away* (1991), points out that adverbs of place always precede adverbs of time. As Heller writes:

> Before an adverb answers "When?"
> it always answers "Where?"
> This ship will sail AWAY TODAY
> It will not sail TODAY AWAY

Lines like these give both native speakers and English learners important insights into how English works.

One fifth-grade teacher reported his students' scores on a standardized language test went up dramatically after he read several of Heller's books and then left them out for his students to read. Students could try to compose their own books about the parts of speech following Heller's model.

Another writer who has produced a series of books on the parts of speech is Cleary. These books with cartoonlike illustrations and simple rhymes are especially appealing to young children. Cleary's book *Under, Over, by the Clover: What Is a Preposition?* (2002) begins with "Prepositions tell us where, like in your bed, beside the chair." Each phrase is accompanied by a colorful illustration that shows the meaning of the preposition. These books would be useful for English learners.

Cleary has written other books, too, including those about adjectives, nouns, and verbs. Each book follows a similar pattern. The title asks, "What Is a Verb?" (or noun, or adjective) and the text answers the question by providing many rhyming examples. The book on verbs, for instance, is titled *To Root, to Toot, to Parachute: What Is a Verb?* (2001). It is filled with verbs: "Verbs are words like sing and dance, pray or practice, preach or prance." Cleary includes a number of unusual words that would pique student interest and help them develop their vocabulary.

Because traditional parts of speech are not clearly defined in a systematic, scientific manner, using children's books to help acquire knowledge of parts of speech is more enjoyable and possibly more effective than traditional methods with worksheets and tests.

Linguistic Approaches to Classifying Words

Even though traditional definitions of parts of speech do not constitute a good scientific method for classifying words, they do provide the vocabulary students need to discuss and analyze language. Without some terms like *noun* and *verb*, it would be almost impossible to talk about the different kinds of words in a language. Linguists have attempted to refine the definitions of these terms and have included additional terms to describe English and other languages.

To classify words, linguists rely to some extent on the meanings of words. This semantic knowledge is what people use when they define a noun as a person, place, or thing, and a verb as a word that shows action. All languages seem to have words that function like nouns and others that serve as verbs. Humans describe their world by naming objects and actions, and these categories may be part of Universal Grammar. In addition, languages have ways to modify both nouns and verbs.

Adjectives serve to describe people, places, and things while adverbs provide extra information about actions. A first step in classifying a word is to use this semantic information. Additional evidence from syntax and morphology can then be used to confirm the category for the word.

Syntactic evidence comes from the position or role of the word in the sentence. Here is a sentence that follows the general pattern or word order of English:

The hungry linguist quickly ate a delicious sandwich before class.

Linguist comes near the beginning of the sentence and serves as the subject. Words in subject position are generally nouns or pronouns. *Ate* serves as the predicate of this sentence. It names the action. Words that serve as predicates are verbs. *Sandwich* follows the predicate and serves as the direct object of the sentence. *Class* comes after the preposition *before* and is the object of the preposition. Words like these that serve as objects are usually nouns. *Hungry* and *delicious* precede and describe nouns. Words that precede nouns are often adjectives. *Quickly* precedes the predicate and describes the action. Words like *quickly* are adverbs. Adverbs can occur in many different positions in a sentence, but they often come near the predicate. The position of these words in the sentence and the roles they play provide syntactic evidence for identifying each part of speech.

Morphological evidence can also be used to help classify words. Both inflectional and derivational suffixes provide clues about parts of speech. For example, it is possible to add the inflectional suffix *-s* or *-es* to a noun to make it plural. This inflectional morpheme can be only added to nouns. Thus, words like *linguists* and *sandwiches* are probably nouns. The derivational suffix *-ly* is added to adjectives in English to make them adverbs. The *-ly* ending signals that a word like *quickly* is an adverb. Figure 7.3 lists morphological evidence that can be used to confirm that a word fits into a certain category.

Evidence from semantics, syntax, and morphology all need to be considered to determine the classification of a word because many English words can be nouns, verbs, or adjectives, depending on how they function in the sentence. For example, *table* functions as a noun in "That is a table," as a verb in "He tabled the motion," and as an adjective in "He has poor table manners."

Content and function words

The kinds of words listed in Figure 7.3 are what linguists refer to as *content words*. These are the words that carry the main meanings in sentences. When people text someone, they include the content words but may omit some function words.

part of speech	can add these inflectional suffixes	can add these derivational suffixes	
noun	-s or -es: plural (*trees / bushes*)	commence**ment**	
	's: possessive (*animal's*)	conven**tion**	
		neat**ness**	
		clar**ity**	
		depend**ence**	
		farm**er**	
		parachut**ist**	
verb	-s: 3rd-person singular (He *walks*.)	class**ify**	
	-*ing*: progressive (He is *walking*.)	characte**rize**	
	-*ed*: past (He *walked*.)	eval**uate**	
	-*en*: past participle (He has *driven*.)		
adjective **adverb**	-*er*: comparative (*bigger / faster*)	mischiev**ous**	
	-*est*: superlative (*biggest / fastest*)	color**ful**	
		fes**tive**	**adjectives**
		reg**al**	
		flex**ible**	
		quick**ly**	**adverb**

Figure 7.3 *Morphological evidence for parts of speech*

Content words are also referred to as *open-class words*, because new words that come into English through processes like borrowing are always content words. English has four types of content words: nouns, verbs, adjectives, and adverbs.

English also has a second group of words called *function words*. Function words serve a variety of purposes. They include determiners, quantifiers, pronouns, auxiliaries, prepositions, conjunctions, intensifiers, interjections, and particles. Some of these terms, like *preposition* and *conjunction*, are probably familiar. Others, such as *determiners* and *intensifiers*, may be new. Figure 7.4 lists examples of each kind of function word.

Determiners and quantifiers are words that precede nouns. In English, every singular common noun has to be preceded by a determiner or a quantifier. An English sentence like "He bought book" doesn't sound right because it lacks a determiner or a quantifier. English speakers say, "He bought that book" or "He bought two books." There are three kinds of determiners: articles like *a, an,* and *the*; demonstratives like *this* and *those*; and possessives like *my* and *their*. In traditional grammar, determiners are often classified as adjectives, but they signal that a noun follows rather than describes the noun. Content adjectives like *green* can take -*er* and -*est* endings, but these endings cannot be added to function words including

type	example	example	example
determiners	the	this	my
quantifiers	one	every	several
pronouns	you	yourself	who
auxiliaries	is	has	might
prepositions	in	before	of
conjunctions	and	if	however
particles	up	down	around
intensifiers	rather	very	so
interjections	Wow!	Absolutely!	Yes!

Figure 7.4 *Types of function words*

determiners. Quantifiers serve much the same purpose as determiners. The difference is that they specify an amount or quantity.

Pronouns are words that are used in place of noun phrases. Pronouns replace whole phrases, not just nouns. The pronoun *her* can replace several words, not just the noun, in the sentence, "I saw the sweet, elderly woman who lives down the street." A speaker would say, "I saw her," not "I saw the sweet, elderly her who lives down the street." Pronouns are considered function words because they do not carry meaning by themselves. Instead, they take their meaning from the noun they refer to. Pronouns are shorthand for referring to a noun phrase. There are different kinds of pronouns including personal pronouns (*I, my*), indefinite pronouns (*someone, anything*), reflexive pronouns (*myself, yourself*), reciprocal pronouns (*each other, one another*), interrogative pronouns (*who, where*), possessive pronouns (*mine, his*), and relative pronouns (*who, which*).

Auxiliaries are often referred to as *helping verbs*. They are words that tell more about the tense or aspect of a verb. This group includes modal auxiliaries like *can* and *would* as well as words like *be* and *have*. English has a complex verb system. Speakers can add inflections to verbs and also use auxiliaries to express shades of meaning. "I should have been asked to go" includes three auxiliaries and the inflection, *-ed*, on the verb *ask*. English learners often find it difficult to master the verb system. Not only can English verb phrases contain several auxiliaries, they occur in a fixed order. For example, a speaker would not say, "I been have should asked to go." The knowledge of the order of auxiliary verbs is acquired, not learned. The verb system alone is too complex to learn.

Prepositions often show place or time. In "The pen is on the table" the preposition *on* shows the relationship in space between the pen and the table. In "I left after the dance" the preposition *after* shows the time relationship between the dance and the leaving. Words like *of* and *with* are also prepositions. Conjunctions also show relationships. For example, in "I read the book, and I ate dinner" the conjunction *and* connects two complete ideas. In "He ran and jumped" the conjunction joins the two verbs.

Two other kinds of function words are *particles* and *intensifiers*. Particles are little words added to verbs to make two- or three-word verbs, sometimes called *phrasal verbs*. For example, in "He ran up a big bill" the particle *up* is part of the verb phrase *ran up*. Together, the two words have a meaning that is different from a combination of the meanings of *run* and *up*. Someone who runs up a bill may not do any physical exercise. The phrase means something like *charged* or *created*. This *up* is not a preposition like the *up* in "He ran up a big hill." In this second sentence *up* shows where he ran, and "up a big hill" is a prepositional phrase. Two-word verbs are very common in English. However, since the meaning has little to do with the individual meanings of the parts, emergent bilinguals are often confused by two-word verbs. The problem is compounded by the fact that different particles are used in different languages. In English, a person can say, "He is married to her," while in Spanish the sentence would be "El se casó con ella" ("He is married with her.")

Intensifiers like *very* and *somewhat* are words used to qualify an expression, making it stronger ("He is very happy") or weaker ("He is somewhat happy"). Interjections are words that show strong emotion. In oral language, they are spoken with strong emphasis. This is represented in written language with an exclamation mark. Interjections may be used in novels as part of dialogue but are seldom used in academic writing.

Function words provide the grammatical connections among the content words. Function words are also referred to as *closed-class words* because languages don't add new words in these categories. Generally, languages have all the conjunctions, prepositions, and so on, that are needed. Even when new function words would be useful, speakers have great difficulty accepting them. For example, in English, third-person pronouns show gender—*he*, *she*, *it*. Writing conventions require writers to avoid sexist language. In the past, *his* in a sentence like "A student should do his best work" could refer to a male or a female student. The masculine term was considered to include both males and females. However, current usage would require a writer to say, "A student should do his or her best work." The use of *his or her* seems awkward, so various alternatives have been proposed, such as *s/he*, but alternatives such as these have not caught on. The failure to accept a new word for a gender-neutral pronoun reflects the fact that, like other function words that are considered closed class, no new words are added even when it would be useful to do so.

And yet, despite this fact, new words are added to the English language all the time, as we discuss later. Dictionaries keep expanding. In fact, English has one of the largest vocabularies of any of the world's languages.

Find dependencies among the units

In phonology, some phonemes depend on other phonemes. For example, the nasal that precedes a stop in a word like *wand* depends on the place of articulation of the stop. Since the /d/ is an alveolar stop, the nasal is /n/, the alveolar nasal.

There are fewer dependencies among morphemes. Bound morphemes must be added to a base or root to form a word. A prefix like *re-* must be attached to a base, such as *search*, or to a root, such as *ject*, to form a word. In the same way, a suffix, such as *-ize*, has to be added to a root or a base word to form an English word. In this respect, bound morphemes depend on roots and bases to form words. However, the only requirement when adding more than one affix is that inflectional suffixes come at the end of a word and follow derivational suffixes, as in *energizes* where the inflectional *-s* follows the derivational *-ize*.

There is no general rule for adding prefixes before suffixes or suffixes before prefixes. In forming a word like *replacement*, the prefix *re-* could be added to form *replace*, and then the suffix *-ment* could be added to form re*placement*, but it would also be possible to add *-ment* first to make *placement*, and then add the *re-*. In forming a complex word with both a prefix and a suffix, adding one doesn't depend on adding the other one first.

Types of Languages

Since linguists find it difficult to define what a word is, it is not surprising that they also find it difficult to classify languages by the ways they combine morphemes to form words. In some languages, like Chinese, almost every word consists of just one morpheme. Some of these are lexical morphemes that carry meaning like *tree*, and others are grammatical morphemes that show things like tense or plurality. Languages that have one morpheme per word are called *analytic*. In analytic languages, morphemes are not bound to one another.

Languages such as Latin are classified as *synthetic*. Synthetic languages add many inflections to words. For example, in Latin *porto* is "I carry" and *portas* is "you carry." One word in Latin carries the meaning of two words in English. Spanish and French are not so heavily inflected as Latin, but they are more inflected than English. One of the difficulties linguists have in classifying languages by the way they combine morphemes is that most languages fall somewhere between pure cases of analytic or synthetic languages. Although English is not as analytic as Chinese, it is not as synthetic as French or Spanish. For that reason, English could be considered an analytic language.

Besides classifying languages as analytic or synthetic, linguists refer to some languages as *agglutinative* and others as *polysynthetic*. Agglutinative languages like Turkish combine many morphemes into a word. Agglutination is also a common feature of Basque. The conjugations of verbs, for example, are done by adding different prefixes or suffixes to the root of the verb: *dakartzat*, which means "I bring them," is formed by *da* (indicates present tense), *kar* (root of the verb *ekarri*—"bring"), *tza* (indicates plural), and *t* (indicates subject, in this case, *I*) (retrieved from http://en.wikipedia.org/wiki/Agglutination on 10/12/2013).

The parts of words in agglutinative languages are "glued" together. However, in this process the morphemes are not changed. In English, the plural morpheme can be /s/ as in *cats*, /z/ as in *dogs*, or /əz/, as in *bushes*, or it can involve a change like the change from *foot* to *feet*. All these variations signal plural. In an agglutinative language, the morpheme that indicates plural is always the same. It doesn't change form when it combines with other morphemes. In general, agglutinative languages have words made up of many morphemes that are combined by placing them together. The difference between a synthetic language and an agglutinative language is that in a synthetic language morphemes change their form more than morphemes in agglutinative languages.

In polysynthetic languages, many more inflections are added than in a synthetic language like Latin. Polysynthetic languages might be considered "super synthetic." Words are made by starting with some base and adding many affixes. Often, each resulting word would be translated as a whole sentence in English. Two examples of words in the polysynthetic Native American language Ojibwe, are:

- baataanitaaanishinaabemong = "being able to speak Ojibwe"

and

- ngiinitaaozhibii'amaadimin = "we used to write to each other" (retrieved from http://en.wiktionary.org/wiki/polysynthetic on 10/12/13)

In polysynthetic languages like Ojibwe, each word translates into English as a sentence. For a polysynthetic language, such as the Native American languages Ojibwe and Navajo, a dictionary has to list morphemes, not words, because every word is made up of many morphemes and represents a whole sentence. Since there are an infinite number of possible sentences, dictionaries list morphemes rather than words. The distinction between a word and a sentence in a language like Navajo is blurred.

Another example of a polysynthetic language is Kivunjo, a Bantu language. The Kivunjo expression *Näïkìm̀lyìïà* translates into the English sentence "He is eating it for her." According to Pinker (1994), this word/sentence consists of the following parts:

N   a marker indicating that this word is the focus of that point in the conversation

ä   a subject agreement marker. It identifies the eater as falling into Class 1 of 16 gender classes, human singular. Other classes include thin objects, animals, several humans, body parts, precise locations, etc.

ï   present-tense marker (other tenses include today, earlier today, yesterday, no earlier than yesterday, yesterday or earlier, in the remote past, habitually, ongoing, consecutively, hypothetically, in the future, at an indeterminate time, not yet, sometimes)

kì   an object agreement marker indicating that the thing eaten falls into gender Class 7

m̀   a benefactive marker indicating for whose benefit the action is taking place—in this case a member of gender Class 1

lyì the verb "to eat"

ï   an applicative marker indicating that the verb applies an additional object (I baked a cake vs I baked her a cake)

à   tells whether this is indicative or subjunctive mood. (127–28)

As this example shows, groups such as the Bantu have developed highly complex language systems. The idea that some people speak a primitive language has been dispelled by modern linguistic studies. Even though this language appears to be extremely complex, children who grow up hearing Kivunjo acquire the language just as easily as other children acquire French or English.

A chapter on Kivunjo morphology would need to be a great deal longer than this chapter on English morphology. English words can contain prefixes and suffixes, but they do not carry the heavy informational load a Kivunjo word carries. Further, polysynthetic languages help show why linguists find it difficult to define the term *word*. However, morphemes are the basic units of meaning in a language, so it is possible to describe and analyze how languages combine morphemes to produce larger units, such as words and sentences.

For teachers, it is important to understand something of the structure of words and sentences in the first languages of their emergent bilingual students. If a student speaks a language that is synthetic, agglutinative, or polysynthetic, then the student's transition to English will need more support than a student who speaks a language that structures words and sentences in similar ways to the way English does. This knowledge of different kinds of words and sentences is part of a teacher's pedagogical language knowledge.

Types of Words and Types of Sentences

One difference between languages that are more analytic and those that are more synthetic is that analytic languages rely on the order of words to show the functions of different words in a sentence. In synthetic, polysynthetic, or agglutinative languages, on the other hand, each word carries more information, so the order of the words is less important although there is a preferred word order even in these languages. A good example of a synthetic language that relies on word endings to signal the function of the different words in a sentence is Japanese. Consider the following four Japanese sentences (Farmer and Demers 1996):

> Watasi-no kodomo-ni sensei-ga sono hono-o ageta.
> Sensei-ga watasi-no kodomo-ni sono hon-o ageta.
> Sono hon-o sensei-ga watasi-no kodomo-ni ageta.
> Sono hon-o watasi-no kodomo-ni sensei-ga ageta. (145)

All four sentences would be translated into English as "The teacher gave that book to my child." What makes it possible for Japanese speakers or writers to express this same sentence in four different ways?

Japanese adds particles to words to indicate the word's function in the sentence. The particle *ga* shows that the noun to which it is attached is the subject of the sentence. As long as the word for teacher, *sensei*, is marked with *ga* it doesn't really matter where it comes in the sentence. Wherever it is placed, the *ga* shows it is the subject. The particle *o* marks the direct object. In this sentence, the direct object is *hon-o* (*book*). The final *o* marks the word as the direct object no matter where it occurs. In addition, *ni* marks the indirect object. In this sentence, the indirect object is *my child*. Again, the word for *child* (*kodomo*) can appear anywhere because the *ni* shows it is the indirect object.

Japanese does have a preferred sequence of words. That is, one sentence pattern is more common than the others. In addition, every sentence ends with the verb. All four of these variations end with *ageta*. Also, the word for *that* or *my* precedes the noun with which it is associated: "that book" and "my child." Although the position of some words in Japanese sentences is fixed, the nouns can be moved around because the word endings show how the nouns function in the sentence.

In contrast, if words are moved around in a more analytic language like English, the meaning changes. In a sentence like "The man chased the dog," the *man* is the subject, the one doing the action, because *man* comes at the beginning of the sentence. In this sentence, the *dog* is the object of the verb because *dog* comes after the verb. In "The dog chased the man," the *dog* is the subject because it comes first, and *man* is the object. English relies on the order of the words to signal the subject or object, not on word endings the way Japanese does. In general, some languages rely more on word endings and others more on word order, but all languages use both endings and order to help convey meaning.

How New Words Enter a Language

One reason that English is not purely an analytic or purely synthetic language is that English vocabulary contains words that come from many different sources. Even though English is a Germanic language, it contains many Latinate words, most of which entered the language during the time the French occupied Great Britain. In this section, we consider the different ways that words enter a language.

"Mrs. Granger, you have so many dictionaries in this room, and that huge one especially . . . where did all those words come from?" (15). Nick, the main character in Clements' delightful book *Frindle* (1996), asks this seemingly innocent question near the end of seventh period. Nick's question is a classic example of communication that has both a direct and an indirect intent. On the surface, this seems like a straightforward question asked of a teacher who loves dictionaries. However, the real purpose of Nick's question is to sidetrack his teacher, to get her talking about dictionaries, so that she won't assign any homework.

"Several kids smiled, and a few peeked at the clock. Nick was famous for doing this, and the whole class knew what he was doing. . . . Unfortunately, so did Mrs. Granger" (15). Not only does Nick's ploy fail, Mrs. Granger assigns Nick an oral report on where words come from due the very next day. Nick gives a good report, but at the end, he asks, this time really wanting to know the answer, "I still don't really get the idea of why words all mean different things. Like, who says that d-o-g means the things that goes 'woof' and wags its tail? Who says so?" (29). Mrs. Granger's answer surprises Nick, "Who says *dog* means dog? You do, Nicholas. You and me and everyone in this class and this school and this town and this state and this country. We all agree" (29).

Mrs. Granger's answer gets Nick thinking, and when his friend, Janet, finds a gold pen, Nick decides to act. This creative fifth grader starts calling the thing his friend found a *frindle*. Not only does Nick call pens *frindles*, he persuades his friends to go along with his plan. If people call the thing they use to write a *pen* just because everyone agrees to call it a *pen*, then that could change if everyone started to call it something else. Nick has his friends sign an oath, "From this day on and forever, I will never use the word *PEN* again. Instead, I will use the word *FRINDLE*, and I will do everything possible so others will too" (38).

The oath launches Nick's campaign to bring a new word into English. Clements' account of Nick's adventures and his battles with Mrs. Granger make wonderful reading for students in upper elementary grades, but the story also makes a serious point about words. The association between a word and an object is arbitrary. It is a social convention. English speakers call the writing instrument a *pen* simply because that is what others call it. There is no physical or logical connection between words and things, between sounds and meanings other than onomatopoeic words like *buzz* and *hiss*.

Frindle is an excellent book that teachers can use to lead students into an investigation of how words enter a language. Some words do enter the way *frindle* does in the story. Someone makes up a name for an object, and the name sticks. This process is called *coining*. But words enter a language in a number of ways. These include compounding, clipping, making acronyms, blending, backformation, and borrowing (Andrews 2001).

Coining

Usually, people coin words to label new inventions or products, not to rename existing objects the way Nick did. Many of these words start as proper nouns and then become common nouns. For example, *kleenex* began as Kleenex, but now the word applies to almost any brand of facial tissue. *Xerox* is the name of a particular type of photocopier, but people use the word *xerox* as a verb to refer to making copies and may call a copy machine a Xerox machine even when it is a different brand.

Many of the new words that have entered English are related to computers. Some of these, like *mouse* or *desktop*, assign new meanings to existing words. Pinker (1994) lists words like *ambimoustrous* and *depediate* as examples of words that appeared in a dictionary of computer terms. A person who is ambimoustrous can use a mouse with either hand, and if the printer cuts off the bottom of a page, it depediates it (takes away the foot). Many computer terms like these are short-lived, but others have entered the language permanently.

Compounds

Earlier we discussed how compounds are formed by joining two free morphemes. English has many compound words like *teacup* and *cupboard*. Some of these are written as one word, or closed. Other compounds like *merry-go-round* and *brother-in-law* are hyphenated. Still others like *sports car* and *grocery store* are written as two words, or open. This variation in spelling reveals an ambiguity. Dictionaries are not consistent in recording the preferred spellings of compounds. Although English spelling of compounds is not consistent, many new words are created by joining existing words. Almost any part of speech can be joined with almost any other part. Figure 7.5 lists examples of compounds made up of different parts of speech.

Compounds are easily confused with noun phrases consisting of an adjective and a noun. For example, the words *high* and *chair* refer to a child's seat or a seat that is tall. The compound *high chair* (a baby's chair) is pronounced with the stress on the first word, *high*, and the noun phrase *high chair* (a tall chair) is pronounced with stress on the noun *chair*. Words like *toothbrush* and *haircut* must be compounds because people brush more than one tooth and cut more than one hair. The usual rules for plural are suspended in a compound.

Clippings, acronyms, blends, and backformations

Both clippings and acronyms are abbreviated forms of words. Clipping occurs when a word is shortened. *Mathematics* becomes *math* and *gasoline* becomes *gas*. Some names of college courses are clipped. *Economics* may be referred to as *econ* and *educational psychology* as *ed psych*. Both *cab* and *taxi* are clipped forms of *taxicab*.

noun + noun	adj + noun	prep + prep	adv + noun	noun + verb
cupboard	highway	into	downfall	sunshine
teacup	hotshot	throughout	upturn	headache

Figure 7.5 *Compounds*

Acronyms are words made up of the first letters of several words. In some cases, such as LED (light emitting diode), just the first letter of each word is used. In other cases, such as Nabisco (National Biscuit Company), the first letters of each word are included. Some acronyms like *scuba* (self-contained underwater breathing apparatus) are pronounced as words. In other cases, like *VIP* (very important person), each letter name is pronounced. This is usually the case for colleges and universities. People say each letter of UCLA (University of California Los Angeles). They don't pronounce it /juklə/. In acronyms like CD-ROM the letters *CD* (compact disk) are each pronounced, and *ROM* (read-only memory) is pronounced as a word. Part of learning a new field of study is learning the acronyms. Students studying second language acquisition (SLA) learn about LEP (limited English proficient) and EBLs (emergent bilingual learners), BICS (basic interpersonal communicative skills), and CALP (cognitive academic language proficiency), L2 (second language) and ELs (English learners). All these acronyms may make students feel as though they are studying a foreign language.

A few words in English are blends created by combining two words. Examples are *brunch* (breakfast + lunch), *smog* (smoke + fog), and *motel* (motor + hotel). A *spork* is that utensil cafeterias pass out when they can't decide whether to give students a spoon or a fork. A blend we have heard more recently is *chillaxin',* which most people are not doing when they study linguistics. Many people use a modem to *modu*late and *demo*dulate a signal for their computer. The writer Lewis Carroll created a number of blends like *slithy* and *chortled* in his poem at the end of *Alice's Adventures in Wonderland* and *Through the Looking Glass* (Carroll 1999). These are words he made up, but readers might recognize them as combinations of *slimy* + *lithe* and *chuckle* + *snort.* However, these blends did not enter into English as regular vocabulary words.

Backformation is a process that has resulted in many new words being added to English. At one time, English had the nouns *peddler* and *beggar* but did not have the verbs *peddle* and *beg*. However, English has many pairs like *teacher-teach* and *worker-work*. These pairs were formed by adding *-er* to the verb to make a noun. Even though there was no verb *peddle* or *beg*, people assumed that *peddler* must have been formed from *peddle* and *beggar* must have been formed from *beg*. People began to use the words *peddle* and *beg*, and these words were easily understood because the words followed the rule in reverse. Rather than going from the verb to the noun (*teach* → *teacher*), they went from the noun to the verb (*peddler* → *peddle*). That is why the process is called *backformation.*

English speakers regularly create verbs from nouns using backformation. Often, this simply involves using the same word for both parts of speech without changing the ending. Almost any noun in English can become a verb through this process. For example, someone can *head* a committee, *table* a motion, and *email* a friend. Recently, we were told to *expense* an organization. Maybe *expense* will replace *bill*, itself a shortened form of "bill of sale."

Even though they are spelled the same, many two-syllable words are pronounced differently depending on whether they function as nouns or verbs. For example, *permit* with the stress on the first syllable is a noun. Shift the stress to the last syllable and it becomes a verb. This is the general pattern. Nouns like *convict* and *subject* change into verbs when the stress shifts to the second syllable.

Borrowings

Many English words were borrowed from other languages. The term *borrow* in linguistics has a slightly different meaning than it does in other contexts. If I borrow a tool or a carton of milk from my neighbor, I now have it and my neighbor doesn't. On the other hand, when English gets a word like *boutique* from French, the French still have the word. Nevertheless, *borrow* is one of the terms linguists use to describe words that come from another language. Words that are borrowed are also referred to as *loanwords*.

Because English has borrowed words from many different languages, the English vocabulary is very large. Figure 7.6 shows the origins of English words. English developed from Anglo-Saxon. In fact, the word *English* is derived from the name of one of the early groups who settled in Britain, the Angles. This analysis of modern English shows that only 15 percent of the words come from Anglo-Saxon. As Figure 7.6 illustrates, modern English is made up of words from many different languages.

Figure 7.7 shows the language families of the languages that make up modern English. English is a Germanic language because it is the language of the people from the lower coastal region of Germany, the Angles, Saxons, and Jutes, who invaded Britain and established their language. Even so, only about 25 percent of English words are from Germanic languages while 58 percent come from Latin and another 5 percent come from the Hellenic languages, principally from Greek.

Figure 7.8 presents a slightly different picture. Although only about 25 percent of modern English words come from Germanic languages, these words make up over half of the most commonly used words in English. These are our everyday words. Words used in academic registers occur less frequently and come primarily from Latin and Greek. Only 3 percent of English words come from sources other than Germanic, Latinate, and Greek languages.

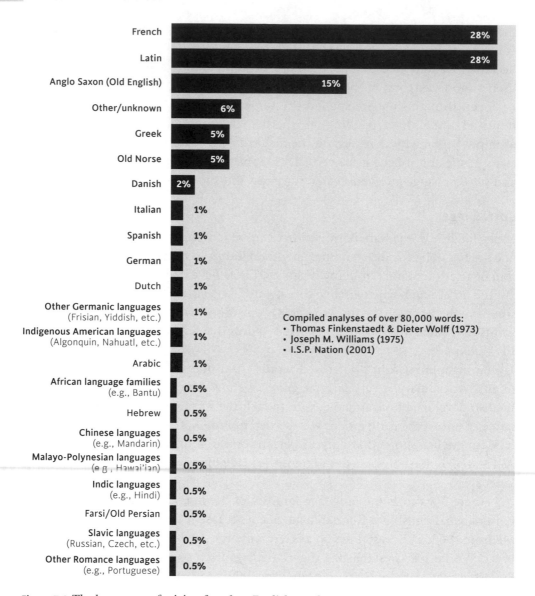

Figure 7.6 *The languages of origin of modern English words*

These figures show the origins of English words. Often, words migrate through several languages to come to English. Sometimes it is difficult to know where a word originated. A word like *yen* started out as a Chinese word and then was borrowed into Japanese. Eventually, it became an English word. Did English borrow *yen* from Chinese or Japanese? The answer is often not clear. The word originated in Chinese but was borrowed from Japanese.

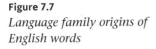

Figure 7.7
Language family origins of English words

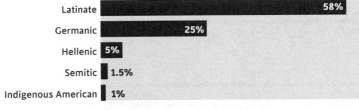

Figure 7.8
Language family origins of the most common English words

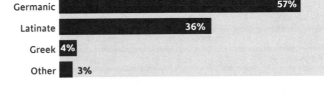

Students may have difficulty in determining where a word came from. It is helpful for teachers to show students how to read the section of a dictionary entry that traces a word's history. For example, the Online Etymology Dictionary lists the following information for *transport:*

> late 14c., from Old French *transporter* "carry or convey across" (14c.), from Latin *transportare*, from *trans-* "across" (see **trans-**) + *portare* "to carry" (see **port** (n.1)). Sense of "carry away with strong feelings" is first recorded c.1500. The meaning "to carry away into banishment" is recorded from 1660s. The noun is attested from mid-15c. originally "mental exaltation"; sense of "means of transportation" is recorded from 1690s. (retrieved from www.etymonline.com/index.php?term=transport&allowed_in_frame=0, 4/24/2014)

As this entry shows, *transport* originated in Latin and came into English from Old French. The *Oxford English Dictionary* is often considered an excellent source for word histories. Figure 7.9 lists words borrowed into English from a number of different languages. Although the figure lists *African* and *American Indian*, those designations cover a great number of different languages.

In addition to researching word etymologies, students can read books about the history of words. One particularly enjoyable read is Bryson's *Made in America: An Informal History of the English Language in the United States* (1994). Bryson's book is full of interesting information that is both historical and linguistic. For example, he explains the origin of the blend, *motel*:

> the first place to style itself a *motel* was the Milestone Mo-tel on Route 101 in San Luis Obispo, California, which opened its doors on December 12, 1925 . . . The term itself appeared a few months earlier in *Hotel Monthly magazine*, in the same article in which *motor hotel* made its debut. (173)

Bryson discusses a variety of topics. One of these is food. He explains that *chicken tetrazzini* was named for the Italian opera singer but was invented in New

Chinese	Greek	Dutch	Persian	Italian
tea	acme	golf	lilac	granite
yen	acrobat	brandy	jasmine	piano
chow	tantalize	yacht	paradise	duet
Spanish	**German**	**French**	**African**	**Am. Indian**
cargo	frankfurter	dime	chigger	skunk
mosquito	sauerkraut	cent	okra	moose
alligator	hamburger	prairie	yam	chipmunk
Polynesian	**Japanese**	**Russian**	**Australian**	**Yiddish**
taboo	kimono	ruble	kangaroo	bagel
tattoo	tycoon	vodka	boomerang	kosher
Slavic	**Malay**	**Bengali**	**Turkish**	**Bantu**
vampire	amuck	bungalow	yoghurt	zebra

Figure 7.9 *Borrowed words*

York. Russian dressing was unknown in Russia. Vichyssoise was invented in New York, not in France. Swiss steak is not from Switzerland. And the Caesar salad was named after Caesar Cardini, a chef in a restaurant in Tijuana, Mexico. Bryson's book provides a great deal of well-researched information about the linguistic history of the United States.

Word Formation Rules

Even though the processes described in the preceding section account for many of the new words that enter English every year, one of the richest sources of new words is the morphological process of *derivation*. Many English words are formed by combining a free morpheme with a derivational affix. Earlier we explained that *teacher* is derived by adding *-er* to the verb *teach*. This is an example of a general pattern. When the suffix *-er* is added to a verb, a new noun is created. English has many words that follow this pattern—*preacher*, *baker*, and *singer*, to name just three.

Words like *teacher* are formed by a process that includes a change in sound, a change in part of speech category, and a change in meaning. Each word that is formed following this pattern undergoes the same sound change, the same category change, and the same meaning change. Figure 7.10 shows the pattern for the formation of *-er* words like *teacher*.

base word	derivational affix	sound change	category change	meaning change
teach	-er	add /ɚ/	verb to noun	one who teaches

Figure 7.10 *Word formation rule for -er suffix*

Linguists refer to patterns like this as word formation rules. These rules are descriptions of regular processes in the language. Every word that follows this rule undergoes the same sound change (add /ɚ/), the same category change (verb to noun), and the same meaning change. Linguists express the meaning change generally for this rule as "one who *X*es." The *X* represents the meaning of the verb. So a teacher is one who teaches, and a singer is one who sings. This is the general meaning change, although there are some words like *islander* and *villager* that refer to someone from an island or a village. Word formation rules like this help people figure out new words. For example, a reader might assume that the nonsense word *glarker* must refer to a person who *glarks*, whatever that is.

New words follow the pattern. A *Xeroxer* is a person who makes copies, and an *emailer* is someone who sends emails. This is a very productive rule because it applies to many verbs in English. However, the rule is blocked when a noun meaning "someone who *X*es" is already associated with a verb. For example, a *chef*, not a *cooker*, is a person who cooks. What is interesting is that people assign a new meaning to words like *cooker*. A *cooker* is a cooking utensil, like a pressure cooker, not a person. Some words derived from Latin, such as *advisor* and *donor*, keep the same sound change but use the spelling *-or* for the suffix rather than *-er*. These words still follow the rule. Some words with the *-er* suffix such as *loafer* could refer to a person who loafs or a type of shoe. The shoe was probably called a loafer to suggest that people could wear it while loafing.

Adding a derivational suffix like *-er* usually results in a word with a different part of speech than the base word. To take a second, very productive word formation rule, *-ly* can be added to adjectives to form adverbs. Thus, English has words like *quickly*, *beautifully*, and *laboriously*. The *-ly* suffix can be added to many different adjectives. In each case, the pattern is the same. The sound change is the addition of /li/, the category change is from adjective to adverb, and the meaning of the new word is "in an *X* manner." If someone does something quickly, they do it in a quick manner. When a reader encounters a new word, like the nonsense word *trebly*, they can assume that this must mean in a *treb* manner. People can determine the probable meaning of the new word by analogy with other words that follow the same pattern.

Not all -*ly* words are the result of this word formation rule. The suffix can be added to nouns to create adjectives, such as *lovely* and *friendly*. The sound change is the same, add /li/, but the category change is noun to adjective, not adjective to adverb. The meanings of *lovely* and *friendly* are related to the base words but they do not indicate a manner of doing something. They mean more generally "having the characteristics of *X*," so a lovely person is one who loves, and a friendly person has the characteristics of a friend. This rule for changing nouns to adjectives is less productive than the rule for changing adjectives to adverbs.

New words can also be derived by adding prefixes to base words. For example, *un-* can be added to adjectives to form new adjectives like *unhappy* and *unusual*. Figure 7.11 shows the pattern for this word formation rule.

Prefixes don't change the part of speech of a word. Although linguists refer to a category change, there is no change with a prefix. The rule simply lists the base as an adjective and the derived word as an adjective. The meaning change could be expressed simply as "not *X*." This would account for any word formed by this rule.

English contains some *un-* words like *uncouth* that at first appear to have been formed by this rule. However, although the word *uncouth* occurs fairly often, the base word *couth* is much less common. It would seem odd to many people to be referred to as *couth* (although it would be a positive remark). In the same way, the word *unkempt* occurs more frequently than *kempt*. If a colleague remarked that he was pleased that his formerly disheveled friend now looked *kempt*, I would have to stop and think about what that meant.

The words *couth* and *kempt* both appear in dictionaries. It may be that they are the result of backformation in the same way that *peddler* and *beggar* are. That is, the language may have had *uncouth* and *unkempt* first and then, by analogy, people formed the words *couth* and *kempt*. Or these words may have been formed by the usual word formation rule for adding the *un-* prefix. Only a historical analysis could determine the process.

There are cases in which only the negative occurs in the language. Your ideas can be *inchoate*, but it would seem strange to say, "I found his ideas to be *choate*." Someone can be *disconsolate*, but not *consolate* (although they can be consoled). A speech can be *impromptu*, but not *promptu* (although the speaker could be prompted). And a person can be *nonchalant*, but not *chalant*. These gaps reflect the

base word	derivational affix	sound change	category change	meaning change
happy	un	add /ən/	adj → adj	not happy

Figure 7.11 *Word formation rule for* un- *prefix*

fact that the lexicon of a language is not completely regular. For this reason, linguists find it difficult to develop a theory of morphology that applies consistently to all the words that make up the lexicon.

Words like *untie* follow a different rule from words like *unhappy* even though the same prefix is involved. In this case, the *un-* has been added to a verb. Although the sound change is the same, the category would be expressed as verb to verb, not adjective to adjective. The meaning change is also different. To untie one's shoes is not the same as to not tie one's shoes. Added to verbs, *un-* has a meaning of something like "to reverse the action of *X*." It is only possible to *undo* something that previously has been done. Thus, a person can *unlock* a door or *unwind* a ball of twine, but a person can't *unplay* a game even though they might wish they could. The verb that takes *un-* expresses an action that is reversible. Some actions are not reversible. However, the word used to describe these actions is *irreversible*, not *unreversible*. More than one prefix can be used to express the negative meaning of *un-*.

Word formation rules account for many of the words in the lexicon of English. Speakers of English create these words by analogy with known words, following the same pattern. People also understand many new words by analogy. If someone knows what the nonsense verb *braf* means, they know that a *brafer* must be a person who *brafs*. They also know that to *unbraf* means to reverse the action of *braffing*. Knowing one word can open up the meanings of many other words formed by adding derivational affixes.

A problem with word formation rules is that there are often different derivational affixes that can be used to achieve the same effect. Both *un-* or *ir-* can signify the negative. A colleague recently used the word *humbleness* to describe a mutual friend. We understood what he meant, but English already has the word *humility*, so the rule for forming nouns from adjectives like *humble* is blocked by the presence of the word *humility*. Despite these problems, word formation rules are used by speakers of a language to create and understand new words.

Conclusion

We began this chapter with the questions:

- How do linguists analyze words?
- How do new words enter a language?

Morphology is the study of words. A morpheme is the smallest meaningful unit or part of a word. Words are made up of free and bound morphemes. Free morphemes can stand alone as words and can serve as bases for complex words. Some complex words are formed by adding an affix to a root word. Bound morphemes are not words by themselves and must be attached to a free morpheme. Bound morphemes are affixes that can be either derivational or inflectional.

Linguists categorize words by their combination of different types of morphemes. Simple words have one free morpheme. Complex words combine free and bound morphemes. Compound words consist of two or more free morphemes. Compound-complex words have two or more free morphemes and a bound morpheme.

Languages differ in the kinds of words they contain. English has only a limited number of inflectional affixes, so it is considered more of an analytic language than a synthetic language. Like other analytic languages, English relies more on the order of words in a sentence than on word endings to signal the role of the word in the sentence. Other languages have many inflections and rely on the inflectional affixes to signal parts of speech rather than relying on the position in the sentence.

Traditional methods of classifying words are not scientifically based, but morphological information can be used along with syntactic and semantic information to determine the part of speech. Words can also be classified as content words or function words. Content words are open-class words because new content words can be added to a language. These words carry the main meanings in a sentence. Grammatical function words are closed class. New function words are not added to a language. The function words show relationships among content words, but they do not carry the same kind of meaning a content word does. In the prepositional phrase "in the chair," *in* and *the* are function words, and *chair* is a content word.

Words enter a language in a number of ways. They include coining, compounding, clipping, blending, making acronyms, and borrowing. Many new words are formed by adding derivational affixes to roots or bases. These word formation rules follow regular patterns. English has a large vocabulary because English borrows words regularly and because many new words are created through word formation rules.

APPLICATIONS

1. Although about 60 percent of the words in an English dictionary have Latin or Greek roots, many words in a text are function words or simple content words. Take a passage of one hundred consecutive words from one of your texts. Working alone or in pairs, classify each word by placing it on the chart that follows. Put all the compound words in the fourth column and

all the function words in the fifth column. For nouns, verbs, adjectives, and adverbs, list each one as simple or complex. If a word is repeated, list it each time it appears. There is an example of each type of word in this chart, but start with a blank chart and then place the words in the right area. You may need to add rows to complete your chart.

	Simple	Complex inflectional	Complex derivational	Compound or compound-complex	Function
Nouns	boy	dogs	national	input	the
				tablecloths	through
					and
Verbs	go	running	prioritize		me
Adjectives	green	taller	unsatisfactory		
Adverbs	fast	slowest	quietly		

Now analyze your results by answering the following questions:

What percent of the words are function words?
What percent are simple words?
What percent are complex words with inflectional suffixes?
What percent are complex words with derivational suffixes?
What percent are compound or compound-complex words?

If each pair or student takes a different passage, the class results would provide a good sample of what students typically read. The class could discuss their findings. Since students may be able to determine the meanings of complex words with derivational affixes by using structural analysis, consider what percent of the words fall into this category. (For example, *unsatisfactory* could be understood by knowing the meanings of *un-* and *satisfactory*.)

2. Two-word verbs like *run across* in the sentence "I ran across an old friend" can be difficult for English learners. Many English verbs combine with particles to form two-word verbs. One very productive particle is *up*. List at least one hundred *up* words. Be careful to distinguish between cases when *up* is a particle ("He ran up a big bill") and when it is a preposition ("He

ran up a big hill"). Two-word verbs have a meaning that is different from the meaning of the individual parts. To *look up* a word has nothing to do with the direction *up*. Create a class composite *up* chart and add words over time. It is easier to *come up* with *up* words than you may realize.

3. Word formation rules are general patterns that follow the same sound change, category change, and meaning change. Following the examples in this chapter, investigate a word formation rule. You might use a prefix like *de-* or *tran-* or a suffix like *-ize* or *-ity*. Do not use an inflectional suffix like *-ing*. Collect several words that follow this pattern and then describe the sound change, category change, and meaning change. Use a chart like the ones in the chapter. Be sure to use a prefix or suffix that was not used in the chapter. Use *X* to represent the general meaning change for all your words. Don't put the specific meaning change for each word. Once you finish, try to find additional words that appear to fit the pattern but are not the same as the other words in some way, following the examples of *friendly* and *untie* that were described in the chapter.

8 /eɪt/

Implications from Morphology for Teaching a Second Language and Teaching Reading

An understanding of morphology is an important part of a teacher's pedagogical language knowledge. Morphology plays a role in both second language teaching and in teaching reading to both native English speakers and emergent bilinguals. In second language teaching, studies of the acquisition of morphemes are the basis of the Natural Order Hypothesis. In addition, methods of teaching a second language based on a learning view give more attention to the direct teaching of morphology than methods based on an acquisition view. In teaching reading, methods based on a learning view teach morphology as a strategy for decoding words while methods based on an acquisition view include morphology as a strategy for constructing meaning and developing academic language.

- **What is the role of morphology in methods of second language teaching?**
- **How can teachers use morphological information as they teach reading?**
- **How can teachers help students acquire academic vocabulary?**

The Natural Order Hypothesis

Morphological concepts are important in understanding second language acquisition. Krashen's Natural Order Hypothesis (1977), discussed in Chapter 3, is based on morpheme studies. Even though language is very complex, it is possible to observe the order in which different common inflectional morphemes appear in an emergent bilingual's speech. In addition to inflectional morphemes, these studies included free morphemes, such as forms of the verb *to be* (*am*, *is*, *are*), articles, and irregular past-tense forms like *came*.

The Natural Order Hypothesis maintains that people acquire parts of a second language in a natural order. For example, some sounds are acquired before others. This hypothesis was based on Krashen's analysis of data from several earlier studies of the order of acquisition of morphemes in oral language, including Dulay and Burt's (1974) study of the acquisition of morphemes by second language adults and children. Some morphemes appear in an English learner's speech before others. Figure 8.1 lists the order of morpheme acquisition of students learning English.

Morphemes within each box in Figure 8.1 may differ in their order of acquisition. For example, the regular past tense *-ed* might come after the third-person singular *-s* morpheme. However, items in the top box are acquired before those in the second box, and so on. This ordering helps account for patterns teachers often observe. Even though the plural and the third-person singular end in *-s*, the plural *-s* appears in speech much sooner than the third-person *-s*. Speakers will acquire the plural *-s* morpheme in *books* as in "I read book*s* in school," before the third-person *-s* morpheme in *reads* as in "He read*s* a book in school."

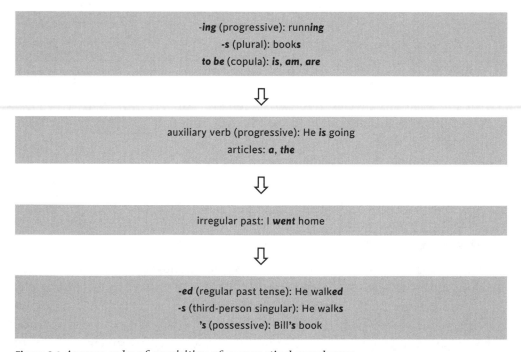

-ing (progressive): runn**ing**
-s (plural): book**s**
to be (copula): **is**, **am**, **are**

⇩

auxiliary verb (progressive): He **is** going
articles: **a**, **the**

⇩

irregular past: I **went** home

⇩

-ed (regular past tense): He walk**ed**
-s (third-person singular): He walk**s**
's (possessive): Bill**'s** book

Figure 8.1 *Average order of acquisition of grammatical morphemes*

The order of acquisition is the same for both children and adults from different language backgrounds. Spanish speakers and Chinese speakers in the Dulay and Burt study acquired English morphemes in this same sequence. The order of acquisition for English as a second language is similar to that of English as a first language. However, Dulay and Burt found that native English speakers acquire auxiliaries and forms of the verb *to be* (the copula) later than English learners.

This order holds for natural learning contexts in which people are acquiring English. Teachers may attempt to teach certain bound morphemes, such as the past tense -*ed*, before students are ready to acquire the morpheme. This will result in a temporary ability to add -*ed* to verbs on an exercise in class. However, students can't fully incorporate the form into their speech or writing until they acquire it.

Direct teaching doesn't change the order of acquisition. Language is complex, and students are acquiring phonology and syntax at the same time that they are acquiring morphology, so this list of morphemes can't be turned into a teaching sequence. Even so, this knowledge of the natural order of acquisition should be part of a teacher's pedagogical language knowledge. Teachers with this knowledge have a general idea of what to expect from their students and can better support students' English language development.

Second Language Teaching Methods and Morphology

Methods of teaching a second or foreign language take different approaches to teaching morphology. Methods based on a learning view either teach morphology directly or contextualize the instruction in drills, role-plays, and other classroom activities. Methods based on an acquisition view assume that morphology will be acquired naturally, or they design lessons to teach morphology through academic content.

Figure 8.2 summarizes the role of morphology in orientations and methods associated with a learning view of second language development.

Orientation	Method	Role of Morphology
Grammar based	Grammar translation	Verb conjugations and other aspects of grammar are taught directly. Morphology plays an important role.
Communicative	Direct method	Morphology is contextualized in activities to improve communicative abilities.
Empiricist	Audio-lingual Method Notional Functional Suggestopedia	Morphology is contextualized in drills, role-play, etc., but not taught directly.

Figure 8.2 *Learning orientations, methods, and role of morphology*

The grammar translation method includes lessons designed to teach different aspects of language, including morphology. Students learn to add the correct endings to show person or tense. These aspects of morphology are taught directly.

In contrast, methods associated with both a communicative and an empiricist view include activities that require students to use correct morphological forms. For example, students might tell a partner what they did yesterday, what they plan to do tomorrow, or even what they would do if they had the time and money. In each case, students would need to use auxiliaries and verbs with the proper suffixes to indicate the time. Students also engage in dialogues in which they need to use inflectional suffixes to indicate person in some languages. A student learning Spanish would use -es to indicate second person *you* and *o* to indicate first person *I* in the following lines:

¿Puedes ir a la tienda? ("Can you go to the store?")
Si, puedo ir. ("Yes, I can go.")

However, in these methods, the grammar is not taught directly.

Figure 8.3 describes the role of morphology in orientations and methods associated with an acquisition view of second language development. These methods either do not teach aspects of grammar at all, or, as in the case of the Silent Way, morphology is included as an aid to forming words.

One feature of the Silent Way is the use of Cuisenaire rods. Students use these rods to represent different parts of a language. In building words, students could use a long orange rod to represent the base of a word like *prevention*, a short green rod for the prefix *pre-*, and a short yellow rod for the suffix *-tion*. Although morphology is not taught directly in this method, students are made aware of word parts and use the rods to visually represent the parts.

In other methods, including Community Language Learning, Problem Posing, and the Natural Approach, the assumption is that students will acquire the language

Orientation	Method	Role of Morphology
Rationalist	Silent Way	Cuisenaire rods are used to indicate morphemes in words.
	Community Language Learning and Problem Posing Total Physical Response Natural Approach	No explicit attention to morphology in these methods.
	CALLA SIOP	Morphology is contextualized in the teaching of academic language.

Figure 8.3 *Acquisition orientations, methods, and role of morphology*

naturally if they receive comprehensible input. Morphology is not taught in these methods.

On the other hand, teachers using methods such as CALLA and SIOP in which language is taught through content include both language and content objectives. Language objectives can focus on word parts. For example, a biology teacher might teach Latin roots of scientific words to help students build science vocabulary. A literature teacher might teach the future tense for students to use in reading and writing during a thematic unit on the future. Language objectives are drawn from academic content, so teachers using these content-based methods may teach aspects of morphology. Any teaching of morphology would be contextualized.

Teaching Reading and Morphology

Insights from linguistic studies of morphology can inform reading instruction. Teachers who employ both methods that are consistent with a learning view and those who take an acquisition view include instruction designed to help students use morphological information as they read. Teachers who have a learning view teach structural analysis to help students decode complex words since those words are difficult to decode using phonics rules. The emphasis in learning classrooms is on helping students identify individual words. Students can then combine the meanings of the words to make sense of sentences, paragraphs, and complete texts.

Teachers who take an acquisition approach also teach students to use information from word parts as one strategy for constructing meaning from texts. Teaching prefixes, roots or bases, and suffixes always occurs in the context of meaningful reading so that readers can combine cues from morphology with graphophonic, syntactic, and semantic cues to make sense of what they read. The suffixes of complex words provide clues as to the word's part of speech. For example, words that end in -*tion* are usually nouns. This morphological information helps readers determine the syntax of a sentence as they read since they know that nouns serve as subjects and objects.

In addition, by reading extensively, readers in acquisition classrooms build vocabulary. When readers come to a word or phrase they don't understand, they can use a number of strategies to make sense of the text, and one of these is to use their knowledge of word parts to comprehend individual words. Since academic texts contain many complex words, knowing some common prefixes, roots, and suffixes helps students build academic vocabulary.

Although using knowledge of word structures during reading is useful, there are several difficulties in applying structural analysis. These include difficulties in recognizing prefixes, roots, and suffixes; a lack of knowledge of some word parts; and the problems with combining word parts to infer the meaning of unknown words. Because of these difficulties, teachers should judge carefully how much time to spend teaching prefixes, roots, and suffixes. While such study can be useful and interesting, teachers always work within time constraints, and time spent teaching word parts is time taken away from having students read.

Teaching vocabulary

In *The Vocabulary Book: Learning and Instruction*, Graves (2006) summarizes the research on vocabulary teaching and learning. Based on his review of the research, he concludes that teachers should follow four procedures to ensure effective vocabulary development:

1. Provide rich and varied language experiences.
2. Teach individual words.
3. Teach word-learning strategies.
4. Foster word consciousness (awareness of, and interest in, words).

The best way to help students build their vocabulary is through class discussions and extensive reading. Research by Anderson and Nagy (1992) shows that students can learn many new words by reading without any explicit teaching. In addition, Krashen (2004) has summarized research studies showing the benefits of free voluntary reading. In their analysis of the international tests of reading, Brozo, Shiel, and Topping (2007/2008) found that engagement in reading was a key predictor of high levels of reading proficiency. When teachers provide rich and varied oral and written language experiences, their students become better readers and build their vocabularies.

In addition, Graves points out that teachers should teach some individual words. These should be words related to the academic subjects students are studying. Marzano and Pickering (2005) outline an approach to teaching words that many teachers have found useful. In teaching linguistics, for example, it would be important to teach words like *phoneme*, *morpheme*, and *syntax*. The key is to embed vocabulary instruction, in meaningful reading.

Graves also emphasizes the benefits of teaching strategies for learning words. One word-learning strategy that Graves discusses is using morphological clues to infer meanings of words. He points out that words that make up the academic vocabulary of English often have Latin or Greek roots as well as prefixes and suffixes. Students can use morphological structural analysis to infer the meaning of words in context.

For example, Thompson and Rubenstein (2000) describe how a math teacher used morphological clues to help her students understand a content-specific math term. The teacher explained, "*Perpendicular* comes from a root, *pend*, meaning 'to hang,' because when a weight hangs freely on a string, it forms a perpendicular to the ground" (571). Then she connected the math term to other, everyday words they knew like *pendant* and *pendulum* to help the students remember the meaning of the Latin root. This teacher used the word root to explain *perpendicular*. She helped her students remember the word by connecting it to other words they knew, and she showed that word histories can be interesting.

Emergent bilinguals also benefit from knowledge of some prefixes and suffixes. These word parts occur frequently and provide consistent clues that help students infer word meanings. In many cases, prefixes and suffixes attach to English base words that students know. If they also know the meaning of the prefix or suffix, they can infer the meaning of the whole word. White, Sowell, and Yanagihara (1989) analyzed words taken from a word-frequency list for school texts in grades 3 through 9. They found that four prefixes (*un-*, *re-*, *in-*, and *dis-*) accounted for 58 percent of the prefixes in their data. They recommend teaching these four prefixes first. Teachers can begin by listing these four prefixes on a chart and having students find words with the prefixes as they read and add them to the chart. Looking at the list of words, the students and teacher can discuss the meaning of each prefix.

Students might notice that *in-* means *not* in a word like *ineligible* and it means *in* for *inside*. The teacher can suggest that students try each meaning to see which one makes sense. The teacher can also add other words to the chart. For example, *impossible* has a prefix that looks like *in-* and means *not* so students could infer that *impossible* means "not possible." Students can gather other words with *im-* and try to make a generalization about when the prefix is spelled *im-*, not *in-*. Activities like these can trigger students' word consciousness.

Teaching these four most commonly occurring prefixes can give students clues to the meanings of many words. In addition, teachers can work with students to create a wall chart listing suffixes that signal that a word is a noun, a verb, an adjective, or an adverb. As students read, they can look for words with suffixes that indicate each of these major parts of speech. For example, the suffixes *-tion* (*attention*), *-ence* (*independence*), and *-ment* (*acknowledgment*) can be added to a base word or a root to make it a noun. Teachers can discuss how knowing whether a word is a noun, a verb, an adjective, or an adverb can help readers figure out its meaning in a sentence. Students will also see that adjectives and adverbs usually provide extra descriptive information and are not as important in understanding the meaning of a sentence as the nouns and verbs.

Teaching word-part clues can be a useful word-learning strategy if used judiciously. Teachers should choose words related to their content area. They should look primarily for words with a recognizable English base that occurs in several words in their field. Then teachers can show students how prefixes modify the meaning of the base and how suffixes provide clues about the part of speech. By teaching students to use morphological clues from prefixes, roots, and suffixes, teachers can help students construct meaning from texts. However, as Graves points out, building students' vocabulary requires involving students in extensive reading and discussions, teaching some individual words, and teaching word-learning strategies such as the use of structural analysis. Graves writes that the goal of vocabulary instruction should be to increase students' word consciousness. Word consciousness is an awareness of and interest in words. Teachers with a knowledge of linguistics can help their students develop word consciousness.

Teaching Latin and Greek roots

One way teachers can help students build academic vocabulary is by teaching Latin and Greek roots since many academic words contain these roots. Rasinski and his colleagues (2011) point out that when students learn Latin and Greek roots, they can apply this knowledge to many words, and this process is more efficient than teaching individual words. For example, if students know that a root like *mis*, which also appears as *mit*, means "send" they can infer the meanings of many words, such as *transmit, transmission, submit, submission, remit, remission, omit, omission, commit, commission, admit, admission*, and *permit, permission*.

As Rasinski and colleagues observe, most of the academic words in English have Latin and Greek roots. They also comment that a "single Latin or Greek root or affix . . . can be found in and aid in the understanding of 20 or more English words" (2011, 134). For example, the Latin root *acu* ("sharp") and the Latin word *acuere* ("to sharpen") give us words like *acupuncture* and *acute* in English. The Latin *ab-, a-,* and *abs-* ("away from") used as a prefix give readers a clue for the meaning of *abnormal, asymmetrical,* and *abstain* in English.

In addition, since Spanish is a Latin-based language, emergent bilinguals who speak Spanish can draw on their native language to determine the meaning of many Latin roots. Often, there is a clear connection between the Latin root and the word in Spanish. For example, *escribir* ("to write") comes from the Latin root *scrib* ("write"), *arbol* ("tree") comes from the Latin root *arbor* ("tree"), and *pasear* ("to walk") comes from the Latin root, *pass* ("pace" or "step"). This knowledge would help them understand English words such as *scribe, arboretum,* or *pace.*

Rasinski and his colleagues give several suggestions for teaching Latin and Greek roots. They list Latin and Greek roots that appear most frequently in English texts for primary, intermediate, and middle grades. These lists are a good starting point for teachers wishing to involve students in morphological study.

Teachers of younger students might begin by having their students look for meaningful word parts in compound words like *sunshine* and *rainbow.* The teacher could have students identify the two words that make up these compound words. Once students have the basic idea that words can have meaningful parts, teachers can have them find the parts in complex words with a common prefix and a recognizable English base, like *uncover.* One meaning of the prefix *un-* means "to reverse an action," so the teacher could explain that *uncover* means "to take off the cover."

After teaching about compound words and words with prefixes and recognizable English bases, teachers can begin to teach Greek and Latin roots. Rasinski and colleagues describe teaching activities for students at different grade levels. For example, for students in grades 1 through 5 they suggest word spokes and word charts. Students and the teacher can use prefixes that have previously been taught for the spoke activity. Students put the prefix in the middle of a chart and then draw lines (spokes) to words around the outside that begin with that prefix. They give an example with the prefix *sub-* in the center and words like *subterranean, subway,* and *submerge* around the outside. The students write a definition of each word on the chart and also draw a picture to show the meaning. This visual display is especially helpful for emergent bilinguals. Students can also create different kinds of word charts with a prefix or root on top and examples with the root or prefix below.

The authors also suggest other activities for older students, such as writing a poem that explains the meaning of a root and uses several examples of words with the root. Another idea is to have students play with affixes and roots to make up their own words and then explain what the word means based on the meanings of the parts. They give the example of the made-up word *automand,* an order one gives to oneself. Although time for teaching vocabulary must be balanced with time for students to read, teachers can teach the morphology of words, including common Latin and Greek roots.

Difficulties in applying structural analysis

Although structural analysis should be one strategy that students use during reading, there are several difficulties in applying structural analysis. These include not recognizing the morphemes in complex words, not knowing the meanings of the word parts, and not being able to combine the meanings of the parts to infer the meaning of a word.

Recognizing word parts

At times, students identify parts of words as morphemes that are not actually morphemes. For example, students might notice the word *hot* in the word *hotel*. However, *hot* is not a base here, so it does not help a reader understand *hotel*. Since *hotel* has only one morpheme, there are no smaller meaningful parts that can be used as clues to word meaning. Or, to take another example, a student could spot *quit* in the word *mosquito*, but this is just a coincidence. There is no relationship between the meanings of *mosquito* and *quit*.

Although students may encounter difficulties applying structural analysis if they are simply told to look for little words inside the big words, they are more successful when teachers introduce and teach common prefixes and roots as one strategy readers can use. As long as students ask themselves the question, "Does this make sense?" they won't be led to think that the meaning of a word like *hotel* is related to the meaning of *hot*.

In some cases, it is fairly easy to divide a word into its meaningful parts, or morphemes. For example, a word like *transportation* has three morphemes. The root is *port*, the prefix is *trans-*, and the suffix is *-ation*. These three parts are fairly easy to recognize. In a word like *reincarnation* students can, with some instruction, identify the prefixes (*re-*, *in-*), root (*carne*, meaning "flesh"), and suffix (*-ation*, meaning "the act of doing something") and use this information to infer the meaning of the word when it appears in a meaningful context.

In other cases, it is not so easy to recognize word parts. Sometimes words are made up of meaningful parts, but it is difficult to decide which part of the word is a prefix and which part is the root. For example, the word *cognate* is made up of a prefix *co-*, which means "with," and a root *gnatus* meaning "to be born." Cognates are English words like *activity* and the Spanish word *actividad*, which come from the same root or are "born together."

There would be other ways to divide *cognate*. One common root is *cogn* meaning "to know" and the suffix *-ate* means "to make." Thus, *cognate* could mean "to make known." The student might know a word like *recognize* and assume that *recognize* and *cognate* are related in meaning. However, the words have different roots. The root of *cognate* is *gnatus* and the root of *recognize* is *cogn*. If students have trouble recognizing the morphemes in a word, then they are not able to use structural analysis effectively. For words like *cognate* it would be better for a teacher to explain the meaning and provide examples than to ask students to use structural analysis.

Recognizing prefixes and suffixes

The word *cognate* illustrates a second potential problem in recognizing word parts. The prefix *co-* means "with." However, this prefix is difficult to identify because the word is pronounced /kɑg neɪt/ (*cog + nate*), not /koʊ gneɪt/ (*co + gnate*). This is a case where the phonology and the morphology don't match. Part of the root is pronounced as part of the prefix.

In addition, this prefix, like many other prefixes in English, changes its pronunciation and spelling to assimilate to the first sound in the root word. The prefix *con-* may be spelled *co, con, com, col,* or *cor*. Usually, *co-* occurs when the root starts with a vowel as in *coauthor* or *coexist*. *Con* is the most common spelling of the prefix, but it changes to *com* when the root begins with a bilabial, as in *commingle, combine,* or *comport*. However, it also changes to *com* in a word like *comfort*. When the root starts with *l* the prefix changes to *col* as in *collate* or *colleague*. Finally, the prefix changes to *r* before roots starting with *r* as in *correct* or *correlate*.

These variations in spelling make it difficult for students to recognize the prefix as the one they studied. On the other hand, students undertaking a linguistic investigation could come to understand these variations as examples of a common process of assimilation that occurs frequently in all languages. The final sound of the prefix assimilates to the first sound of the root, and the current spellings reflect this process. Knowing that *con-* means "with" can help students understand complex words (like *complex*), but only if they can recognize the prefix as one of the variants of *con-*.

Some prefixes are even more difficult to recognize than *con-*. One of the most complicated prefixes is *ad-*, a prefix that means "to, toward, or near." An analysis of this prefix using a large dictionary yields the data shown in Figure 8.4.

In addition to these changes, scribes added a *d* to words like *avance* because they thought the word came from Latin and originally had a *d*. As a result, *advance* looks like it has the *ad-* prefix when it really doesn't. Even if a student recognized one of these variations, it would still be hard to use this knowledge to figure out the word meaning. For example, how does the meaning of *ad* as "to, toward, or near" apply in a word like *adopt* or *assist*? The *con-* and *ad-* examples show that prefixes may be difficult to recognize, and even if a student recognizes the prefix, the meaning it carries may not unlock the meaning of the entire word. Many of the words in Figure 8.4 have Latin roots that students may not know.

No assimilation before	Assimilates before other consonants	Assimilates to *a* before 2 consonants
d – ad + dition = addition	ad + breviate = abbreviate	ad + scend = ascend
h – ad + here = adhere	ad + cent = accent	ad + spire = aspire
j – ad + judicate = adjudicate	ad + firm = affirm	ad + stound = astound
m – ad + mit = admit	ad + gressive = aggressive	
v – ad + verb = adverb	ad + literation =alliteration	
vowels – ad + opt = adopt	ad + nounce = announce	
	ad + pear = appear	
	ad + tempt = attempt	
	ad + quit = acquit	
	ad + range = arrange	
	ad + sist = assist	

Figure 8.4 *Assimilation of* ad- *prefix*

Suffixes undergo fewer spelling changes than prefixes. However, the /ʃən/ suffix undergoes various spelling changes. Consider the words in Figure 8.5.

prefix plus root or base	suffix	word
prevent	ion	prevention
repress	ion	repression
imagine	ation	imagination
inspire	ation	inspiration
compile	ation	compilation
redeem	tion	redemption
evade	ion	evasion
invert	ion	inversion

Figure 8.5 *Assimilation of* -tion *suffix*

As Figure 8.5 shows, this suffix has several possible spellings. Some words ending in *t* like *prevent* or ending in *s* like *repress* just add -*ion*, but others like *invert* change the *t* to *s* in *inversion*. Similarly, in a word like *evade*, the *d* becomes *s* to form *evasion*. *Redeem* is unusual because a *p* is added, and the vowel in *redeem* is shortened. Some words add an *a* between the base word and the suffix, as in *imagination*, while others don't. What happens when -*tion* is added to *revolt*? It appears that two possible words result, *revulsion* and *revolution*. In addition, the sound of the first consonant in all of these suffixes changes to the /ʃ/ sound.

The situation is further complicated by the fact that in some cases the last phoneme of the base or root word becomes the first phoneme of the suffix. In both *prevention* and *repression*, for example, the last phoneme of the base, /t/ or /s/, is pronounced as the first phoneme of the suffix. Here again, there is a split between the morphology and the phonology. The morphological analysis of *prevention* is *prevent + ion*, but the phonological analysis would be *preven + tion*. The syllables of the spoken word don't match the morphemes that make up the word. This makes it more difficult to recognize the suffix.

Combining meanings of morphemes

Students can learn the meanings of prefixes and suffixes as well as the meanings of common root words with good instruction as discussed earlier. However, even if they know the meaning of the parts, students may find it difficult to determine the meaning of the whole word. The problem is that the meaning of the whole is often more than the sum of the meanings of the parts. When someone knows the meaning of the whole, the meanings of the parts can make sense. However, going from whole to part is easier than going from part to whole. Trying to put the meanings of the parts together to come up with the meaning of the whole is a much more difficult task.

Figure 8.6 lists the meanings of some common prefixes, roots, and suffixes. These parts can be combined in different ways. For example, a word could start with two of these prefixes and end with two of these suffixes to produce a word like *unconditional*. However, even if students recognize these morphemes and know their meanings they may

Prefix	Root	Suffix
re – back, again	cogn – know	ize – to make
con – with	bene – good	tion – state or condition
un – not	dic(t) – say	al – relation to
de – down, from	greg – flock	ate – to make
	capit – head	able – able to

Figure 8.6 *Prefixes, roots, and suffixes*

have difficulty determining the meaning of words like the following (note: if you know the meaning of the whole word, the parts make sense; it's going from knowledge of the parts to inferring the meaning of the whole that is difficult):

> *con + greg + ation + al* = relation to the state or condition of being with the flock
>
> *un + re + cogn + ize + able* = not able to make known again
>
> *bene + dict + ion* = the condition of saying something good
>
> *de + capit + ate* = to make the head go from

The meanings of these words do seem to be at least roughly a combination of the meanings of the parts. In the case of *congregational* one would need to use the metaphorical meaning of the church group as a flock. But, in general, there is a relation between the meanings of the parts and the meaning of the whole. As these examples demonstrate, it is possible to use knowledge of word parts to determine word meanings.

In other cases it is much more difficult. For example, the word *product* is made up of the prefix *pro-* meaning "forward" and *duc*, which means "lead." In this case it is difficult to connect the meaning of *product* with "lead forward." Or to take one more example, *factor* has a root *fact*, which means "to do or make," and a suffix, *-or*, which means "one who." So a factor is "one who does or makes." This does seem to relate to the meaning of factor, which means "something that contributes to a result," but the connection is not entirely clear. In math, *factor* has a related meaning, but the meaning is not easily discerned from the parts.

As these examples show, it is important for students to use a combination of strategies, including structural analysis, to make sense of texts as they read. Structural analysis is a useful strategy because it enables readers to use their knowledge of common prefixes, roots, and suffixes to infer the meanings of complex words. However, students often have difficulty recognizing the parts of complex words and then combining the meanings of prefixes, roots, and suffixes to determine the meaning of the whole word. In addition, it takes time to teach the meanings of prefixes, roots, and suffixes, and time spent on teaching word parts is time taken away from students' being engaged in meaningful reading.

Academic Vocabulary

Despite the difficulties in using structural analysis during reading, both emergent bilinguals and native English speakers can benefit from some knowledge of word parts to help them read academic texts. Structural analysis is one strategy students can use to comprehend the complex vocabulary in these texts. As Rasinski and his colleagues suggest, students can benefit from some carefully planned activities to help them build knowledge of Latin and Greek prefixes and roots as they study different academic subjects.

The vocabulary in academic texts contains many polysyllabic words, which are comprised of prefixes, roots or bases, and suffixes. The academic language register of English, which includes words used in academic texts and discussions, contains many words from Greek and Latin. Linguists studying academic language have examined different *corpora*, very large collections of data with words from different sources such as recordings of conversations and academic textbooks.

One such corpus study was conducted by Corson (1997), who analyzed English vocabulary. He examined two different collections of words for his study. When Corson examined the Birmingham corpus, which lists words that emergent bilinguals, children and adults, need for daily communication, he found that only two of the 150 most frequent words, *very* and *because*, have Latin or Greek roots. The rest are drawn from Anglo-Saxon vocabulary. This study shows that the vocabulary of everyday English comes primarily from Anglo-Saxon words. These are short words like *bread* and *house*. This is the vocabulary that makes up most of the conversational language that emergent bilinguals acquire.

In contrast, academic texts contain a high number of words with Greek and Latin roots, such as *transportation* and *sympathetic*. Corson also examined the 150 most frequent words in the University Word List. This list includes words students need to read academic texts. Corson found only two words with Germanic roots and four others that entered English from French. The rest had Greek and Latin origins.

English vocabulary, then, can be divided into two types, words with Anglo-Saxon origins used in everyday conversation and words from Latin and Greek sources that occur frequently in academic texts. (The University Word List has been refined and updated by Averil Coxhead. The result is the Academic Word List: www .uefap.com/vocab/select/awl.htm.)

The historical development of academic vocabulary

A brief review of the history of the English language shows how morphologically complex words entered into English at different times (Tompkins and Yaden 1986). The Romans occupied Britain from 43 to 410 AD, and during this time a few Latin words, such as *camp* and *port*, were added to Celtic. During the Old English period, from about 450 to 1100, the Angles and Saxons invaded Britain and drove the Celts into the northern and western areas. The mixture of Germanic tribes spoke *Englisc*. Few words from Old English remain. Some of these are basic words such as *child*, *hand*, *foot*, *mother*, and *sun*. These words form part of the conversational English register. The Englisc speakers borrowed some words from the Celts such as *Britain*, *cradle*, *London*, and *babe*, including words the Celts had borrowed from Latin.

Additional Latin words came into English through contact between Roman soldiers and traders and the Germanic tribes in England and also on the continent. Missionaries who reintroduced Christianity to Britain in 597 brought in religious Latin words like *angel*, *disciple*, *hymn*, and *priest*. In 787, the Vikings invaded from the north and ruled England for three centuries. The Vikings contributed pronouns including *they*, *their*, and *them* and many everyday words like *husband*, *low*, *ugly*, and *window*.

In 1066 the Norman-French invaded England and ruled for three centuries, contributing many words to English, such as *army*, *navy*, *peace*, and *stomach*. Most of the Norman-French loanwords were derived from Latin. These morphologically complex words make up much of the current academic vocabulary in English. About 10,000 Norman-French words were added, and many Old English words were lost. Sometimes, both the Old English and Norman-French words stayed but took on differentiated meanings. One example is that the names for animals are based on Old English, but the word for the meat from the animals is Norman-French. This reflects the fact that English peasants cared for the animals, and the Norman-French rulers ate the meat in their castles. Figure 8.7 lists some of these pairs of words.

Old English	Norman-French
steer	beef
sheep	mutton
calf	veal
pig	pork
deer	venison

Figure 8.7 *Old English and Norman-French words*

By about 1400, English was restored as the main language. During the Renaissance, from about 1500 to 1688, many Greek and Latin scholarly terms were added to the English vocabulary, words like *congratulate*, *democracy*, and *education*, along with many scientific terms such as *atmosphere*, *pneumonia*, and *virus*. During this period, additional morphologically complex words were added to the vocabulary of English.

Brook (1998) points out that because of this infusion, especially of Latin terms, "One basic meaning could be expressed by three different English words that come from three sources—Anglo-Saxon, French, and Latin" (26). Brook provides some examples listed here in Figure 8.8.

Anglo-Saxon	French	Latin
fear	terror	trepidation
win	succeed	triumph
kingly	royal	regal
holy	sacred	consecrated

Figure 8.8 *Words from different languages*

English has many sets of words like these. Latin- and Greek-based words, including words from French, seldom occur in everyday conversation, but they are typical of academic discourse. One way to infer the meaning of the Latin- and Greek-based words is by using morphological information.

Strategies for Teaching Academic Vocabulary

All students, including emergent bilinguals, need to develop academic vocabulary to succeed in school. The best way to increase vocabulary is through extensive reading (Krashen 2004, 2013). Since morphologically complex words occur much more often in academic texts than in casual conversations, students can only acquire academic language through engagement with academic texts and academic discussions. In addition, teachers can use new Internet tools, such as WordSift, to help students build vocabulary, and they can expand students' vocabulary through the study of cognates.

Using WordSift to build academic vocabulary

An Internet tool that can be used to build academic vocabulary for emergent bilinguals is WordSift, a program developed by Hakuta and his colleagues at Stanford University. As the designers explain:

> WordSift was created to help teachers manage the demands of vocabulary and academic language in their text materials. We especially hope that this tool is helpful in supporting English Language Learners. We want WordSift to be a useful tool, but we also want it to be fun and visually pleasing. We would be happy if you think of it playfully—as a toy in a linguistic playground that is available to instantly capture and display the vocabulary structure of texts, and to help create an opportunity to talk and explore the richness and wonders of language! (retrieved from www.wordsift.com, 10/16/2013)

A visual tour of the website demonstrates many of the useful features of this "toy in a linguistic playground." A teacher can copy and paste a section of text into a box. Then the fifty most frequent words are displayed as a tag cloud. The words in the tag cloud can be sifted in different ways. They can be displayed so that the words that occur most frequently are the biggest words. Teachers can also click on a word and then click on a link to do a visual search for images that represent the word. Visuals are particularly helpful for emergent bilinguals.

There are several other options. Any of the words can also be linked to a visual thesaurus. A user can choose a word from the tag cloud, and the display will show sentences where the word appears with the word highlighted. The words can also be sorted against lists from different content areas. For example, if a teacher chooses the science list, all the science words will be highlighted in one color. The words can also be sorted from the most common to the rarest, and the size of the word will show how common or rare it is.

There are a number of suggestions for creating lesson plans using WordSift. Teachers can click on words from the tag cloud and drag them along with pictures from the visual search to make semantic webs for key words. There are other suggestions as well for using WordSift to create visual displays of the words in a passage. This would be an excellent tool for students to play with. Students could take different key passages from their textbooks to enter into WordSift and work in small groups to create innovative ways to display the words, complete with pictures from the visual search and information from the visual thesaurus. This activity could stimulate students' interest in words and help them focus on the important academic vocabulary from the texts they are reading.

Teaching cognates to increase academic vocabulary

Another way that teachers can help students use their knowledge of morphology to develop academic vocabulary is through the study of cognates. Cognates are words that come from the same root, that were literally "born together." If emergent bilinguals speak a Latinate language, they may understand many academic English words when they connect those words to related words they know in their first language. A Spanish speaker could understand the English word *hypothesis* by associating it with the Spanish cognate *hipótesis*. Knowledge of the Spanish word transfers to reading in English.

Support for the idea that what a person knows in one language can transfer to a second language comes from Cummins' (2000) theory of a common underlying proficiency. Cummins cites research that shows an interdependence among the concepts, skills, and linguistic knowledge in two languages. If a student understands the concept of the water cycle in one language, that concept transfers into a second language. If a student knows how to summarize a chapter, that skill also transfers. Linguistic knowledge transfers as well. Emergent bilinguals who have developed knowledge of prefixes, roots, and suffixes in their first language can transfer that knowledge to an additional language.

Since many words that make up academic English have Latin roots, students who speak a Latinate language such as Spanish or French already know related words. By accessing these cognates, English learners can rapidly increase their academic English vocabulary. Figure 8.9, taken from the *NTC's Dictionary of Spanish Cognates Thematically Organized* (Nash 1990), lists some cognates from social studies and science.

Many everyday Spanish words are part of the academic language register in English. However, as they read or interact in classrooms, Spanish-speaking students

Social Studies		Science	
English	*Spanish*	*English*	*Spanish*
civilization	civilización	geography	geografía
history	historia	biology	biología
past	pasado	analysis	análisis
pioneer	pionero	diagram	diagrama
colonial	colonial	experiment	experimento
diary	diario	formula	fórmula

Figure 8.9 *Spanish–English cognates*

often fail to draw on this knowledge base. Teachers can help students access cognates by engaging them in activities that increase their awareness of similar words across languages. Williams (2001) explains several strategies teachers can use. For example, a teacher might begin by projecting book pages on a screen and having students find cognates. Then students could work in pairs to identify cognates. The teacher could also create a cognate wall. Pairs of students could add the cognates they find to the wall. This activity could extend throughout a unit of study, and students could list as many cognates as possible related to the topic. The class could also develop a cognate dictionary, using the words from the cognate wall.

Rodríguez (2001) suggests that once students identify cognates, they can work together to categorize them. This is an excellent activity to raise word consciousness and increase the important academic skill of categorization. Rodríguez's students found several ways to classify cognates. For example, some cognates like *colonial* have the same spelling. Others like *civilization* and *civilizacíon* have a predictable variation in spelling. As we discussed in Chapter 6, the derivational suffix *-tion* in English is spelled *-cíon* in Spanish. The suffix *-ly* in English is *-mente* in Spanish. As students become aware of these consistent differences, they can use morphological knowledge from their first language as they read in English.

Other cognates like *sport* and *deporte* have the same root. Knowledge of the meanings of common Latin and Greek roots transfer across related languages. In addition, some cognates share only one of the meanings of the word. An example is that *letter* in English can refer to a letter of the alphabet or a business letter, but in Spanish, the cognate *letra* only means a letter of the alphabet. As students collect cognates, they can categorize them. This exercise helps make them more aware of the different cognates that exist. Students can then apply their knowledge of cognates to academic English reading.

Students do need instruction in recognizing cognates. Teachers can use WordSift, described earlier, to help students find cognates in a text. WordSift can be customized, and teachers can input a list of cognates as one of the word lists. Using this feature, a student or a teacher can then have WordSift find the cognates in a passage and put those words in a tag cloud. In addition, many lists of Spanish–English cognates can be found on the Internet. One of the best sites is Colorín Colorado! (www.colorincolorado.org/educators/background/cognates/), which includes both an extensive list of cognates and helpful tips for teaching cognates. In addition, teachers can use Google Translate to create bilingual word walls, even in languages the teacher does not speak.

Conclusion

In this chapter, we addressed these questions:

- What is the role of morphology in methods of second language teaching?
- How can teachers use morphological information as they teach reading?
- How can teachers help students acquire academic vocabulary?

A knowledge of morphology aids in both teaching and learning a second language and in teaching and learning reading. Evidence from studies in the acquisition of morphemes form the basis for Krashen's Natural Order Hypothesis.

Methods of teaching a second language vary in the attention they give to morphology. Methods based on a learning view give more attention to morphology than methods that take an acquisition view. Morphology is taught directly in the Grammar Translation method and is taught in the context of communication in other empiricist methods. Rationalist methods, such as the Natural Approach, assumed that morphology would be acquired without direct teaching. Methods such as CALLA and SIOP call for language objectives and these may include teaching prefixes, roots, and suffixes to help students develop academic language.

Morphology also plays a role in reading. Students learning to read should develop strategies for constructing meaning from texts. One strategy is the use of structural analysis. However, inferring word meanings through structural analysis can be difficult because it is sometimes hard to recognize word parts, learn the meanings of the parts, and combine the parts to determine the meaning of a word.

Nevertheless, structural analysis is useful for reading academic texts that contain morphologically complex vocabulary. Students can build academic vocabulary through the study of prefixes, roots, and suffixes. Internet tools, such as WordSift, can also be helpful in deciding what vocabulary to teach and in teaching and learning new vocabulary. If emergent bilinguals speak a language related to English, they can also engage in study of cognates to expand their academic vocabulary.

APPLICATIONS

1. Many prefixes assimilate to the root of the word. Study a prefix like *in-* to find how it changes as it is attached to different roots. A comprehensive dictionary can provide information about prefixes.

2. Go to the WordSift website, copy and paste in a passage from an academic text, and then try out the different tools that are available. Be prepared to report your results.

3. We list several activities for investigating cognates. Try out some of these activities with emergent bilinguals. Be prepared to share what you and your students did and how the students responded to the activities.

4. Looking at the second language population in your area, which of their languages would have cognates in English and which do not? For the languages that do have cognates use the Internet to find resources with lists of the cognates.

9 /naɪn/

English Syntax

*S*yntax is the study of how words are combined to create phrases and clauses in the sentences of a language. All languages have content words for naming people, places, and things. And, all languages have content words to indicate actions and states of being. Further, all languages have content words that describe both things and actions. Finally, all languages have grammatical function words to show relationships among the content words and to indicate shades of meaning of the content words.

> • How have people viewed grammar?
> • What are some basic aspects of English syntax?

Although all languages have these same building blocks, they arrange them differently. For example, some languages begin clauses by naming a subject, a person, place, or thing, which is the topic of the sentence. Other languages begin clauses with words that name the action in the sentence. In some languages, adjectives precede nouns and in others adjectives follow nouns. A study of the syntax of a language entails specifying the order of the words. That is, syntax looks at the organization of the parts of a language.

This chapter describes the syntax of English. For many linguists syntax is synonymous with grammar. However, people have different views of grammar. In the following sections we consider four different views of grammar.

Four Views of Grammar

Most linguists, especially those whose work is based on Chomsky's theories, consider *grammar* to be the study of syntactic structures. However, the word *grammar* has other meanings. Some people would say that grammar is the built-in, subconscious knowledge of a language that enables people to communicate in that language. Still other people who studied rhetoric in college might say that *grammar* refers to the effective use of syntactic structures in writing or speaking. In the minds of most people, though, the word *grammar* brings back memories of worksheets and tests based on rules or on knowing the parts of speech. Most people admit they never really understood grammar very well or that they have forgotten it. Weaver (1996) lists these four definitions of grammar:

- the functional command of sentence structure that enables us to comprehend and produce language
- a description of syntactic structure
- rhetorically effective use of syntactic structures
- prescriptions for correct use. (2)

The first three definitions define grammar in terms of syntax. All three definitions are based on current studies in linguistics. The fourth definition, grammar as prescriptions for correct use, reflects a traditional approach to teaching language designed to enable students to speak and write using conventional forms.

Grammar as the *functional command of sentence structure*

One view is that a grammar is a set of internalized rules that people acquire. These are the rules that allow humans to communicate in a language. Chomsky and other linguists argue that humans have an innate capacity for language. They are born with Universal Grammar, a set of mental structures that enable them to use language input to form subconscious rules to understand and produce one or more languages. The internal grammar includes a syntactic component along with a knowledge of phonology, morphology, semantics, and pragmatics. Over time, humans develop a full command of the grammar of their community of speakers and this allows them to function effectively.

Grammar as *a description of syntactic structure*

A second view is that a grammar is a description of these rules that humans acquire. Although linguists study all the different aspects of language, the major area of study in recent years in the U.S. has been syntax. Syntax is one component of the grammar of a language. Other areas include phonology, morphology, semantics, and pragmatics. Together, these components enable humans to communicate in language. A grammar, then, from this perspective is a description of these rules.

In their study of syntax, linguists have attempted to make explicit the implicit rules that humans have acquired that allow them to comprehend and produce language. Chomsky argued that there must be a small set of rules that can generate an infinite number of sentences. If there were a large set of rules, people could not acquire them. In earlier studies linguists had attempted to describe the syntactic structures in samples of speech that people produced. Chomsky argued that these descriptions of speech were too complex to have been produced by rules that humans could learn.

To solve this problem, Chomsky distinguished between two levels of language. The level represented by people's language output he called the *surface structure* of language. However, below this surface structure, according to Chomsky, is a deeper level of language, which he called the *deep structure*. Chomsky's claim was that a few simple rules can generate all the deep structure sentences, and that people produce variations on these deep structures using a second set of rules to transform the deep structures into different surface structures.

For example, a statement is considered to represent the deep structure. Statements can be changed to questions in different ways. Questions represent surface-structure transformations of a deep-structure statement. Thus, the statement "Today is Tuesday" could be changed into the question "Is today Tuesday?" or the question "Today is Tuesday, isn't it?" These questions are created by transforming the deep-structure statement. Chomsky's theories of syntax have evolved over time, but the goal has remained: to provide a description of syntactic structure.

Grammar as rhetorically effective use of syntactic structures

A third view of grammar is that it is the rhetorically effective use of syntactic structures. Studies in rhetoric examine the ways that speakers and writers can use language effectively for different purposes, such as describing, explaining, or persuading. Current studies in rhetoric build on the work of Aristotle and Plato. These Greek philosophers studied the ways language could be used for persuasion and reasoning.

Teachers who teach grammar in the context of students' writing and speech build on the tradition of the early studies in rhetoric. Weaver (1996) provides a number of useful minilessons teachers can use to teach language in context. When instruction applies directly to student writing, it helps them produce more effective pieces. Students need many opportunities for meaningful writing, and when they have produced a good piece of writing they are motivated to edit it to ensure that the grammar and spelling are conventional. Students can also be shown how to enhance the rhetorical effects of their writing through careful organization and choice of examples.

Grammar as prescriptions for correct use

For most people, the word *grammar* means studying rules for correct speaking and writing. In Chapter 7 we explained that at one time schools were conducted in

Latin. Teachers in these grammar schools taught Latin grammar. When the language of instruction shifted to English, these same teachers applied their knowledge of Latin grammar to English and began to teach English grammar. Since students could already understand and speak English, the focus was on written language. Teachers believed that their job was to prescribe the rules of the language, and if students learned grammar, they could apply this knowledge to both writing and speaking.

Despite this tradition, research has consistently shown that students have trouble learning traditional grammar or applying grammar rules when they write or speak. In the first place, students find it difficult to learn and retain concepts from traditional grammar. In one series of studies, Macauley (1947) tested the grammar knowledge of students in schools in Scotland. At the time of these studies, grammar was taught in both elementary and secondary schools for an average of thirty minutes a day. At the elementary level, the lessons emphasized knowing parts of speech and their functions. For example, students were taught to identify nouns in a sentence, and they learned that nouns served as subjects and objects in sentences.

Macauley tested students at the end of elementary school. The test required students to read fifty sentences and decide whether the underlined word in each sentence was a noun, verb, pronoun, adjective, or adverb. Even though all students had had several years of daily study of parts of speech, the average score for the 131 students was a mere 27.9 percent right. Macauley had set 50 as a passing score. Students could get about 11 percent right just by guessing, but only one student scored 50 percent or better on all five parts of speech. When Macauley tested secondary students, they did somewhat better, but the mean for the top classes at the end of their third year of secondary school had only risen to 62 percent. Macauley's studies, with students who received intensive training in traditional grammar, showed that students have a great deal of difficulty even learning basic parts of speech.

Krashen (1998) has also reviewed research on the teaching of grammar. His conclusion is blunt: "Research on the relationship between formal grammar instruction and performance on measures of writing ability is very consistent: There is no relationship between grammar study and writing" (8). For example, in a three-year study comparing the effects of traditional grammar, transformational grammar, and no grammar on high school students in New Zealand, Elley and Barton (1976) concluded that whether grammar study is traditional or transformational, it has almost no influence on the language growth of secondary students. This study found that students could not apply knowledge of grammar to their speech or writing.

One of the strongest statements on the teaching of grammar comes from a report issued by the National Council of Teachers of English, an organization with many members vitally interested in grammar and in the teaching of writing. The authors of the report state:

> In view of the widespread agreement of research studies based upon many types of students and teachers, the conclusion can be stated in strong and unqualified terms: the teaching of formal grammar has a negligible or, because it usually displaces some instruction and practice in actual composition, even a harmful effect on the improvement of writing. (Braddock and Lloyd-Jones 1963, 37–38)

None of these are new studies. There are no current studies that dispute the early findings. Despite the research consensus, teachers continue to teach traditional grammar. Weaver (1996) lists several reasons:

- Teachers may not be aware of the research.
- They may not believe the research.
- They believe grammar is interesting and teach it simply for that reason.
- They notice that some students who are good readers and writers are also good at grammar, so they assume that this correlation shows cause and effect.
- They are required to teach grammar.
- They feel pressure to teach grammar from parents or other community members.
- They feel that although grammar may not help the average student, it still may help some students.

Teachers do need to know about grammar. This should be part of their pedagogical language knowledge. However, teachers should not expect that teaching traditional grammar will improve their students' speech or writing.

Introduction to a Theory of Syntax

The first three definitions of grammar connect grammar with syntax. Syntax refers to the order of words in sentences. To develop a theory of syntax, linguists follow the same four steps that we described for the study phonology and morphology. These include:

1. Break the speech stream into discrete units.
2. Categorize the units.
3. Group the units.
4. Find dependencies among the units.

In the case of syntax, the basic units are words. Syntax is the study of the order of the words in a clause. Each sentence in English is composed of one or more clauses. A clause is a group of words with a subject and a predicate. For the study of syntax, clauses, rather than sentences, are used, since the clause is a complete unit that contains the syntactic structures of English. A simple sentence has just one clause, and compound and complex sentences are simply combinations of clauses.

In developing a theory of syntax, one could begin by simply saying that a clause is an unstructured string of words, like "The teacher has developed creative linguistics lessons," but it is quickly apparent that for the words to make sense, they must be put in some sequence. If we said, "Developed has teacher lessons linguistics the creative" the sequence would make no sense and would be considered ungrammatical because it doesn't follow the rules of English syntax. An important assumption in developing a theory of syntax is that the linear order of the words needs to be considered.

The second step is to recognize that the words in a sentence are not all the same. Words serve different functions. A word like *creative* is different from one like *lessons*. This observation leads to the need to categorize the words. In Chapter 7 we distinguished between content words (noun, verbs, adjectives, and adverbs) and function words, such as determiners and pronouns. Morphological evidence can be used to help identify content words. For example, only nouns add a plural *-s*, as in *lessons*. The words in the sentence above could be categorized as shown in Figure 9.1.

A third step in developing a theory of syntax would be to group the words. Some of the words seem to go together. This sentence could be divided into the following groups: "The teacher—has developed—creative linguistics lessons." Groups of words, or phrases, include noun phrases, verb phrases, adjective phrases, adverb phrases, and prepositional phrases. For example, in this sentence, both *The teacher* and *creative linguistics lessons* are noun phrases. Linguists identify phrases by their function. Noun phrases name people, places, and things. Verb phrases name actions or states of being. Adjective, adverb, and prepositional phrases all function to describe either noun phrases or verb phrases.

In addition to having a semantic function, such as naming a person, place, or thing, phrases serve as constituents in a sentence. A *constituent* is a group of words that serves a specific function, such as subject or object. In this sentence, *the teacher*

nouns	auxiliary	determiner	verb	adjectives
teacher lessons	has	the	developed	creative linguistics

Figure 9.1 *Categories of words*

functions as the subject, *has developed* is the predicate, and *creative linguistics lessons* is the object of the verb. Building a theory of syntax involves determining the possible functions constituents play in a sentence.

The final step is to find connections among the constituents of a clause. Some constituents depend on others. For example, the auxiliary verb form *has* is used because the subject *teacher* is singular. If the subject were plural, *teachers*, then the auxiliary would be *have* to agree with the subject. There is a dependency between the subject and the verb.

Developing a theory of syntax involves all four steps: determining the basic units, categorizing the units, grouping the units, and finding dependencies among the units. In the case of syntax, it is also important to consider the linear order of the words and the roles that constituents play in the clause. Linguists such as Chomsky follow this sequence of steps in developing a theory.

Generative Grammar

Chomsky' theory of syntax is referred to as *generative grammar* because it is an attempt to develop a small set of rules that could be used to produce, or generate, any sentence in a language. Rather than trying to find a new way to describe the sentence patterns of oral language, Chomsky began to consider a more complex model that contains both a surface structure (what we say or write) and a deep structure (roughly, what we mean, our basic ideas). He argued that there are only a limited number of these deep-structure patterns. Speakers learn how to move around, or transform, these basic structures to produce a great number of different surface structures. The task of learning a few basic structures and some rules governing how to move the elements of the base structures around to produce different surface structures is much easier than learning all the possible surface structures.

Chomsky's idea that language is best described by a model with both a surface level and a deep level came from his observation that many sentences are ambiguous. Some sentences are ambiguous because an individual word has multiple meanings. For example, if I say, "There's a fork in the road," I might mean that the road divides or that I see an eating utensil on the road. This sentence is ambiguous because *fork* has two possible meanings.

Other sentences are ambiguous not because of the multiple meanings of individual words, but because the sentence has two possible underlying structures corresponding to the two meanings. For example, "Visiting linguists can be boring" is a surface structure that could have come from one of two underlying or deep structures corresponding roughly to the meanings: "Linguists who visit can be boring" and "Visiting a linguist can be boring."

Even though the original sentence is ambiguous, listeners could discern the intended meaning by using context cues. Many other ambiguous sentences can be found. When someone says, "The chicken is too hot to eat," a listener has to decide whether the chicken is going to eat once she cools off, or if a person is going to eat the chicken once it cools. In these sentences, the words are not ambiguous, but the sentences could be interpreted in two ways. Chomsky developed his theory of syntax with both a surface and a deep structure based on the presence of structurally ambiguous sentences such as these. Ambiguous sentences can be represented as shown in Figure 9.2.

Not only do some surface-structure (SS) sentences relate to (or map on to) two deep structures (DS), but two surface-structure sentences could be derived from one deep structure. For example, if a DS sentence was "Her favorite teacher gave her an A," someone could say, "She was given an A by her favorite teacher." The meaning of the DS and SS are the same. Speakers can choose different surface structures to emphasize different things and for stylistic variation. For example the statement could be turned into the question "Did her favorite teacher give her an A?" Figure 9.3 represents cases where two surface structures are derived from one deep structure.

The process of changing a deep structure into a surface structure is referred to as a *transformation*. Sentences can undergo different kinds of transformations. In the example given above, one transformation forms a passive sentence and the other forms a question. Linguists have to decide which forms represent the deep structure or meaning of a sentence and which forms are derived as the result of transforming the sentence. Transformations can involve moving parts of the sentence or adding or deleting parts.

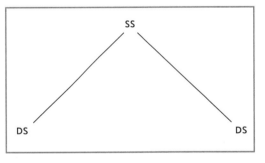

Figure 9.2 *Deep structures and surface structure of ambiguous sentences*

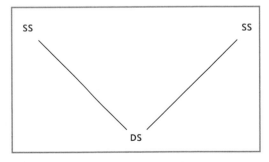

Figure 9.3 *Deep structure and surface structures of transformed sentences*

Generally, linguists assume that active sentences such as "My favorite teacher gave me an A" are basic, and passive sentences such as "I was given an A by my favorite teacher" are the result of a transformation of the basic sentence. Active sentences are more common in the language, and passive sentences seem to be a variation. Children acquire active sentences earlier than passives. Forms that are acquired earlier are considered more basic. Variations on basic sentence forms allow speakers and writers to create rhetorical effects. For example, by using the passive in the sentence above, the speaker emphasizes him- or herself instead of "my favorite teacher."

Chomsky's two-level theory seems to work well. Rather than trying to describe all the different possible surface structures for a deep structure, this theory attempts to discover a few basic deep structures and then specify how these can be changed to produce different surface structures. To take one more example, if all sentences at deep structure level are statements, one change to surface structure would result in a question. There is a consistent relationship between statements such as "Juan can pass the linguistics test" and questions such as "Can Juan pass the linguistics test?" Chomsky and other linguists first attempted to specify the exact process of each type of transformation. At a later time, Chomsky shifted his research to determine the limits on possible variations. Rather than specifying the exact changes involved, he attempted to determine the changes that are not possible. This approach may reflect more accurately what children do when they acquire a language. They develop a general set of rules for generating deep structures and another for limiting possible ways the elements of the deep structure can be moved around to form different surface-structure sentences.

This line of research was elaborated as Chomsky's government binding theory. Both transformational grammar and government binding theory are theories of syntax. Linguists continue to attempt to understand the underlying rules humans use to produce and comprehend language. For example, following the development of Government Binding theory, Chomsky shifted to a new theory referred to as the Minimalist Program.

Since later theories of syntax were built on Chomsky's early theory, it is useful to begin the study of syntax by looking at some basic concepts from transformational grammar. A good way to do this is to examine a transformational rule carefully to better understand the process linguists use to describe syntactic structures. Akmajian and colleagues (1979) write, "One of the most important ways of discovering why and how sentences must be structured is to try to state explicitly some grammatical rules for a given language" (140).

They offer the example of the rule for forming yes/no questions in English. For linguists, a rule is simply a description of some aspect of a language. The question rule describes the relationship between statements and questions that can be answered with *yes* or *no*. The assumption is that statements and questions have the same deep structure. Questions are formed by changing a statement in some way to produce a different surface structure. Investigating this rule involves examining the structure of English sentences.

The question rule

There are different ways that a linguist might try to discover the rule for forming questions from statements. A first attempt might rely on the linear order of the words. For example, one could number the words in the following sentence:

> The teacher has developed creative linguistics lessons.
>   1   2   3   4   5   6   7

Then, it would be possible to state a rule for changing the statement into a question. This first attempt at the rule might look like this:

> 1   To change a statement into a question, move word 3 to the front of the sentence.

This rule works fine for this sentence. If word 3 is moved to the front, the result is "Has the teacher developed creative linguistics lessons?" However, for the rule to be adequate, it must apply to other statements. The scientific process involves forming a hypothesis and then looking for counterexamples. Are there statements that could not be turned into questions by following this rule? It is quickly apparent that a rule that relies only on the order of the words is not adequate. For example, if the rule is applied to the following sentence,

> Some great teachers have developed creative linguistics lessons.
>   1   2   3   4   5   6   7   8

and then the third word was moved to the front, the question would be, "Teachers some great have developed creative linguistics lessons?" It is easy to find many other examples of sentences for which Rule 1 would not work. This suggests that the hypothesis would need to be refined to take into account more than the linear order of words in a sentence.

It appears that the word that gets moved to the front of the sentence is an auxiliary verb like *has* or *have*, not a noun like *teachers*. To state the rule, then, one must rely on the morphological categories of words as well as the order of words. The second try for this rule could then be stated as:

> 2   To change a statement into a question, move the first auxiliary verb to the front of the sentence.

Applying this rule would produce the desired result and change "Some great teachers have developed creative linguistics lessons" into "Have some great teachers developed creative linguistics lessons?"

Rule 2 works for many English sentences. Nevertheless, it is still possible to find counterexamples, statements that can't be turned into questions by following this rule. Take, for example, the following sentence: "Teachers who have read this book can develop creative linguistics lessons." Moving the first auxiliary verb to the front produces, "Have teachers who read this book can develop creative linguistics lessons?" Obviously, this is the wrong result. The question that corresponds to "Teachers who have read this book can develop creative linguistics lessons" is "Can teachers who have read this book develop creative linguistics lessons?"

The rule needs to be stated in a way that the right auxiliary verb gets moved. In a simple sentence, the right auxiliary is the first one, but in a complex sentence, the right auxiliary verb might be the second or third one. English allows very long sentences like this one: "Teachers who have read this book and have attended courses that have enabled them to learn a great deal about linguistics can develop creative linguistics lessons." Here, *can* is the fourth auxiliary verb. There doesn't seem to be any limit, except for a listener's memory span, on how long sentences can be, and the auxiliary verb that moves to the front can be any of the auxiliary verbs in the sentence. Trying to specify that it is the first, second, or third verb doesn't result in the desired rule.

A better statement of the rule involves reference to the subject of the sentence (*Teachers*) and the predicate of the main clause (*have developed*), which corresponds to this subject. Rather than only referring to morphological categories, it is necessary to refer to sentence constituents like subject and predicate to state the rule. The revised rule would then read:

> 3   To change a statement into a question, move the first auxiliary verb in the predicate of the main clause to the left of the subject.

Even Rule 3 can't account for all the possible sentences in English. It is easy to find a counterexample, such as "Often, teachers have developed creative linguistics lessons." Applying Rule 3 would produce the question, "Often have teachers developed creative linguistics lessons?" Although this sentence seems to be a counterexample, rather than refining the rule at this point, a linguist might point out that the surface structure of a sentence starting with *often* does not match the deep structure. At the deep-structure level, *often* would be next to the main verb, and the sentence would read "Teachers have often developed creative linguistics lessons." Applying Rule 3 to this sentence would produce the desired question, "Have teachers often developed creative linguistics lessons?" Rule 3 seems to work consistently when it is applied to the deep structure form of a statement.

In cases involving adverbs like *often* the difference between the deep structure and the surface structure involves the position of the adverb in the sentence. Adverbs like *often* can move to a variety of positions. However, moving an adverb like *often* to the left of the main verb in the deep structure of this sentence results in a sentence that can be changed into a question by the application of Rule 3. This fact could be used to argue that adverbs in deep structure always occur before verbs. As this example shows, linguistic rules apply to deep structures, and one task for a linguist is to determine the deep structure of a sentence.

Rule 3 refers to auxiliary verbs. However, some sentences lack auxiliary verbs at the surface-structure level. For example, there is no auxiliary in the sentence "Joan developed a creative linguistics lesson." At one point in the history of English, questions were formed by moving the main verb in sentences like this, as anyone who has read Shakespeare can attest. However, "Developed Joan a creative linguistics lesson?" doesn't sound like a modern English question. In modern English, some form of the auxiliary *do* is used to form a question in sentences with no auxiliaries in the surface structure. In this case, the form used is *Did* because the sentence is in past tense. If the statement were "The teacher develops creative linguistics lessons," the question would be "Does the teacher develop creative linguistics lessons?"

Since there is an auxiliary in the related question "Did Joan develop a creative linguistics lesson?" linguists hypothesize that at deep structure all sentences contain an auxiliary. In some cases, the auxiliary is deleted at surface structure. However, a theory of syntax would include a deep-structure auxiliary since it shows up in questions. Native speakers of English automatically supply some form of *do* to form yes/no questions in sentences that lack an auxiliary verb. They also supply a form of *do* to form negatives, such as "Joan didn't develop a creative linguistics lesson."

Even Rule 3 is subject to change. If there is a sentence that can't be transformed into a yes/no question by this rule, then the rule would need revision. Linguists try to state rules that govern language processes as clearly as possible so that they can be tested against new sentences. The scientific process that linguists follow is to identify a question (How are statements transformed into yes/no questions?), gather data in the form of sentences that native speakers judge to be grammatical, and state a rule to account for the data. This rule becomes a hypothesis. Then the hypothesis is tested against additional sentences in a language. Each time a counterexample is found, the hypothesis is refined. The goal is to develop a small set of rules that account for all the possible sentences in a language. The rules for a transformational theory of syntax would describe how sentences are structured at a deep level and the changes that take place to produce surface-level variations, such as questions.

Rule 3 could be amended as follows:

4   To change a statement into a question, move the first auxiliary in the predicate of the main clause immediately to the left of the subject. If there is no auxiliary in the sentence, supply the appropriate form of *do*.

Syntactic Structure

A theory of syntax is based on the linear order of words, the morphological categories of words, and the constituents of sentences. Using these constructs, linguists attempt to describe the structure of English sentences at a deep level. Linguists hypothesize that sentences are structured because this allows them to explain why a series of unambiguous words like "The chicken is too hot to eat" can have an ambiguous meaning. The surface structure of this sentence can be associated with two different deep structures. In addition, if sentences are structured, then linguists can explain a rule like the question rule. Only by appealing to syntactic structure can such rules be stated.

Linguists have developed a set of rules to describe the structure of English sentences. The rules presented in this section provide an introduction to the kinds of rules linguists have written. Linguists have continued to refine their descriptions of the grammar of languages in their attempt to make explicit the implicit rules that allow people to comprehend and produce sentences. The rules presented here should be considered the beginning of a description of English syntax.

Grammatical Acceptability

In describing the syntactic structure of English, we have said that a phrase or sentence "doesn't sound like English." This phrasing may not sound very scientific. A linguist would say that the syntactic structure is ungrammatical. Linguists use intuitions of native speakers to determine grammatical acceptability. Even though people cannot explain most of the rules they have internalized, they can judge whether or not a sentence or phrase sounds right in the variety of the language spoken in their community. For example, most native speakers of English would say "a tall green tree" not "a green tall tree." They could make judgments about grammatical acceptability even though they couldn't explain why "tall green" sounds better than "green tall."

Often, people studying a new language are frustrated when native speakers tell them they have used the wrong word or phrased things incorrectly but then can't explain the rule for determining which wording to use. For example, Spanish has two words, *por* and *para,* that translate into English as *for.* However, native Spanish speakers know that it is fine to say, "Lo compré para ti" ("I bought it for you"), but it is not acceptable to say, "Lo compré por ti" if you want to say that you are buying a gift to give someone. "Lo compré por ti" means "I bought it on your behalf." Even though both *por* and *para* translate as *for,* they convey different meanings. The rule for their use is fairly complex. Native Spanish speakers will often say, "Give me a sentence, and I'll tell you if it's right," but they find it difficult to state an explicit rule.

In the same way, English has three words, *at, in,* and *on,* that can all be translated into Spanish as *en.* English speakers say "in the city," "at the airport," and "on the train." However, "at the city" or "in the train" sounds wrong and "at the airport" and "in the airport" mean two different things to most native English speakers. This is frustrating for Spanish speakers who translate all three prepositions as *en.* Why do English speakers say they got "in a car" but "on a bus"? If we say "I got on the car," it would mean that I was on top of the car. Most native English speakers can make these grammaticality judgments, but they would find it difficult to explain why one sentence is right and the other is not. Linguists rely on these grammatical intuitions to describe language structures.

Judgments of syntactic acceptability are not the same as traditional grammar rules. Telling someone not to end a sentence with a preposition or not to use two negatives in a sentence is different from saying something sounds like English. Teachers can tell students that periods go inside quotation marks. That is a rule to be learned. It is a convention of formal written language. Students can learn such rules and apply them in certain situations, such as when they edit their writing. However, in attempting to describe syntactic structure, linguists are attempting to describe how the language works based on grammatical acceptability judgments of native speakers. They are not attempting to prescribe correct usage.

Phrase Structure Rules

The rules used in the following description of syntactic structure are referred to as *phrase structure rules* because they attempt to specify how the phrases in a clause are structured and ordered. Phrase structure rules, like other scientific notations, are written following certain conventions. For example, the rule for the structure of a simple sentence is:

$$S \rightarrow NP-AUX-VP$$

This notation can be read as a sentence (S) consists of a noun phrase (NP), an auxiliary verb (AUX), and a verb phrase (VP). The arrow can also be translated as "can be expanded into." In other words, every simple sentence (S) can be expanded into, or rewritten as, a series that includes a noun phrase (NP), an auxiliary (AUX), and a verb phrase (VP). These elements appear in this linear order. For example, the sentence "Melinda has studied syntax" follows this pattern. The claim is that every clause or simple sentence in English at a deep-structure level follows this pattern.

Noun phrases

Syntactic structure can further be described by writing a phrase structure rule for each type of phrase. For example, an NP can contain several elements. Linguists would describe an NP as follows:

$$NP \rightarrow (DET)-(Q)-(ADJP)-N-(PP)$$

This is a shorthand notation for the components of a noun phrase. It can be read as "A noun phrase can be expanded into a determiner, a quantifier, an adjective phrase, a noun, and a prepositional phrase." The parts of the NP go in the linear order specified by the formula. The abbreviations for determiner (DET), quantifier (Q), adjective phrase (ADJP), and prepositional phrase (PP) are placed in parentheses to show that they are optional. Only a few NPs have all of these elements. Every NP has a noun so the N is not put in parentheses. Figure 9.4 illustrates some possible NPs that contain these different components.

As Figure 9.4 shows, an NP can have some or all of the elements.

DET	Q	ADJP	N	PP
the	two	rather hungry	boys	in the kitchen
that		creative	teacher	
	several	very lazy	linguists	at the conference
		green	trees	
			dogs	

Figure 9.4 *Noun phrases*

However, the elements must occur in the specified order. An NP like "two rather the hungry boys" or "hungry the rather two boys" would not sound like English. An NP could simply be a noun, like *dogs*. In addition, an NP could contain any of the optional elements. By writing the rule to show that the noun is obligatory and the other elements are optional, it is possible to write just one rule to cover all cases. By doing this, linguists can avoid writing a whole series of rules, such as:

$$NP \rightarrow N \text{ (dogs)}$$

$$NP \rightarrow DET-N \text{ (the dogs)}$$

$$NP \rightarrow DET-ADJP-N \text{ (the big dogs)}$$

$$NP \rightarrow DET-ADJP-N-PP \text{ (the big dogs in the yard)}$$

In general, in describing a language, linguists attempt to write the fewest rules necessary to account for all the possible cases. The rule represents the subconscious rule English speakers acquire that lets them produce sentences with NPs and other elements that follow the conventions of English syntax.

It is possible to replace an NP with a pronoun. For example, a person could say, "My neighbor is very talkative." This sentence has the NP *my neighbor* as the subject. Since NPs can be replaced with pronouns, it would also be possible to say, "She is very talkative." The phrase structure rule for nouns could be written to indicate pronouns. On the other hand, we could argue that at deep-structure level, all sentences have NPs as subjects, and pronouns are a surface-structure variation. Speakers only use a pronoun if both the speaker and listener (or writer and reader) know what or who the pronoun refers to, so the referent must exist at a deep level. However, for simplicity sake, if a sentence has a pronoun, when we discuss diagramming sentences later in the chapter we use the rule $NP \rightarrow PN$.

Adjective phrases

The rule for an NP contains two other phrases, ADJP and PP. Each of these also has an internal structure that can be defined. The rule for an ADJP could be written as follows:

$$ADJP \rightarrow (INT)-ADJ$$

An adjective phrase can include an intensifier like *very* or *somewhat*. The INT is an optional element. Thus, two possible ADJPs are *very hungry* and *hungry*. In addition, an ADJP can have more than one adjective. A speaker can refer to "an energetic, creative teacher" using two adjectives. In this case, the speaker could have also referred to the teacher as "a creative, energetic teacher." That is, the order of the adjectives could be reversed. This is because *creative* and *energetic* are the same kind of adjective. However, consider the adjectives in the NP "the tall green tree." In this case, reversing the order of the adjectives and saying, "the green tall tree" produces a phrase that does not sound like English. As children or emergent bilinguals acquire a language, they acquire the syntactic structure of sentences, phrases, and the elements within phrases. For adjectives, it appears that adjectives of size, like *tall*, occur before adjectives of color, like *green*. This example also shows that in the rule for adjective phrases, one or more adjectives can occur.

The order of adjectives is a good example of an aspect of syntax that is acquired rather than taught, although it may be included as a topic in some books on English grammar for students learning English. One website, http://web2.uvcs.uvic .ca/elc/studyzone/410/grammar/adjord.htm, identifies different types of adjectives and explains the order of the adjectives. The types in order include opinion (*difficult*), size (*big*), age (*old*), shape (*round*), color (*red*), origin (*Greek*), material (*iron*), and purpose (*sleeping*). The website offers exercises to practice the order. For native English speakers, the answers are easy and come naturally, but for emergent bilinguals, they might be quite difficult.

It would be unusual to have a sentence with all these kinds of adjectives. However, it would be possible to describe something as an "ugly big old long green French cloth sleeping bag." What is important is that when two or more adjectives of different types occur in an NP, they follow a fixed order. No one made up or prescribed this order. It has just become the conventional way of speaking, signing, and writing. Linguists studying syntax would attempt to describe the order, and to do that they would need to categorize adjectives into different types. The typology presented here is not the only one possible, but it does seem to account for most adjectives that occur commonly in English.

Prepositional phrases

An NP also may contain a prepositional phrase (PP). The rule describing a PP is:

$$PP \rightarrow P - NP$$

Both elements of the PP, the preposition P and the NP, are obligatory. Every PP has a preposition followed by a noun phrase. Figure 9.4 lists two PPs, "in the kitchen" and "at the conference."

The rule for NP includes PP as optional. At the same time, the rule for a PP includes an obligatory NP. As a result, English syntax places no length limits on NPs. The upper limit is only imposed by the memory or attention span of the listener; for example, the sentence "I saw the boy in the yard of my neighbor down the street near the corner with the big tree raking leaves" would stretch any listener's memory (and patience).

Including so many PPs would not be considered good writing, but English syntax allows such phrases. The rules for NP and PP are recursive since NPs can include PPs and PPs must include NPs. Recursive structural rules are those for which the output of one rule forms the input for the other. A recursive rule is like a circular reference in a formula. Computers can't handle such formulas because they are potentially infinite. English sentences can be infinitely long. Of course, a speaker would die before producing an infinite sentence.

A rule of traditional grammar is "Don't end a sentence with a preposition." The structural description of a PP as a preposition followed by a noun phrase seems to support this rule, and it is a rule of English. However, as we discussed earlier, many sentences that appear to end with prepositions actually end with verb particles. English has many two-word verbs like "look up" or "write down." If a sentence ends with one of these two-word verbs, the particle (*up*, *down*) may be mistaken for a preposition. In questions such as "What word did you look up?" or "Which definition did you write down?" the last word is a particle. Trying to move the particle to a different position would produce questions like "Up what word did you look?" and "Down which definition did you write?" Clearly, these questions do not sound like English. The words *up* and *down* are particles that attach to the verbs, not prepositions that can be moved.

Other sentences that may appear to end with prepositions actually end with adverbs. For example, if we say, "He walked in," the *in* serves as an adverb telling where. Similarly, if we say "She walked over," meaning "She walked over to our house," then *over* is an adverb. English sentences don't end in prepositions, but they do end in particles and adverbs. The confusion comes because the same lexical form (*over*, *in*, *up*) can function as a preposition, a verb particle, or an adverb.

Auxiliary verbs

English sentences begin with an NP. The second constituent is the auxiliary (AUX). As we discussed earlier, even though many clauses do not have an AUX at the surface level, every clause in English has an AUX at the deep-structure level, and this is shown when statements are transformed into questions or negatives.

English has a complex system of auxiliary verbs. This category includes modal auxiliaries like *should* and *can* along with forms of *have*, *be*, and *do*. Pinker (1994) estimates that, "There are about twenty-four billion logically possible combinations of auxiliaries . . . of which only a hundred are grammatical" (272). For example, it is possible to say, "The linguist might have been napping," but other combinations of these three auxiliaries are not grammatical. Sentences like "The linguist have might been napping" or "The linguist been have might napping" are ungrammatical. Part of what a child or an emergent bilingual acquires is this implicit knowledge of the order of auxiliary verbs. Linguists try to specify the order of the kinds of auxiliary verbs. For example, modals (*can*, *might*, etc.) precede auxiliaries showing tense like *have*, and forms of *be* that indicates passive come last.

Verb phrases

The third main constituent in every English sentence is the verb phrase. The rule describing the verb phrase is:

$$VP \rightarrow V - (NP) - (PP) - (ADVP)$$

This rule specifies that a VP must have a verb and can have one or more NPs, one or more PPs, and one or more adverb phrases. An adverb phrase, like an adjective phrase, can include an intensifier and must include an adverb. Thus, both *fast* and *very fast* can serve as ADVPs. Figure 9.5 shows some possible VPs. Note that we list two-word verbs as verbs here although they could be further divided into verb and particle.

In some sentences, like "Birds sing," the VP consists of just the verb. In other sentences, the verb is followed by one or more NPs. Thus, "The bird sang a song" has a VP with one NP, and "The student gave the linguist his homework" has two NPs, *the linguist* and *his homework*. Some verbs, called intransitive verbs, do not take a following NP. For example, no NP follows a verb like *go*.

V	NP	NP	PP	ADVP
sing				
look up	a difficult word		in the dictionary	
study	linguistics			very diligently
give	the student	his homework	during class	daily

Figure 9.5 *Verb phrases*

Prepositional phrases can be part of an NP or part of a VP. The following sentence illustrates the difference between these two roles of a PP: "The teacher assigned the problems in the book at the end of the class period." This sentence has three PPs. The first one, "in the book," is a PP that is part of the NP "the problems in the book." A way to test for whether this is one NP is to ask whether it can be replaced by a pronoun like *them*. The sentence could read, "The teacher assigned them at the end of the class period," so this is one NP. The last PP, "of the class period," is also part of an NP, "the end of the class period." However, the whole PP "at the end of the class period" is not part of any NP. Instead it is an independent part of the VP.

Prepositional phrases that are part of NPs function like adjectives. They describe the noun. For example, "in the book" tells which problems the teacher assigned. The PP describes or modifies the noun *problems*. On the other hand, a PP that is part of the VP acts like an adverb. It usually tells when or where. The PP "at the end of the class period" tells when the teacher assigned the problems. It does not describe or define which problems the teacher assigned.

A VP can also contain an ADVP. The rule lists the ADVP at the end of the VP, but it can occur in almost any position in the VP. In English, both adverbs and PPs that function like adverbs can occur in different positions. We can say "He often goes to the store" and "He goes to the store often," and both would be acceptable.

A PP phrase that functions as an adverb can also be moved. For example, the sentence used earlier could read "The teacher assigned the problems in the book at the end of the class period." But it would also be grammatical to say "At the end of the class period, the teacher assigned the problems in the book" or "The teacher, at the end of the class period, assigned the problems in the book."

However, PPs that serve as adjectives, like "in the book," cannot move out of the NP. The NP (*the problems in the book*) includes the PP. A sentence like "In the book, the teacher assigned the problems at the end of the class period" does not sound like English. Another way of stating this is that PPs that are part of a VP can be moved around at surface level, but PPs that are part of an NP cannot be moved out of the NP.

The phrase structure rules in this section describe the syntactic structure of sentences in English. The rules should account for all the possible simple sentences in English at the deep-structure level. Together, these phrase structure rules constitute a theory of syntactic structure. Combined with a set of transformational rules, they should account for any and all the grammatical sentences that English speakers produce.

Language Functions and Tree Diagrams

Linguists differentiate between syntactic structures and their functions. An NP like "the creative teacher" is a noun phrase. That is its structure. However, that same structure can function in different ways in a sentence. For example, in the following sentences this NP serves as a subject, as the object of the verb, as a subject complement (sometimes referred to as a *predicate noun*), and as the object of a preposition:

(1) The creative teacher developed exciting linguistics lessons. (as subject)
(2) The principal admired the creative teacher. (as object of the verb)
(3) The yearbook advisor is a creative teacher. (as subject complement)
(4) The student spilled her lunch on the creative teacher. (as object of the preposition)

This NP serves as a different constituent of each of these sentences. Its function is determined by its position in the overall sentence structure. Subjects come at the beginning of a sentence. Objects of verbs follow action verbs. Subject complements follow linking verbs. And objects of prepositions follow prepositions. Constituents such as subject and object are determined by their position in the sentence. Syntax has to do with the order of words, and the order of words signals which constituents are subjects and objects.

Linguists use tree diagrams, sometimes called *phrase markers*, to represent visually the structure of sentences and the functions of phrases, such as NPs, within a sentence. These diagrams are different from the Reed Kellog diagrams taught in traditional grammar classes. The tree diagrams make it easier to see that the subject of a sentence is the first and highest up NP in the diagram, the NP that follows the verb is the direct object or the subject complement, and the NP that is part of a PP is the object of the preposition. The four sentences above can be represented by the tree diagrams listed below as Figures 9.6, 9.7, 9.8, and 9.9.

These visual representations are called *tree diagrams* because they look somewhat like upside down trees. They branch out as they move from the level of the sentence to the phrases and down to the words. At the top level, every diagram begins with S for simple sentence. The next level has the three components of the sentence, an NP, an AUX, and a VP. The first NP under the S is the subject of the sentence. Thus, the function of a constituent is defined structurally, not just semantically, as is often done in schools when students learn that the subject is "the doer of the action." In the same way, the object of the verb (the direct object) is the first NP under the VP.

Diagrams represent the different levels of sentence structure. At the top level, every S has an NP, an AUX, and a VP. This represents the deep structure even though the AUX may not appear at the surface level. If the AUX is not represented in the surface structure, it is indicated with a zero. At the next level, each of those parts of the sentence is expanded. For example, in 9.6 the first NP is made up of a DET, an ADJP, and an N. In Figures 9.7 and 9.8 the first NP consists of a DET and an N. All these expansions of the subject NP follow the phrase structure rules. The differences come because different phrases contain different optional elements. The level below

the phrase level contains word categories like N or DET. At the bottom level are the lexical items, or words, that make up a particular sentence.

Tree diagrams, like other graphic organizers, are useful because they help show relationships among parts of a structure. For example, in Figure 9.6, it is possible to see that *exciting linguistics* is an adjective phrase. The two words are grouped together under one heading. In addition, the diagram shows that this ADJP is part of the NP that it is placed under. In Figure 9.9 the words "on the creative teacher" are all part of one PP, and that PP phrase forms part of the VP. These relationships are more evident because of the visual display.

Sometimes students worry about having to learn how to diagram sentences. However, if sentence diagramming is considered just another kind of graphic organizer, students may be

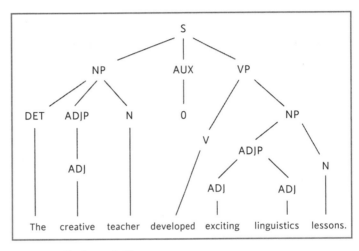

Figure 9.6 *Sentence 1 diagram*

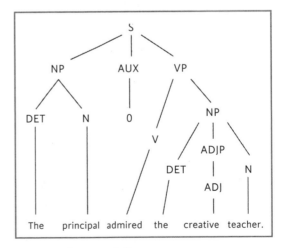

Figure 9.7 *Sentence 2 diagram*

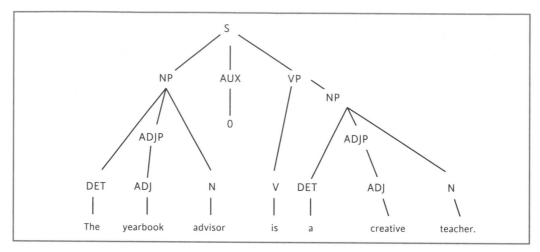

Figure 9.8 *Sentence 3 diagram*

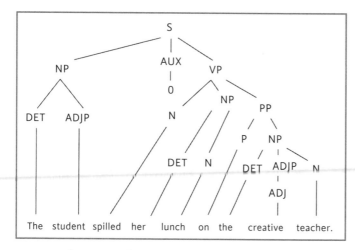

Figure 9.9 *Sentence 4 diagram*

less apprehensive. In fact, some students who have difficulty reading about syntactic structure find that they can grasp many of the concepts more easily when they see them in a diagram. The diagram captures linear order, grouping of words into constituents, and labels for morphological categories of words. Such diagrams help students understand the structure of sentences and phrases. The best procedure is to write the sentence but then start the diagram at the top and, following the phrase structure rules, work down to the individual words. It is much more difficult to go from the words up to the top of the diagram. Working from the top down helps students understand the constituents of the sentence and the elements in the different phrases.

Using the morphological categories described in Chapter 7 and the rules listed in this chapter, students should be able to diagram any simple sentence. However, it is important to remember that diagrams represent the structure of sentences at the deep level, *not* at the surface structure. Some sentences have to be rearranged into their deep structure before they can be diagrammed. For example, a sentence that begins with a prepositional phrase like "After class, the students will hold a meeting" must be a surface-structure variation since at deep-structure level, sentences start with an NP, not a PP. If a student attempted to diagram

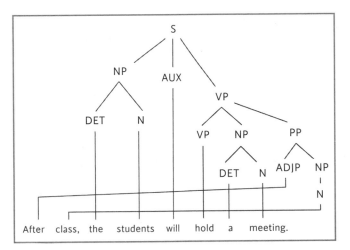

Figure 9.10 *Diagram with crossing lines*

the surface-structure transformation beginning with "After class" he would have to draw crossing lines. In tree diagrams, lines don't cross. Figure 9.10 shows an incorrect representation of this sentence with lines that cross.

Moving the PP to the end would produce the deep-structure sentence "The students will hold a meeting after class." This sentence can be diagrammed following the rules listed previously. Figure 9.11 shows the correct diagram. The lines in this tree diagram don't cross over one another.

This section provides an introduction to the syntax of simple sentences. Many more details would need to be included to fully describe the structure of English sentences. However, linguists use the approach outlined here. The goal is to develop a small set of rules that can produce an infinite number of sentences. A description of syntax that contains this small set of rules would be psychologically real if it is the best hypothesis

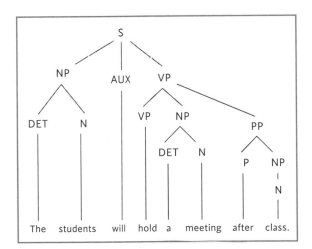

Figure 9.11 *Diagram drawn correctly*

to account for observable behavior, in this case, the speech and sign that humans use to communicate.

Even though most linguists argue that humans have an innate capacity to acquire language, and even though language is complex, the underlying structure must not be so complex that it would be impossible to acquire. The phrase structure rules outlined here can account for the deep structures of clauses (simple sentences) in English. The small set of rules listed earlier can account for the structure of an infinite set of English sentences.

Complex and Compound Sentences

The preceding sections described the structure of simple sentences in English. Simple sentences have one clause—one subject and predicate. Compound and complex sentences contain two or more clauses. The internal structure of each clause in a compound or complex sentence is the same as the structure in a simple sentence. The same phrase structure rules can be used to describe any English sentence. However, additional rules are needed to describe the organization of clauses in compound and complex sentences.

Compound sentences

Compound sentences consist of two or more simple sentences joined by a *coordinate conjunction*. The three most common coordinate conjunctions in English are *and*, *or*, and *but*. These three words capture the possible logical relationships between two ideas. The second idea can be an addition (*and*), an alternative (*or*), or an opposite (*but*).

A coordinate conjunction shows that two statements are of equal importance. This is why these conjunctions are labeled *coordinate*. A compound sentence can be represented in a tree diagram in which the two simple sentences are at the same level with the conjunction between them, as shown in Figure 9.12. The conjunction connects the two simple sentences but is not part of either one.

In Figure 9.12, the top level S represents the whole sentence. It branches into two Ss representing the two independent clauses. The conjunction is in the middle joining the two clauses. Each of these lower clauses can be expanded using the phrase structure rules shown earlier. The simple sentences in this compound sentence consist of an NP, an AUX, and a VP. In each one the NP is an N (*birds*) (*dogs*), and the VP is a V (*sang*) (*barked*). Students writing compound sentences should use parallel structure in the two simple sentences. The diagram in Figure 9.12 shows the parallel structure.

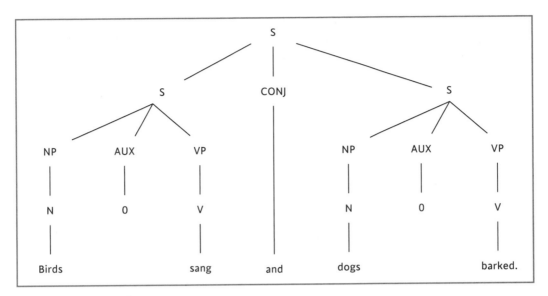

Figure 9.12 *Compound sentence*

Complex sentences

Beginning writers often string together their ideas with *and*. They present a series of equally important ideas in their writing. As writers develop, they learn to subordinate one idea to another. They structure their sentences to show that some ideas are subordinate to or dependent on other ideas. Rather than using a series of simple sentences or stringing together several ideas joined by *and*, they start writing complex sentences.

Complex sentences consist of a main clause and one or more subordinate clauses. The main clause may also be referred to as an *independent clause* because it can stand alone as a complete sentence. The subordinate clauses may be referred to as *dependent clauses* because they depend (literally "hang from") an independent clause. Just as complex words can consist of free and bound morphemes, complex sentences contain independent and dependent clauses.

Dependent clauses begin with a subordinate conjunction. Unlike coordinate conjunctions, subordinate conjunctions form part of the clause they attach to. Consider the following two sentences:

(1) Students represent syntactic structures when they draw tree diagrams.
(2) Students draw tree diagrams when they represent syntactic structures.

In sentence (1), the subordinate conjunction, *when* attaches to "they draw tree diagrams." In sentence (2) *when* attaches to "they represent syntactic structures." The clause with *when* is the subordinate or dependent clause. It represents a less important idea than the idea in the main clause. Thus, sentence (1) emphasizes representing syntactic structures, and sentence (2) foregrounds drawing tree diagrams.

As people speak or write, they signal the important ideas by placing them in main clauses. They add extra information related to the idea in *subordinate clauses*. The subordinate conjunction shows the relationship between the ideas. In the sentences above, the relationship is one of time. A different conjunction could show a different relationship. For example, using *if* would show a condition: "Students represent syntactic structures if they draw tree diagrams." A conjunction like *because* signals cause and effect: "Students draw tree diagrams because those diagrams represent syntactic structures." Effective writing involves deciding which ideas to emphasize and choosing the right conjunction to show the relationship between the ideas.

Adverb clauses

Dependent clauses can function in a sentence in the same way that an adverb, an adjective, or a noun functions. The clause is then represented in a tree diagram in the same position as the corresponding adverb phrase, adjective phrase, or noun phrase. However, since these are clauses, they are represented as an S rather than as an ADVP, ADJP, or NP.

Adverb clauses tell when, where, why, how, or under what conditions. They answer the same questions that adverbs do. The conjunctions that begin adverb clauses are words like *after*, *since*, and *if*. On the surface-structure level, adverb clauses can appear at the beginning or end of a sentence, just like prepositional phrases that function as adverbs. However, at deep-structure level, sentences begin with the main clause, and the adverb clause forms part of the VP because it functions to modify or add information to the VP just as an adverb does.

Figure 9.13 illustrates how sentence (1) above would be represented by a tree diagram. The subordinate adverb clause is part of the VP. The rule for the VP with an adverb clause is VP→V–(NP)–(PP)–S. The S is a clause that begins with a conjunction, and then the conjunction is followed by NP–AUX–VP. The rule for a subordinate clause could be written S→CONJ–NP–AUX–VP. This rule adds the conjunction to the rule for main clauses. The subordinate clause appears further down in the tree than the main clause. Adverb clauses are placed under the VP of the main clause, just as adverb phrases are.

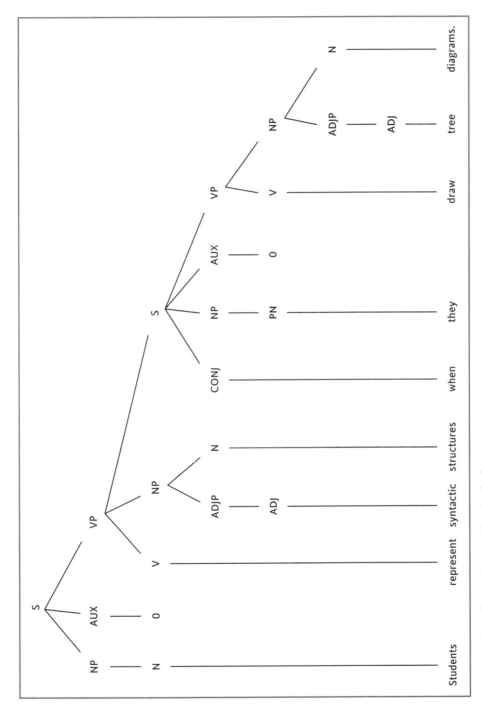

Figure 9.13 *Complex sentence with adverb clause*

Adjective clauses

Adjective clauses function as part of a noun phrase just as an adjective phrase does. Subordinate adjective clauses begin with one of the relative pronouns, *who*, *whom*, *whose*, *which*, or *that*. The following sentences contain adjective clauses:

(1) Students who draw tree diagrams represent syntactic structures.

(2) Diagrams that represent syntactic structures are often found in linguistics books.

(3) I made an error in this tree diagram, which I drew yesterday.

Adjective clauses can occur in NPs at any point in a sentence where an NP can occur. Thus, the adjective clause can be part of the subject, the object of the verb, or the object of a preposition. The rule for an NP with an adjective clause is $NP \rightarrow (DET) - (Q) - (ADJP) - N - (S) - (PP)$. The S of this subordinate adjective clause is then expanded as $S \rightarrow NP - AUX - VP$. In adjective clauses, the NP is a PN. This pronoun serves as both a conjunction and as the subject of the adjective clause. For example, in sentence (1) the adjective clause "who draw tree diagrams" *who* is a conjunction and the subject of the verb *draw*. Figure 9.14 shows how sentence (1) above would be diagrammed. Notice that *who* is listed as a PN even though it serves two functions.

Sentences (2) and (3) exemplify one convention used with adjective clauses. When the clause contains information that is necessary to identify the noun that precedes it, *that* is used. In sentence (2) the words "that represent syntactic structures" is needed to identify which diagrams are being referred to. This type of adjective clause is called a *restrictive clause* because the words in the clause restrict the meaning of the preceding noun.

Sentence (3) contains the adjective clause "which I drew yesterday." The information in this clause is not needed to identify the diagram because the speaker uses the words "this diagram." The use of *this* indicates that it is clear which diagram is being referred to. When a clause, such as this one, contains extra information that is not needed to identify the preceding noun, it is introduced with *which* and set off by commas. This is called a *nonrestrictive clause* because it isn't needed to restrict or identify the noun (in this case, the diagram) being referred to. Since the listener or reader knows which diagram the speaker or writer is referring to, the fact that it was drawn yesterday is incidental information. The use of *which* and the commas rather than *that* is a social convention used in formal writing. Teachers often give minilessons on conventions like these, and students can use this information when editing their writing.

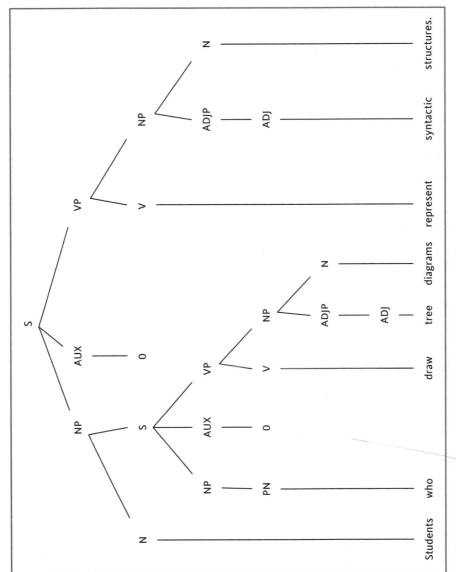

Figure 9.14 *Complex sentence with adjective clause*

Noun clauses

The third kind of subordinate clause is a noun clause. Noun clauses replace noun phrases and serve the same functions. The following sentences contain noun clauses:

(1) What Evelyn does is up to her.
(2) Gustavo bought whatever appealed to him.
(3) The teacher knew that Juan studied hard.
(4) You can be what you want to be.
(5) I wonder where he went.
(6) He didn't tell me whether he would go.

Noun clauses can start with *that, if, whether, wh* words (*how, when, where, why, what, who, whose, whom, which*), and *wh -ever* words (*whatever, however, wherever, whenever, whoever*) (retrieved from http://faculty.deanza.edu/flemingjohn/stories /storyReader$23, 4/25/2014). These words are referred to as *noun clause markers*. They can be classified as relative pronouns like the relative pronouns that introduce adjective clauses. They also function as conjunctions.

Noun clauses serve the same functions as noun phrases. In sentence (1) the noun clause is the subject of the sentence. In sentences (2) and (3) the noun clauses are the objects of the verbs. In sentence (4) the noun clause is a subject complement. In sentences (5) and (6) the noun clauses are also objects of the verbs.

There are two things to notice about noun clause markers. The only one that can be omitted is *that*. It is possible to say either "The teacher knew that Juan studied hard" or "The teacher knew Juan studied hard." At deep structure, the noun clause marker is present, but it may be omitted at the surface level. This also holds true for *that* in adjective clauses, such as "I bought a book (that) I liked" where *that* can be omitted.

The second thing to notice is that in sentences like (5) "I wonder where he went" the noun clause is part of an indirect question. The sentence is made up of two clauses: "I wonder" and "Where did he go?" Putting these two together creates an indirect question in which the original question is in statement form ("where he went") rather than question form ("Where did he go?"). Students learning English often produce sentences such as "I wonder where did he go" using the form of a direct question. Indirect questions are quite complex and are acquired late.

When diagramming sentences with noun clauses, we label the noun clause markers as PNs even though they also function as conjunctions. The rule that describes a noun clause is the same as the rule that describes a noun phrase except that S replaces NP, and the NP is a PN.

Sentences with noun clauses are diagrammed like the corresponding sentences with NPs. For example, sentence (2), "Gustavo bought whatever appealed to him," corresponds to the simple sentence "Gustavo bought a linguistics book." However, instead of an NP ("a linguistics book"), there is a clause with a subject and predicate ("whatever appealed to him"). Sentence (2) would be diagrammed as shown in Figure 9.15.

In Figure 9.15 the noun clause serves as the direct object. It is part of the verb phrase. The two-word verb in this sentence, *appealed to*, contains a verb and a particle. We have represented this by the rule V→V—PART to show that this is a two-word verb. It would also be possible to draw a line from V to both words, *appealed to*.

This section provides a brief outline of the way linguists analyze and represent compound and complex sentences. Compound sentences contain equally important ideas, so the two or more clauses are drawn at the same level in a diagram. Complex sentences contain a main idea and one or more subordinate ideas. These less important ideas are placed lower on the tree. They are subordinated to and dependent on the main clause structure. Tree diagrams represent the relationships among the clauses in a compound or complex sentence. However, the structure of each clause in these longer sentences is the same as the structure of a simple sentence with the addition of a conjunction to introduce the clause.

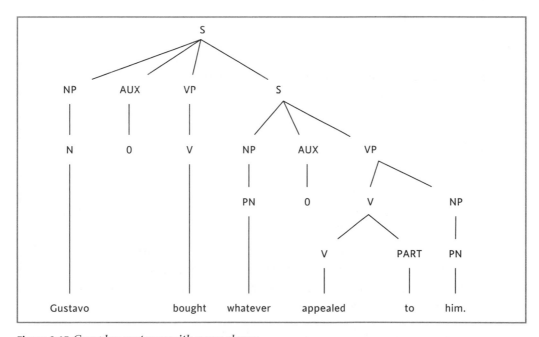

Figure 9.15 *Complex sentence with noun clause*

Conclusion

In this chapter, we considered these two questions:

- How have people viewed grammar?
- What are some basic aspects of English syntax?

For linguists, grammar can refer to the internal rules native speakers construct. The word *grammar* can also refer to the descriptions of syntactic structures that linguists develop. In addition, grammar can mean the rhetorically effective use of syntactic structures. However, for many people, grammar refers to a set of traditional rules to be learned in school. Research has shown that traditional approaches to teaching grammar have not been effective in improving students' speech or writing. However, targeted minilessons based on students' writing are useful. Students can apply this knowledge as they edit their writing.

In this chapter, we have provided a brief introduction to syntax. Syntax is a complex subject. Linguists continually revise their theories of how language is structured. Their goal is to describe syntactic structure using a relatively small number of rules that would generate an infinite number of sentences. The description would account for the implicit rules that native speakers of a language acquire that enable them to comprehend and produce that language.

To describe the syntax of English, linguists use concepts such as linear order, morphological word categories, and sentence constituents. These concepts help linguists describe the structure of the phrases that make up simple sentences at the deep structure level. Further, linguists analyze the structure of compound and complex sentences to show the relationships among the clauses. An understanding of syntax is an important part of a teacher's pedagogical language knowledge.

APPLICATIONS

1. Survey several colleagues. Ask them what *grammar* means to them. How do their definitions match up with the Weaver list on page 234? Discuss your results with classmates.

2. The position of a word in a sentence can change its function. *Only* is a function word that would be classified as a quantifier (derived from *one + ly*). Its position in a sentence determines which word or phrase it modifies. Consider the following set of sentences:

   (1) Only he said that he loved linguistics.
   (2) He only said that he loved linguistics.

(3) He said only that he loved linguistics.
(4) He said that only he loved linguistics.
(5) He said that he only loved linguistics.
(6) He said that he loved only linguistics.
(7) He said that he loved linguistics only.

Discuss the meaning of each sentence. Do some sentences mean the same thing? How does changing the position of *only* change the meaning? What does this suggest about the relationship of syntax and semantics? If some classmates learned English as an additional language, do they reach the same conclusions about the meanings of these sentences as native speakers of English do? Test this by checking their interpretation of sentence (2).

3. In this chapter, we describe how a linguist would formulate a rule for changing statements into questions. Using a similar procedure develop a rule for changing an active sentence into a passive sentence. For example, your rule should be able to change

(1) The linguist described the new language

to

(2) The new language was described by the linguist.

Use linear order, word categories, and sentence constituents in forming your rule.

4. An example of structural ambiguity is the saying "Time flies like an arrow." A humorous reply that shows the ambiguity is "Yes, and fruit flies like a banana." The surface structure, "Time flies like an arrow," has several deep-structure meanings. Some of these are not likely, but they are possible. Pinker (1994) lists five possible meanings of this sentence.

(1) Time proceeds as quickly as an arrow proceeds. (The usual meaning.)
(2) Measure the speed of flies in the same way that you measure the speed of an arrow.
(3) Measure the speed of flies in the same way that an arrow measures the speed of flies.
(4) Measure the speed of flies that resemble an arrow.
(5) Flies of a particular kind, time flies, are fond of an arrow. (209)

Write the five deep-structure sentences that correspond to these five meanings. Use the words "Time flies like an arrow" and add any missing words that are not in the surface structure but are understood. For example, the first meaning could be written as "Time flies like an arrow flies." The second and third meanings are commands, so you would need to start with *You*. Once you write the five sentences, then determine the part of speech for each word and write it under the word. The first sentence could be written as:

Time flies like an arrow flies.
N   V   CONJ DET N   V

Be prepared to share your results with your classmates.

10 /tɛn/

Implications from Syntax for Teaching a Second Language and Teaching Reading

Syntax refers to the order of words and phrases in sentences. Teachers can draw on their knowledge of syntax as they teach a second language or as they teach reading. An understanding of syntax forms an important part of a teacher's pedagogical language knowledge. In this chapter, we discuss the implications from syntax both for teaching second language and for teaching reading. In addition, we describe features of syntax that are found in academic texts and provide suggestions for teaching academic language at the sentence and text levels.

- How is syntax used in different methods of teaching a second language?
- What are some strategies for helping students use syntactic cues as they read?
- What are some features of the syntax of academic language and what are some strategies for teaching academic language?

Syntax in Second Language Teaching Methods Based on a Learning View

Insights from linguistic studies have informed methods of teaching English as a second language or teaching a foreign language. Methods based on a learning view of language development generally include exercises to help students learn the syntax of the target language. The grammar translation method attempts to teach syntax explicitly, while other methods teach syntax implicitly. Figure 10.1 summarizes the role of syntax in orientations and methods associated with a learning view of second language development.

Orientation	Method	Role of Syntax
Grammar based	Grammar translation	Syntax is taught directly. Students study the order of words and the structure of phrases in the new language.
Communicative	Direct method	The focus is on vocabulary rather than syntax, but exercises contextualize vocabulary in sentences, so syntax is taught inductively.
Empiricist	ALM	Basic sentence patterns are contextualized in dialogues, drills, and role-play, but not taught directly.
	Notional Functional	The focus is on notions and functions of language. These are contextualized in role-plays and exercises, but syntax is not taught directly.
	Suggestopedia	Syntax is not taught directly but is contexturalized in exercises and role-plays.

Figure 10.1 *Learning orientations, methods, and role of syntax*

As Figure 10.1 shows, syntax is only taught directly in the grammar translation method. Other methods include many classroom drills, exercises, and role-plays designed to help students communicate using different syntactic structures. For example, a role-play might be based on asking and answering questions to help students learn the syntax of questions, such as "Do you live on Elm Street?" Later, students might learn to use tag questions, such as "You live on Elm Street, don't you?" And still more advanced students would study the structure of indirect questions like "I wonder if he lives on Elm Street."

Audio-lingual Method

One of the most widely used methods of teaching a second or foreign language is the Audio-lingual Method (ALM). This method is based on behaviorist psychology and structural linguistics. Structural linguists carried out studies in contrastive analysis between different European languages (Lado 1957). Lado and other linguists developed the Contrastive Analysis Hypothesis (CAH). According to Brown (2007):

> CAH is a claim that the principal barrier to second language acquisition is the interference of the first language system with the second language system, and that a scientific structural analysis of the two languages in question would yield a taxonomy of linguistic contrasts between them which in turn would enable linguists and language teachers to predict the difficulties a learner would encounter. (248)

The taxonomy of linguistic contrasts that Brown refers to has six levels of difficulty ranging from the least interference, *transfer*, when there is no difference between the structures in the two languages all the way to the most interference, *split*, when one item in the native language becomes two or more items in the target language. Using the example of a Spanish speaker learning English, an example of transfer would be that both languages have subject–verb–object word order. An example of split is that in Spanish an adjective generally goes after the noun (*casa nueva*), but it can also precede the noun (*nueva casa*). The change in position changes the meaning. If it follows the noun it is a new creation. So a *casa* nueva is a house that has just been built, while a *nueva casa* would be a house that is new to me, although it may have been built several years ago. Since in English adjectives usually precede nouns (except in questions and when the adjective is a predicate adjective as in "Roses are red"), the CAH would predict that an English speaker learning Spanish would have difficulty with the position of adjectives since there is one position in English but two possibilities in Spanish.

These studies in contrastive analysis helped form the basis for ALM syllabuses. ALM includes dialogues, role-plays, and drills designed to help students learn English sentence patterns, especially those that are different from the patterns of their native language. Lessons start with a dialogue. Then students practice the sentence patterns and vocabulary of the dialogue with different kinds of role-plays, exercises, and drills.

Substitution drills require students to put a target word into a sentence slot. The drills follow this format: The teacher holds up a pencil and says, "This is a pencil." The teacher then holds up a pen and points to a student. The expected response is "That is a pen." The teacher continues with other classroom objects. Students give complete sentence answers to practice both the vocabulary and the syntax of the new language. This is a simple substitution drill.

To help students learn the syntax of long sentences, teachers can use a backward buildup drill. In this drill the teacher gives one word or phrase at a time starting with the end of the sentence and building up to the complete sentence. Students repeat after the teacher:

TEACHER: Linguistics classes	*Students:* Linguistics classes
TEACHER: In linguistics classes	*Students:* In linguistics classes
TEACHER: Syntax in linguistics classes	*Students:* Syntax in linguistics classes
TEACHER: Study syntax in linguistics classes	*Students:* Study syntax in linguistics classes
TEACHER: Students study syntax in linguistics classes.	*Students:* Students study linguistics in linguistics.

Some exercises require students to transform patterns. For example, in one drill students change statements into questions. Given the prompt "Today is Tuesday" students would respond with "Is today Tuesday?" transforming the statement into question form. The drill continues with more statements that students turn into questions. In other exercises students might change active sentences into passives or direct speech into reported speech. All these drills would require students to transform syntactic patterns in Spanish.

In ALM, students are expected to learn the syntax without explicit instruction. This approach contrasts with the earlier grammar translation method in which students are given the rule and then practice it. In ALM the grammar is presented inductively. The assumption is that students develop good language habits by memorizing and repeating dialogues as well as by completing drills and exercises. Teachers provide immediate correction of errors. Every lesson focuses on a specific grammar point.

Although ALM and other methods are based on scientific studies on contrastive analysis, the predictions of difficulty from the contrastive analysis hypothesis proved inaccurate. Many items that were predicted to be easy to learn turned out to be difficult, and items that were predicted to be difficult were often learned quickly.

In addition, even though the grammar teaching in ALM classrooms is implicit, the underlying assumption is that students learn a language, not acquire it. For that reason, very little attention is given to the meaning of the sentences in the exercises and drills. It doesn't really matter whether students can understand the words as long as they put them into the sentence following the pattern to be practiced. If a teacher who is conducting a drill gives the example "The teacher writes on the board with chalk" and then gives the prompt "whiteboard marker," a student can give the correct response, "The teacher writes on the board with a whiteboard marker" without understanding what the sentence means. According to Krashen (1982), this focus on form over meaning blocks acquisition. People acquire language when they receive messages they understand.

A second problem is that the exercises focus on the surface-level features of language. Students are expected to learn the patterns through repetition. However, acquisition only takes place when a person uses the surface structure (what they hear or read) to construct a deep-structure meaning. Language is not developed by imitating what people say. Children use what they hear to develop rules for how a language works at a deep-structure level, and then they use these rules to generate sentences. That is why children produce sentences like "I bringed it with me," sentences they could never have heard, but sentences that reflect the rules children are constructing. Second language learners also need to construct rules so that they can comprehend and produce the new language. They use the surface structure to formulate rules for how the language works. They don't simply imitate what they hear.

There is an old joke about a student who goes to Mexico after studying Spanish using ALM. When he returns, the teacher asks him if he used his Spanish. The student replies, "I'm afraid not. Nobody ever gave me the first line of the dialogue."

Syntax in second language teaching methods based on an acquisition view

In general, methods of teaching a second language based on an acquisition view of language development focus on communication and on teaching content rather than on grammar. Recently, some content-based methods have started to include language objectives as well as content objectives. In these methods syntax may be included. The instruction on syntax is contextualized within the academic content being studied.

Figure 10.2 describes the role of syntax in orientations and methods associated with an acquisition view of second language development. These methods vary in their approach to syntax.

In classes using the Silent Way, grammar is taught inductively. This method includes colored Cuisenaire rods. These rods can serve as visual aids in forming sentences. The different-colored rods can represent parts of speech, so students can use the rods as they make sentences. For example, a green rod could be used to represent adjectives, and a red rod could represent nouns. In representing a sentence in English, students would learn to put the green rod before the red rod. A yellow rod might be used to represent verbs, and the sentence pattern of noun–verb–noun would be represented by a red rod, a yellow rod, and another red rod. The colors are intended to help the students visualize patterns in a new language.

Orientation	Method	Role of Syntax
rationalist	Silent Way	Cuisenaire rods may be used to indicate word patterns in a sentence.
	Community Language Learning Problem Posing Total Physical Response Natural Approach	No explicit attention to syntax in these methods
	CALLA SIOP	Syntax may be taught in specific lessons and contextualized in academic content.

Figure 10.2 *Acquisition orientations, methods, and role of syntax*

In other methods, including Community Language Learning, Problem Posing, and the Natural Approach, grammar is not taught because the assumption is that the syntax of a language is acquired in the process of using the language.

Content-based methods such as CALLA and SIOP include specific lessons to help students comprehend academic language. Teachers develop both content objectives and language objectives. For example, in teaching a lesson on the westward migration in the U.S., a teacher could include the language objective "Students will be able to use subordinate conjunctions to combine simple sentences to form complex sentences as they describe the westward migration." Students could then combine sentences such as "Eastern cities were crowded" and "New territories opened in the west," using words like *since* or *therefore* to create complex sentences such as "Since Eastern cities were crowded, people migrated when new territories opened in the West."

The practice of writing and teaching language objectives is quite different from the early direct teaching of grammar in the grammar-translation method. In grammar translation, often used in foreign language classes, teaching the grammar point is the goal of the lesson. On the other hand, in content-based methods, there is a dual objective of teaching the academic content and, at the same time, teaching the language students need to comprehend and produce the content.

Syntax and the Two Views of Reading

An understanding of syntax can inform teachers as they teach reading. Each of the two views of reading assigns syntax a different role. From a learning perspective, syntax plays a limited role. Since the focus of instruction is at the word level, little is written about the sentences. The five areas that are emphasized are phonemic awareness, phonics, fluency, vocabulary, and comprehension. Comprehension does include levels beyond the word level.

In their discussion of comprehension, Armbruster and Osborn (2001) discuss literal and inferential questions, metacognitive strategies, and the use of graphic organizers among other things. Nowhere in the discussion of comprehension do they discuss syntax in any detail. While students need to use syntactic information to comprehend texts, the focus in discussions of comprehension from a learning view is not specifically on syntax.

In contrast, those who take an acquisition view of reading regard syntax as an important component. Syntax is one of the three cueing systems. Readers use acquired knowledge of syntactic patterns to predict upcoming words. Proficient readers use syntactic cues to predict, and they often make substitutions that maintain the sentence syntax. For example, they substitute nouns for nouns and determiners for determiners.

In English, sentences follow the general pattern of NP–AUX–VP. Even though there are surface variations, this is the pattern readers predict. They also know that in an NP there may be a determiner, an adjective, and a noun, in that order. They use this subconscious knowledge to help them predict. If they see a preposition, they expect a noun phrase will follow.

To illustrate how readers use syntax, consider the following sentence that contains nonsense words: "A phev was larzing two sleks." Readers of English predict that sentences will start with a noun phrase. "A phev" is probably a noun phrase. It begins with a determiner, *A*, that is followed by *phev*, a word that looks like a noun. Next, *was* is an auxiliary verb so *larzing* is probably a verb. It follows the auxiliary verb and has an *-ing* ending. Finally, "two sleks" must be a noun phrase. The first word, *two*, is a quantifier, and *sleks* has an *s* at the end, so the *s* must indicate a plural noun. This sentence follows the normal pattern of English (NP–AUX–VP), and, as a result, readers can *read* this sentence with good intonation since they can make use of syntactic cues as they read. Of course, since the content words are nonsense words, the sentence doesn't make sense, and a person is really just pronouncing nonsense words and not really reading. Readers need all three cueing systems, including semantics, to actually read a sentence.

Part of knowing a word is understanding how the word functions in a sentence. This knowledge goes beyond being able to categorize a word as a noun or a verb. It includes knowing what other kinds of words will follow. Linguists refer to the lexico-syntax to show the link between words or phrases (lexical items) and syntactic patterns. In English, verbs are especially important. Consider the following sentences:

(1) The linguist went to the lecture.
(2) The teacher put her keys on her desk.
(3) The student gave the teacher her homework.

A reader who has acquired knowledge of each of these verbs can predict other constituents that will occur in the sentence. For example, forms of the verb *to go* including *went* are usually followed by a prepositional phrase that indicates location, what linguists call a *locative*. Readers can use this knowledge of the lexico-syntax to predict a following prepositional phrase in sentence (1).

The verb *put* is followed by both an object and a locative. People usually put something somewhere. With lexico-syntactic knowledge a reader can correctly make predictions of the sentence constituents that follow *put* in sentence (2). *Give* requires two objects because people give something to someone. Thus readers can predict that two NPs will follow *give* in sentence (3). This is not conscious knowledge. Good readers cannot usually explain that forms of *go* are usually followed by locatives. However, readers use this subconscious knowledge to make predictions of syntactic structures as they read.

Strategies for using syntactic cues

Teachers who take an acquisition view of reading can provide strategies for using syntactic cues. The goal is for students to use these cues during independent reading to construct meaning from texts. Three teaching activities that help readers draw on syntactic cues as they read include using predictable books, using sentence frames, and using cloze activities.

Many books for beginning readers follow a predictable pattern. For example, one book about *Mom* (Randell, Giles, and Smith 1996) follows a consistent pattern. On page one, the text reads, "Mom is cooking" (2). Each of the following pages shows a picture of Mom doing a different activity, and the text follows the same pattern. For example, pages include "Mom is painting" (4), "Mom is swimming" (8), and "Mom is reading" (14). This book is predictable because only the verb changes, and the syntactic pattern is constant.

Books for slightly more advanced readers can be used to introduce more varied syntactic patterns. For example, in the book *I Love You More* (Duksta 2007), the mother compares her love for her child using comparatives in complex structures like "I love you higher than the highest bird ever flew" (3). Each page contains another comparison using the same syntactic structure. Children hearing or reading this book will acquire this syntactic structure over time. Poems like "Mary Had a Little Lamb" and songs like "Old McDonald Had a Farm" have predictable, repeated patterns, and during singing and shared reading, students can join in on the repeated sections.

Predictable books provide the support that beginning readers need to make good predictions as they begin to acquire literacy. A teacher can follow up a shared reading of a predictable book with a discussion of how students can predict the kind of word that will follow some part of a text. Students can also make their own predictable books following the pattern of a book the teacher has read. For example, after reading the book about Mom, students can make a similar book about a member of their family and then share it with the class.

Teachers can also scaffold instruction for beginning writers with activities that provide syntactic support. One simple strategy is to give students sentence frames to guide their writing. For example, one teacher read the story *Mañana Iguana* (Long 2004) with her class. In this story, modeled on *The Little Red Hen*, Iguana asks her friends to help with preparing for a party, but they all reply that they will help *mañana* (tomorrow). The teacher then divided the students into groups and gave each group a word like *exhausted* or *frustrated*. She also wrote this sentence frame on the board, "Iguana was ____ because _____." Students in each group completed the sentence using their word and put the sentence up on a web pocket chart that had *Iguana* in the middle and a place for each group to put their sentence around the chart. One group wrote, "Iguana was frustrated because she did everything for the party." Another group wrote, "Iguana was exhausted because she had to do all the work." Sentence frames can provide students with opportunities to use different syntactic patterns as they write.

Another activity that helps students develop the ability to use syntactic cues is a cloze procedure. In a cloze procedure, students are given a passage with some words deleted and are asked to supply the missing words. Teachers can create passages with different types of deletions to help students focus on different aspects of syntax. There are also several websites that offer cloze passages to use for different purposes. By searching for cloze exercises, a teacher can find many such passages. However, cloze passages are easy to create. For example, a teacher might delete adjectives that precede nouns. Or a teacher might take out the conjunctions.

Students can work together to figure out what words could go in the blank. It is important for students to discuss why they chose the words they did. Consider the following short passage:

> The linguist began to study a new language. He wanted to learn about the syntax of sentences in this language. He began by collecting a large corpus of language samples. Then he began to analyze the language to find the syntactic patterns.

A teacher could delete the verbs to create this cloze exercise:

> The linguist _____ to _____ a new language. He wanted to _____ about the syntax of sentences in this language. He _____ by _____ a large corpus of language samples. Then he began to _____ the language to _____ the syntactic patterns.

Normally, a longer passage would be used. Students can work in groups to guess the words that go in the blanks. Then each group can report back telling the class the words they chose and the cues they used to decide on particular words. Students can also compare the words they chose with the original passage.

In the follow-up discussion of the passage earlier, a teacher could point out that the missing words are verbs and then talk with students about the clues that readers use to predict a verb. Through a series of lessons, a teacher can introduce different aspects of English syntax. What is important is for students to think about the clues that tell them what kind of word might fit a particular blank. Getting the right word is not important as long as the word makes sense. What is important is developing a strategy to be used later during silent reading.

One source for cloze exercises is *The Reading Detective Club* (Goodman 1999). This book contains a series of clever, contextualized cloze activities. Students are invited to become detectives and solve the mystery of the missing words. Helpful suggestions for follow-up discussions are included. This book is a resource for lessons that would help students use both syntactic and semantic cues during reading.

By using cloze activities, sentence frames, and predictable books, teachers can help students use syntactic cues as they read and write. All of these activities make students more aware of syntactic structures. Teachers should embed this strategy instruction in meaningful contexts as students read and write different kinds of texts.

Syntax in Academic Texts

In the course of their schooling, students are expected to read and write texts written in the academic registers of schooling. A *register* is the language used in a specific context, what Halliday and Hassan (1989) refer to as a "context of situation." As we discussed in Chapter 1, the context of situation has three components: field, tenor, and mode. The *field* refers to the subject being discussed. For example, the field could be algebra. The *tenor* is the relationship between the speaker and listener or reader and writer. In academic registers, the speaker or writer assumes the role of the person in authority with greater knowledge of the subject than the listener or reader. The *mode* refers to the means of communication, oral, signed, or written. The mode can be studied by examining the devices speakers or writers use to make texts (oral, signed, or written) coherent and cohesive. Together, the field, tenor, and mode constitute the register of language used in a certain context. When students read academic texts in history, math, science, and language arts, they must learn to comprehend the academic registers of these different subject areas.

Fang (2004) points out that texts written in academic registers are characterized by technicality, authoritativeness, informational density, and abstraction. Technicality is reflected in the specialized vocabulary found in academic writing. Authoritativeness is the tone achieved by using dense, abstract, technical writing.

Both informational density and abstraction are the result of the syntax of academic texts, which differs from the syntax of conversational language.

Lexical density

Although the basic syntactic structure of clauses in academic texts is the same as the structure in conversational texts, academic texts contain many complex sentences, and the syntax of the noun phrases is complex. Noun phrases in academic writing are often very long. This leads to greater density. Linguists measure informational density, often referred to as *lexical density*, by determining the number of lexical words in each clause. Lexical words are content words—nouns, verbs, adjectives, and some adverbs—that occur in texts. Texts are made up of content words and grammatical function words. Halliday (1989) has demonstrated that written language is lexically denser than spoken language. Conversational language has about 2.5 lexical items in each clause while academic written language has almost double that amount.

Consider the following passage taken from a ninth-grade biology text (Biggs et al. 2004):

> Like many <u>organisms</u> <u>studied</u> in this <u>chapter</u>, <u>planarians</u> <u>are</u> <u>hermaphrodites</u>. During <u>sexual</u> <u>reproduction</u>, <u>individual</u> <u>planarians</u> <u>exchange</u> <u>sperm</u>, which <u>travel</u> along <u>special</u> <u>tubes</u> to <u>reach</u> the <u>eggs</u>. <u>Fertilization</u> <u>occurs</u> <u>internally</u>. The <u>zygotes</u> are <u>released</u> in <u>capsules</u> into the <u>water</u>, where they <u>hatch</u> into <u>tiny</u> <u>planarians</u>. (707)

These four sentences contain six clauses. The passage has 44 words, and 27 of these are content words, which we have underlined. On average, then, each clause contains 4.5 content words, about twice as many content words as would be found in a speech sample.

Because texts written in the academic register, such as this one, have more content words in each clause, the information load is greater than the information load of conversational registers. This lexical density makes academic texts more challenging for readers.

Abstraction

Academic registers also contain certain features that make the language abstract. Two of these features are passive constructions and complex noun phrases that result from the process of nominalization. The first clause in the last sentence in the passage about planarians is written in passive voice: "The zygotes are released in capsules into the water."

The surface-level syntactic structure of passive sentences differs from the syntax of active sentences. Sentences in passive voice are also more abstract than those in active voice. Consider sentences (1) and (2):

(1) Francisco wrote this children's book.
(2) This children's book was written by Francisco.

Sentence (1) is written in active voice. The logical subject, the doer of the action, is also the grammatical subject of the verb *wrote*. This sentence reports events in a way that corresponds to our understanding of how things occur in the world. Our everyday experience is that people write books, and the order of words in sentence (1) reflects our experience. Since the words map on to our experience, active voice is concrete.

Now consider sentence (2). Here the grammatical subject of the verb *was written* is *This children's book*. We know *This children's book* is the grammatical subject because subjects and verbs agree, and if we change the noun phrase to *These children's books* we would need to change the verb to *were written*. Even though *This children's book* is the grammatical subject, it is not the logical subject because it is not the doer of the action. Passive sentences are therefore abstract because they do not correspond to our experiences in the world. The syntax of the passive voice results in a more abstract way of expressing an idea.

The sentence about zygotes illustrates another feature that makes the sentences in academic texts abstract. This sentence reads, "The zygotes are released in capsules into the water." Here, we are not told who or what releases the zygotes. In passive constructions writers or speakers can omit the *by* phrase in cases where it is not clear or not important to state who carried out an action. Often, this is the case in science. In the clause "When petroleum products and coal are burned" the writer wants to report the effect of burning these products. It is not important to state who burns them. The passive construction is more abstract because in our direct experience, people burn coal and petroleum products. By removing the actor, a writer can make the event more abstract.

Academic registers also make frequent use of nominalization, which makes texts abstract as well. *Nominalization* is the process of turning verbs or adjectives into nouns. Two examples of nominalization in the passage about planarians are *reproduction* and *fertilization*. Both of these words are nouns. Yet the concepts these words express would normally be conveyed by verbs and adjectives. *Reproduce* refers to an action. By adding a suffix, the writer has converted this word into a noun. *Fertilization* has the adjective *fertile* as its base. *Fertile* can be turned into a verb, *fertilize*, and then that word can be changed into a noun, *fertilization*. In other cases, adjectives are converted directly into nouns. For example, the adjective *sincere* can be changed into the noun *sincerity*.

In English, nouns usually name the actors or participants in a sentence, verbs describe the actions, and adjectives modify nouns. A more direct way to express the ideas in the paragraph would be to use the verb forms of *reproduction* and *fertilization* to express the actions: "Individual planarians *reproduce* when they exchange sperm. The sperm *fertilize* the eggs." When we talk, we usually use sentences like this in which the nouns name the actors and the verbs express the actions. The syntax reflects our experience with the world.

Nominalization not only makes academic texts more abstract, this process also increases the lexical density. In our discussion of syntax, we gave the description for noun phrases as follows: NP→(DET or Q)–(ADJP)–N–(PP)–(S). A noun phrase has several optional elements, a determiner or quantifier, an adjective phrase, a prepositional phrase, and a relative clause (S) along with the obligatory noun. The process of nominalization allows writers to create complex noun phrases that include more of these optional elements, and these NPs are typical of academic texts. Fang (2004) gives the following example, "This effect of Earth's rotation on the direction of winds and currents is called the Coriolis effect" (340). The underlined initial noun phrase with the nominalization *rotation* has twelve words, half of which are content words. As this example shows, nominalization allows writers to create lexically dense texts.

Cummins (2000) defines academic registers as being context reduced and cognitively demanding. Academic texts that are lexically dense, such as this one, are cognitively demanding because of the number of content words in each clause. At the same time, such writing is context reduced because it presents ideas in an abstract way, using both nominalization and a passive construction. The sentence above and the passage about planarians use syntax that is typical of the academic registers of schooling, and without scaffolded instruction most students, and particularly emergent bilinguals, are not able to comprehend such texts or to write texts in the academic register.

Scaffolding the Writing of Academic Texts

Teachers can scaffold instruction for emergent bilinguals to help them read academic texts as well as help students write more complex texts that have some of the features of academic registers. Emergent bilinguals often begin by writing simple sentences. At a later stage, they may begin to produce complex sentences using a few conjunctions, such as *because* and *when*. Sentence-combining activities have been shown to be an effective activity to help students move from writing simple sentences to writing more complex sentences (Kilgallon and Kilgallon 2007).

In sentence combining, students are given a series of simple sentences and asked to combine them into a more syntactically complex sentence. For example, students are asked to combine sentences like the following:

(1) Members of political parties introduce bills in Congress.
(2) Members of Congress vote on the bills.
(3) Some bills receive many votes.
(4) These bills pass.
(5) They may become laws.

Students can learn to write complex sentences that combines ideas from several simple sentences. Students can compare their answers with those of classmates. They can discuss which sentences they think are most effective. Students can also work in small groups to produce their sentences.

Another way to help students write more complex sentences is to build their vocabulary by introducing other, more precise, words to show the relationships between ideas. These transition words are often referred to as *signal words* because they signal to the reader how two ideas are related.

Fisher, Rothenberg, and Frey (2007) explain how a team of ninth-grade teachers worked to help their emergent bilinguals develop their vocabulary of signal words to link ideas. The teachers examined student writing and found that their students often left out signal words. The teachers found a word list that grouped signal words by function. The functions included addition, example, comparison, contrast, cause and effect, concession, and conclusion.

The teachers then listed several words for each function. For example, for addition, the list included *also, and, besides, furthermore, in addition, indeed, in fact, moreover, so,* and *too* (52). The teachers posted this list in their rooms as a word wall. They took time on a regular basis to review the words with their students. As they read aloud to their students, they made a point of emphasizing words in the texts that were on the list.

According to Fisher, Rothenberg, and Frey (2007), "Over time, students started to notice the terms in their reading and began incorporating them into their writing" (51). The process the teachers used enabled the emergent bilinguals in these ninth-grade classes to enrich their vocabulary by adding words that show logical connections between ideas. The signal words the teachers Fisher and Frey worked with were subordinate conjunctions that connect clauses or sentences. Teachers can also help students understand the effects created by combining clauses in different ways.

A teacher might begin with two simple sentences logically related by cause and effect, such as "There was a prolonged drought in the area. Many of the plants died," and discuss different ways these sentences can be combined. Students might write, "Because there was a prolonged drought, many of the plants died." They can also discuss the difference between this sentence and one that begins with the clause about plants dying, "Many of the plants died because there was a prolonged drought." The teacher can help the students understand that the order of clauses can be changed.

The class can also discuss the idea that the clause that comes first is the one the writer wants the reader to focus on. One order puts the focus on the drought and the other emphasizes the effect on the plants. After students have practiced with other pairs of sentences showing cause and effect, the teacher can introduce embedded relative clauses. The teacher might give students two sentences such as "The plants received adequate sun and water" and "The plants were healthy." First, students can discuss how these two sentences can be combined to show cause and effect. Then, the teacher can show them that the sentences can also be combined by putting one clause inside the other to produce, "The plants that received adequate sun and water were healthy."

Next, students can practice this new way of combining clauses with other sentence pairs. After showing students these two basic ways of combining clauses, teachers can have students analyze passages in their textbooks to see how writers vary the syntax as they combine ideas into complex sentences. Students can also begin to use these kinds of sentences in their own writing.

Fang (2008) suggests a kind of sentence-combining activity that he calls Deconstruct–Reconstruct. This activity can help students read and write academic texts. The teacher begins with a short passage taken from a student textbook. This should be a key passage so that students can learn both the academic content and the academic language needed to comprehend it and produce similar content.

For example, a teacher might begin with the following passage from a social studies text:

> The early colonists who settled in the new land struggled to become self-sufficient because they lacked familiarity with local conditions. As a result, many of the early colonies failed when colonists planted the wrong crops or planted them at the wrong times.

The first step in this activity is for the teacher to work with the students to *deconstruct* the passage. This involves rewriting the passage as a series of simple sentences. For this passage, the sentences might be the following:

> The early colonists settled in the new land.
> They struggled to become self-sufficent.
> They lacked familiarity with local conditions.
> The colonists planted the wrong crops.
> They planted them at the wrong time.
> Many of the early colonies failed.

This step helps students identify the ideas in the passage. The second step is to have the students work in pairs to *reconstruct* the passage into more complex language. What is important here is for students to come up with new ways of combining the sentences, rather than simply trying to replicate the original passage. For that reason, students should not have access to the original passage as they combine the sentences.

When they finish, the groups can write their results on the board or project them on a whiteboard and explain the process they went through. The class could also create a composite paragraph using ideas from the different groups. What is important here is for students to talk about how and why they combined sentences as they did. Students can also compare their reconstructed paragraphs with the original. In some cases, students may decide they like their version better than what the published author wrote. Sentence-combining activities such as this one help students understand how the different syntactic structures of English can be used to write effectively.

Advanced academic writing

More advanced students can benefit from examining how writers of academic texts use nominalizations in their writing. A careful analysis of the differences between everyday writing and academic writing can help students as they read. They begin to see that advanced academic writing contains fewer conjunctions and action verbs and more nominalizations and being verbs.

The teacher would need to guide the instruction carefully. After the students have deconstructed and reconstructed passages, such as the history passage about the colonists, the teacher could take one of the reconstructed passages and change some of the verbs or adjectives into nouns and use these nominalized forms in a rewrite of the passage. For example, here is the original passage about the colonists:

The early colonists who settled in the new land struggled to become self-sufficient because they lacked familiarity with local conditions. As a result, many of the early colonies failed when colonists planted the wrong crops or planted them at the wrong times.

The first sentence contains the verbs *struggled* and *lacked* and the adjective *self-sufficient*. These can be converted into the nouns *struggle*, *lack*, and self-sufficiency. The original sentence could be rewritten to include one or more of these nominalizations. One possible way to rewrite this sentence would be: "The early colonists' struggle for self-sufficiency in the new land was impeded by their lack of familiarity with local conditions." In its rewritten form, this sentence has one clause rather than two. Advanced academic writing packs more information into each clause and uses nominalizations rather than conjunctions.

The same process could be used with the second sentence. Here, the verb *failed* can be changed to the noun *failure*, and *planted* can be made a nominal form, *planting*. One possible rewrite would be "The failure of the early colonies was the result of the colonists' planting the wrong crops or planting them at the wrong time."

The teacher can show students the two versions, the one with conjunctions and the rewritten sentences with nominalizations, and guide the students in a discussion of the differences between the two passages. This can be followed by a careful analysis of a passage from a student text used in class that contains nominalizations. Although students would not be expected to write using nominalized forms, it is important for them to be able to read passages that contain this advanced academic syntax.

Writing cohesive paragraphs

Students also need to be able to write cohesive paragraphs in which sentences are logically connected. Often, teachers tell students that all the sentences should develop one main idea, but this advice can be difficult for students to apply. The difficulty comes when deciding whether one or more sentences they wrote contribute to the central idea.

Brown (2009) explains a more concrete way to help students write cohesive paragraphs. First, teachers can present several simple sentences and explain that sentences in English have two parts, a topic and a comment. For example, in the sentence "Emergent bilinguals can succeed with good instruction," the topic is "Emergent bilinguals" and the comment is "can succeed with good instruction."

This division of simple sentences into topic and comment is similar to dividing a sentence into its subject and predicate. When people talk or write, they begin by identifying a topic. Then they say something about that topic; they comment on it. This is not a difficult concept, and students can grasp it quickly. Once students understand that sentences consist of a topic and a comment, then teachers can explain that there are three ways to create cohesive paragraphs.

One way to make a paragraph cohesive is to start each sentence with the same topic. Consider the following paragraph, taken from Guthrie and Davis (2003):

> Struggling readers tend to be notably unmotivated. They are especially likely to have low confidence in their reading, which is termed *self efficacy* in the research literature (Wigfield, Eccles, and Rodriguez 1998). These students are likely to lack confidence in their ability to read or even to improve their reading skill. In addition to a lack of belief in their reading capability, struggling readers in middle school are more likely to be extrinsically motivated than intrinsically motivated. These students report that their incentive for reading consists of grades and meeting teachers' requirements. They are unlikely to read for their own enjoyment, seek satisfaction of their curiosity through books, or enjoy the challenge of a complex plot or intricate knowledge in books. (60)

We have underlined the topic of each sentence in the paragraph. The topic of the first sentence is *struggling readers*. The next sentence starts with the pronoun *they*, which refers to *struggling readers*. The third sentence begins with *These students* to link again to *struggling readers*. The topics of the next three sentences follow a similar connective pattern: *struggling readers*, *These students*, and *they*. The subject or topic of each sentence is linked to the topics of the other sentences. This is a pattern that Brown refers to as *constant topic*. Since all the sentences in the paragraph have the same topic, they are related.

It is easy for students to decide whether or not each sentence has the same topic. This is a good starting point, but there are other ways to write cohesive paragraphs. If each sentence is making a comment on the same topic, after a while, a writer needs to move on to a new topic. Otherwise, the writing may become repetitive.

Brown (2009) describes two other ways that writers can create cohesive paragraphs: *derived topic* and *chained topic*. In a paragraph with derived topics, the topic is a derivation or example of the topic of the first sentence. The derived topic pattern is similar to the constant topic. However, instead of being identical, the topic of one sentence is related to or derived from the topic of the first sentence. For example, if the topic of the first sentence is *emergent bilinguals*, a derived topic might be a type of emergent bilingual, such as an adequate formal schooling student. Here is an example of a paragraph with a derived topic pattern:

<u>Emergent bilinguals</u> can become engaged readers with the right instruction. <u>Limited formal schooling students</u> may need to learn the Roman alphabet. <u>Adequate formal schooling students</u> may need to learn how to take multiple-choice tests. <u>Long-term English learners</u> may need reading comprehension strategies.

The derived topic pattern is commonly used when students develop a paragraph using examples.

Brown (2009) refers to the third pattern as a *chained topic*. In this pattern the topic of one sentence links to the comment from the preceding sentence. This pattern allows a writer to present a series of related ideas. For example, here are two chained sentences: "Struggling readers can become <u>engaged readers</u> with the right instruction. <u>Engaged readers</u> enjoy reading a variety of books." In this example, the comment of the first sentence, *engaged readers*, becomes the topic of the second sentence. This chaining process may be illustrated as follows:

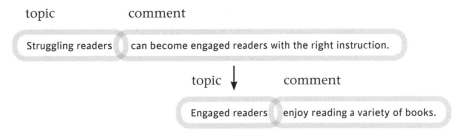

Brown describes three types of chaining. The first, which is shown in the previous example, is *repetition*. Key words from the comment of the first sentence are repeated as the topic of the second sentence. Too much repetition, of course, would become monotonous, so writers use two other ways to chain ideas. One of these is to *substitute* a word or phrase for the key words in the comment. For instance, the writer could have written the second sentence as "These students read a wide variety of books." In doing so, the writer substitutes *These students* for *Engaged readers*. The result is shown as follows:

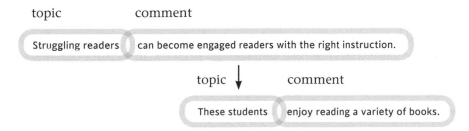

Brown explains, "To substitute, you can use a synonym for one of the key words in the Comment, use a pronoun, or summarize the main idea of the Comment" (2009, 93).

A third way to chain ideas is to use *nominalization*. Rather than repeating keywords from the previous comment or substituting for those words, a writer can change an adjective or a verb in the comment of the first sentence to a noun in the topic of the next sentence. To continue with our example, we could focus on the key words *engaged readers* and use the nominalized form *engagement* as the topic of the following sentence, thus creating a sentence such as "Engagement leads students to read a wide variety of books." This can be illustrated as follows:

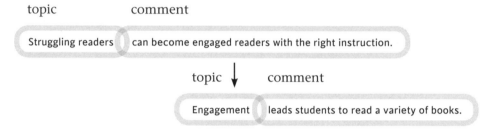

Most cohesive paragraphs use a combination of constant, derived, and chained topics. Academic writing uses all these ways of connecting sentences to create cohesive paragraphs. Of the three, though, chaining using nominalization is the most common since nominalization allows writers to pack more information into each sentence.

In the example we gave to demonstrate chaining, we used a simple sentence with just one clause. However, the three patterns we have described apply to complex sentences with more than one clause as well. For example, in the sentence "Engaged readers enjoy reading so they read a variety of books," the second clause uses a pronoun (*they*) to refer to the topic of the first clause (*engaged readers*). The pattern here is constant topic.

The derived topic pattern could be shown with a sentence like "Engaged readers enjoy reading, and Mary's students read a variety of books." Here *Mary's students* is a derivation of *engaged readers*. The third pattern, chained topic, is shown in this sentence: "Alexander Graham Bell invented the telephone, and this invention changed how people communicate." Here the verb *invented* from the first clause becomes the noun, *invention* in the second clause.

As these examples show, writers can use the same devices to link clauses in a sentence or sentences in a paragraph. Consider the following paragraph taken from an integrated physics and chemistry textbook (McLaughlin, Thompson, and Zike

2002). It uses a combination of the patterns Brown describes to give it cohesion. In some cases, a topic or comment from one sentence relates to an earlier sentence rather than the one immediately preceding it. We have reformatted the paragraph, listing each nonembedded clause separately.

1. Although fossil fuels are a useful source of energy for generating electricity and providing the power for transportation,
2. their use has some undesirable side effects.
3. When petroleum products and coal are burned,
4. smoke is given off that contains small particles called particulates.
5. These particulates cause breathing problems for some people.
6. Burning fossil fuels also releases carbon dioxide.
7. Figure 9 shows how the carbon dioxide concentration in the atmosphere has increased from 1960 to 1999.
8. The increased concentration of carbon dioxide in the atmosphere might cause Earth's surface temperature to increase. (296)

Clause 1 has the topic *fossil fuels*. Clause 2 uses *their* to refer to *fossil fuels*. In addition, *use* in clause 2 connects with *useful* in clause 1. The topic of clause 3, *petroleum products and coal*, is derived from *fossil fuels*, the topic of clause 1, since petroleum products and coal are types of fossil fuels. The topic of clause 4, *smoke*, is connected to the comment of clause 2, *undesirable side effects*. This is an example of chaining using the process of substitution. The topic of clause 5, *These particulates*, is connected to the comment of 4. In this case, the chaining uses repetition. The topic of clause 6, *Burning fossil fuels*, connects to the previous *are burned*, the comment in clause 3, since *burning* is a nominalization. In addition, *fossil fuels* connects to the topic of clause 1. The topic of clause 7, *carbon dioxide concentration*, relates to the comment of clause 6 through chaining, and the topic of clause 8, *concentration of carbon dioxide*, is a variation of the topic of clause 7.

The analysis of this paragraph shows how the clauses are closely linked using many of the devices that Brown identifies. The paragraph has the characteristics of academic writing that we have already discussed. It is technical, abstract, dense, and authoritative (Fang 2008). For example, the last sentence contains a complex noun phrase, "The increased concentration of carbon dioxide in the atmosphere." *Concentration* is a nominalized form. It is modified by the participle *increased* and by the following prepositional phrase *in the atmosphere*.

It is clear that emergent bilinguals need scaffolded instruction to read and write texts like these. This paragraph also shows that the syntax of academic texts is different from the syntax of conversational language. Academic texts contain complex noun phrases, passive constructions, and complex sentences with both subordinated and embedded clauses. When teachers develop a good understanding of syntax, they can better assist their students in reading and writing academic texts.

Conclusion

The questions we addressed in this chapter were the following:

- How is syntax used in different methods of teaching a second language?
- What are some strategies for helping students use syntactic cues as they read?
- What are some features of the syntax of academic language and what are some strategies for teaching academic language?

Methods of teaching a second language differ in how they teach syntax. In the grammar-translation method syntax is taught directly and explicitly. Other methods based on a learning view teach syntax inductively. The syllabus for a class using the Audio-lingual Method is based on a contrastive analysis of the language students are learning and their native language. Dialogues, exercises, and drills are designed to give students practice in items that are predicted to be difficult because of the differences between the two languages.

Methods of second language teaching based on an acquisition view do not teach grammar directly. The assumption is that students will acquire the grammar of a language as they use the language to communicate. More recent content-based methods include both content and language objectives. Different aspects of language, including syntax, are taught in the context of learning academic content.

Teachers with a learning view of reading focus instruction on words and phrases and seldom include lessons that deal with syntax. Teachers with an acquisition view assume that much of grammar is acquired in the process of reading. However, they also use predictable books and teach strategy lessons to help their students use syntactic cues as they read. Strategies include using predictable books, cloze activities, and sentence frames.

There are differences in syntax between the academic registers of schooling and the registers of conversational language. Academic texts contain passive constructions and complex sentences. In addition, academic language contains nominalizations and complex noun phrases. These features make academic language lexically dense and abstract.

Teachers can help students read and write in academic registers through different activities, such as sentence combining and deconstructing and reconstructing key passages from their textbooks. Teachers can also instruct students in different ways to write cohesive paragraphs using constant topics, derived topics, and chained topics. With carefully scaffolded instruction all students can succeed in developing proficiency in the academic registers of schooling.

In this book we have discussed some important aspects of linguistics including phonology, morphology, and syntax. For each of these topics, we considered implications of teaching second languages and teaching reading to help teachers make informed decisions about the methods they use. Knowledge of linguistics is the basis for pedagogical language knowledge, an understanding of how to meet the language demands of the academic content subjects.

We began this book by writing that many students enter a linguistics class thinking it would be difficult and would not include anything relevant to their teaching. Our hope is that you have not found the topics in this book to be too difficult and that you have gained information that you can use daily in your teaching.

APPLICATIONS

1. Students frequently have difficulty writing cohesive paragraphs. Try explaining constant, derived, and chained topics, giving students examples. Ask them to write paragraphs using these devices. Be prepared to share with classmates the result of your instruction.

2. Analyze a paragraph from your own writing. How did you connect the sentences in that paragraph? Use the fossil fuel paragraph analysis from this chapter as a model for your explanation.

3. Choose a key passage from a class textbook and work with students to deconstruct and reconstruct the passage. What did your students learn from this?

4. In this chapter we describe how teachers can use cloze activities to help students use syntactic cues as they read. Prepare a cloze passage and use it with your students. What did they learn from this lesson?

References

Adams, Marilyn. 1990. *Beginning to Read: Thinking and Learning About Print*. Cambridge, MA: MIT Press.

Agee, Jon. 1999. *Sit on a Potato Pan, Otis! More Palindromes*. New York: Farrar, Straus & Giroux.

Akmajian, Adrian, Richard Demers, and Robert Harnish. 1979. *Linguistics: An Introduction to Language and Communication*. Cambridge, MA: MIT Press.

Anderson, Richard, and William Nagy. 1992. "The Vocabulary Conundrum." *American Educator* Winter: 14–18, 44–47.

Andrews, Larry. 2001. *Lingustics for L2 Teachers*. Mahwah, NJ: Lawrence Erlbaum Associates.

Armbruster, Bonnie, and Jean Osborn. 2001. *Put Reading First: The Building Blocks for Teaching Children to Read*. Washington, DC: U.S. Department of Education.

Asher, James. 1977. *Learning Another Language Through Actions: The Complete Teacher's Guide*. Los Gatos, CA: Sky Oaks.

Atwell, Nancie. 1998. *In the Middle: New Understandings About Writing, Reading, and Learning*. 2d ed. Portsmouth, NH: Heinemann.

Bach, Kent, and Robert Harnish. 1979. *Linguistic Communication and Speech Acts*. Cambridge, MA: MIT Press.

Baker, Colin. 2011. *Foundations of Bilingual Education and Bilingualism*. Bristol, UK: Multilingual Matters.

Baugh, Albert, and Thomas Cable. 2012. *A History of the English Language*. 6th ed. Englewood Cliffs, NJ: Prentice-Hall.

Berdiansky, Betty, Bruce Cronnell, and John Koehler. 1969. "Spelling–Sound Relations and Primary Form-Class Descriptions for Speech Comprehension Vocabularies of 6–9 Year Olds." Inglewood, CA: Southwest Regional Laboratory for Educational Research and Development.

Bergmann, Anouschka, Kathleen Currie Hall, and Sharon M. Ross. 2007. "Theories of Language Acquisition." In *Language Files: Materials for an Introduction to Language and Linguistics*, 311–18. Columbus: The Ohio State Press.

Biggs, Alton, Whitney Crispen Hagins, Chris Kapicka, Linda Lundgren, Peter Rillero, Kathleen G. Tallman, and Dinah Zike. 2004. *Biology: The Dynamics of Life*, ed. Glencoe. New York: McGraw-Hill.

Boeckx, Cedric, and Victor Longa. 2011. "Lenneberg's Views on Language Development and Their Relevance for Modern Biolinguistics." *Biolinguistics* 5 (3): 254–73.

Braddock, Richard, and Richard Lloyd-Jones. 1963. *Research in Written Composition*. Urbana, IL: National Council of Teachers of English.

Brook, Donna. 1998. *The Journey of English*. New York: Clarion.

Brown, David. 2009. *In Other Words: Grammar Lessons for Code-Switching, Composition, and Language Study*. Portsmouth, NH: Heinemann.

Brown, H. Douglas. 2007. *Principles of Language Learning and Teaching*. 5th ed. White Plains, NY: Pearson Education.

Brown, Roger. 1973. *A First Language: The Early Stages*. Cambridge, MA: MIT Press.

Brozo, William, Gerry Shiel, and Keith Topping. 2007/2008. "Engagement in Reading: Lessons Learned from Three Pisa Countries." *Journal of Adolescent & Adult Literacy* 51 (4; December/January): 304–17.

Bryson, Bill. 1994. *Made in America: An Informal History of the English Language in the United States*. New York: HarperCollins.

Bunch, George. 2013. "Pedagogical Language Knowledge: Preparing Mainstream Teachers for English Learners in the New Standards Era." *Review of Educational Research* 37 (February): 298–341.

Calkins, Lucy. 1991. *Living Between the Lines*. Portsmouth, NH: Heinemann.

Calmenson, Stephanie. 1993. *It Begins with an* A. New York: Scholastic.

Carroll, Lewis. 1999. *Through the Looking Glass and What Alice Found There*. New York: Dover.

Chamot, Anna, and Michael O'Malley. 1989. "The Cognitive Academic Language Learning Approach." In *When They Don't All Speak English: Integrating the ESL Student into the Regular Classroom*, ed. Pat Rigg and Virginia Allen, 108–25. Urbana, IL: National Council of Teachers of English.

Chomsky, Noam. 1959. "Review of Verbal Learning." *Language* 35: 26–58.

———. 1975. *Reflections on Language*. New York: Pantheon.

Clark, Kevin. 2009. "The Case for Structured English Immersion." *Educational Leadership* April: 42–46.

Cleary, Brian. 2001. *To Root, to Toot, to Parachute: What Is a Verb?* Minneapolis: Carolrhoda.

———. 2002. *Under, Over, by the Clover: What Is a Preposition?* Minneapolis: Carolrhoda.

Clements, Andrew. 1996. *Frindle*. New York: Simon and Schuster.

Clymer, Theodore. 1963. "The Utility of Phonic Generalizations in the Primary Grades." *The Reading Teacher* 16 (January): 252–58.

Cornman, Oliver. 1902. *Spelling in the Elementary School*. Boston: Ginn.

Corson, David. 1997. "The Learning and Use of Academic English Words." *Language Learning* 47: 671–718.

Cummings, D. W. 1988. *American English Spelling*. Baltimore: Johns Hopkins University Press.

Cummins, Jim. 2000. *Language, Power and Pedagogy: Bilingual Children in the Crossfire*. Tonawanda, NY: Multilingual Matters.

———. 2007. "Rethinking Monolingual Instructional Strategies in Multilingual Classrooms." *Canadian Journal of Applied Linguistics* 10 (2): 221–40.

Curran, Charles. 1976. *Counseling-Learning in Second Languages*. Apple River, IL: Apple River Press.

Derewianka, Beverly. 2007. "Changing Approaches to the Conceptualization and Teaching of Grammar." In *International Handbook of English Language Teaching*, ed. Jim Cummins and Chris Davison, 843–58. New York: Springer Science+Business Media.

Diller, Karl. 1978. *The Language Teaching Controversy*. Rowley, MA: Newbury House.

Duksta, Laura. 2007. *I Love You More*. Naperville, IL: Jabberwocky.

Dulay, Heidi, and Mariana Burt. 1974. "Natural Sequences in Child Second Language Acquisition." *Language Learning* 24: 37–53.

Edelsky, Carole. 1986. *Writing in a Bilingual Program: Había Una Vez*. Norwood, NJ: Ablex.

Elley, Warwick, and Ian Barton. 1976. "The Role of Grammar in a Secondary School Curriculum." *Research in the Teaching of English* 10: 5–21.

Ellis, Rod. 2005. "Principles of Instructed Language Teaching." *System* 33: 209–24.

Fang, Zhihui. 2004. "Scientific Literacy: A Systemic Functional Linguistics Perspective." *Wiley InterScience* 89 (2): 335–47. doi:10.1002/sce.20050.

———. 2008. "Going Beyond the Fab Five: Helping Students Cope with the Unique Linguistic Challenges of Expository Reading in the Middle Grades." *Journal of Adolescent and Adult Literacy* 51 (6): 476–87.

Farmer, Ann, and Richard Demers. 1996. *A Linguistics Workbook*. Cambridge, MA: MIT Press.

Fernandes, Eugenie. 1996. *ABC and You*. Boston: Houghton Mifflin.

Fillmore, Lily Wong. 1991. "Second-Language Learning in Children: A Model of Language Learning in Context." In *Language Processing in Bilingual Children*, ed. Ellen Bialystok, 49–69. Cambridge, UK: Cambridge University Press.

Fillmore, Lily Wong, and Catherine E. Snow. 2002. "What Teachers Need to Know." In *What Teachers Need to Know About Language*, ed. C. T. Adger, C. E. Snow, and D. Christian, 7–53. Washington, DC, and McHenry, IL: Center for Applied Linguistics and Delta Systems.

Fisher, Douglas, Carol Rothenberg, and Nancy Frey. 2007. *Language Learners in the English Classroom*. Urbana, IL: National Council of Teachers of English.

Fountas, Irene, and Gay Su Pinnell. 2012–2013. "Guided Reading: The Romance and the Reality." *The Reading Teacher* 66 (4): 268–84.

Freeman, David E., and Yvonne S. Freeman. 2009. *Academic Language for English Language Learners and Struggling Readers: How to Help Students Succeed Across Content Areas*. Portsmouth, NH: Heinemann.

Freeman, Yvonne S., and David E. Freeman. 2006. *Teaching Reading and Writing in Spanish and English in Bilingual and Dual Language Classrooms*. 2d ed. Portsmouth, NH: Heinemann.

———. 2009. *La enseñanza de la lectura y la escritura en español y en inglés en clases bilingües y de doble inmersión*. Segunda edición revisada ed. Portsmouth, NH: Heinemann.

Freeman, Yvonne S., David E. Freeman, Margo Gottlieb, Robert Marzano, Mary Lou McCloskey, Lydia Stack, Cecilia Silva, and Aurora Garcia. 2011. *On Our Way to English Teachers' Resource Guide of Language Transfer Issues for English Language Learners*. Boston: Houghton Mifflin Harcourt.

García, Ofelia. 2009. *Bilingual Education in the 21st Century: A Global Perspective*. Malden, MA: Wiley–Blackwell.

———. 2010. "Misconstructions of Bilingualism in U.S. Education." *NYSABE News* 1 (1): 2–7.

Gattegno, Caleb. 1972. *Teaching Foreign Languages in Schools: The Silent Way*. Reading, UK: Educational Explorers.

Gibbons, Pauline. 2002. *Scaffolding Language: Scaffolding Learning*. Portsmouth, NH: Heinemann.

———. 2009. *English Learners, Academic Literacy, and Thinking: Learning in the Challenge Zone*. Portsmouth, NH: Heinemann.

Goodman, Debra. 1999. *The Reading Detective Club*. Portsmouth, NH: Heinemann.

Goodman, Kenneth S. 1996. *On Reading*. Portsmouth, NH: Heinemann.

Goodman, Yetta M., and Kenneth S. Goodman. 1990. "Vygotsky in a Whole Language Perspective." In *Vygotsky and Education: Instructional Implications and Applications of Sociohistorical Psychology*, ed. Luis C. Moll, 223–50. Cambridge, UK: Cambridge University Press.

Goswami, Dixie. 1986. "Children's Use of Analogy in Learning to Read: A Developmental Study." *Journal of Experiemental Child Psychology* 42: 73–83.

Gottlieb, Margo. 2004. *English Language Proficiency Standards for English Language Learners in Kindergarten Through Grade 12*. Madison: Wisconsin Department of Education.

Graves, Donald. 1994. *A Fresh Look at Writing*. Portsmouth, NH: Heinemann.

Graves, Michael. 2006. *The Vocabulary Book: Learning and Instruction*. New York: Teachers College Press.

Grice, Herbert P. 1989. *Studies in the Way of Words*. Cambridge, MA: Harvard University Press.

Grosjean, François. 2010. *Bilingual: Life and Reality*. Cambridge, MA: Harvard University Press.

Guiora, Alexander, Robert Brannon, and Cecelia Dull. 1972. "Empathy and Second Language Learning." *Language Learning* 22 (1): 11–130.

Guthrie, John, and Marcia Davis. 2003. "Motivating Struggling Readers in Middle School Through an Engagement Model of Classroom Practice." *Reading & Writing Quarterly* 19: 59–85.

Gwynne, Fred. 1988a. *A Chocolate Moose for Dinner*. New York: Aladdin.

———. 1988b. *The King Who Rained*. New York: Aladdin.

Halliday, Michael. 1984. "Three Aspects of Children's Language Development: Learning Language, Learning Through Language, and Learning About Language." In *Oral and Written Language Development Research: Impact on the Schools*, ed. Yetta M. Goodman, Myna M. Haussler, and Dorothy S. Strickland. Urbana, IL: National Council of Teachers of English.

———. 1989. *Spoken and Written Language*. Oxford, UK: Oxford University Press.

———. 1994. *An Introduction to Functional Grammar*. 2d ed. London: Edward Arnold.

Halliday, Michael, and Raquiah Hassan. 1989. *Language, Context, and Text: Aspects of Language in a Socialsemiotic Perspective*. 2d ed. Oxford, UK: Oxford University Press.

Heath, Shirley B. 1983. *Ways with Words: Language, Life, and Work in Communities and Classrooms*. Cambridge, UK: Cambridge University Press.

Heller, Ruth. 1987. *A Cache of Jewels and Other Collective Nouns*. New York: Grosset and Dunlap.

———. 1988. *Kites Sail High: A Book About Verbs*. New York: Grosset and Dunlap.

———. 1989. *Many Luscious Lollipops: A Book About Adjectives*. New York: Grosset and Dunlap.

———. 1991. *Up, Up and Away: A Book About Adverbs*. New York: Grosset and Dunlap.

Hughes, Margaret, and Dennis Searle. 1997. *The Violent E and Other Tricky Sounds*. York, ME: Stenhouse.

Hymes, Del. 1970. "On Communicative Competence." In *Directions in Sociolinguistics*, ed. John Gumperz and Dell Hymes, 35–71. New York: Holt, Rinehart and Winston.

Johnson, Karen E. 1995. *Understanding Communication in Second Language Classrooms*. Cambridge, UK: Cambridge University Press.

Kilgallon, Don, and Jenny Kilgallon. 2007. *Grammar for High School: A Sentence-Composing Approach*. Portsmouth, NH: Heinemann.

Krashen, Stephen. 1977. "Some Issues Related to the Monitor Model." In *On Tesol '77: Teaching and Learning English as a Second Language; Trends in Research and Practice*, ed. H. Douglas Brown, Carlos Alfredo Yorio and Ruth H. Crymes, 144–58. Washington, DC: Teachers of English to Speakers of Other Languages.

———. 1982. *Principles and Practice in Second Language Acquisition*. New York: Pergamon Press.

———. 1998. "Teaching Grammar: Why Bother?" *California English 3* (3): 8.

———. 2003. *Explorations in Language Acquisition and Use*. Portsmouth, NH: Heinemann.

———. 2004. *The Power of Reading: Insights from the Research*. 2d ed. Portsmouth, NH: Heinemann.

———. 2009. "The Comprehension Hypothesis Extended." In *Input Matters in SLA*, ed. Thorsten Piske and Martha Young-Scholten, 81–94. Bristol, UK: Multilingual Matters.

———. 2013. "The Sullivan and Brown Reading Study: New Evidence for the Power of Reading, the Effect of Reading on Poverty, and Evidence for Late Intervention." Retrieved from http://skrashen.blogspot.com/2013/09/new-evidence-for-power-of-reading.html.

Krashen, Stephen, and Tracy Terrell. 1983. *The Natural Approach: Language Acquisition in the Classroom*. Hayward, CA: Alemany Press.

Kucer, Stephen, and Jenny Tuten. 2003. "Revisiting and Rethinking the Reading Process." *Language Arts* 80 (4): 284–90.

Lado, Robert. 1957. *Linguistics Across Cultures*. Ann Arbor: University of Michigan Press.

Lederer, Richard. 1991. *The Miracle of Language*. New York: Pocket Books.

————. 2012. *Amazing Words: An Alphabetical Anthology of Alluring, Astonishing, Beguiling, Bewitching, Enchanting, Enthralling, Mesmerizing, Miraculous, Tantalizing, Tempting, and Transfixing Words*. Portland, OR: Marion Street Press.

Lenneberg, Eric. 1967. *The Biological Foundations of Language*. New York: Wiley.

Lindfors, Judith. 1987. *Children's Language and Learning*. 2d ed. Englewood Cliffs, NJ: Prentice-Hall.

Long, Ethan. 2004. *Mañana Iguana*. New York: Holliday House.

Long, Michael. 1983. "Does Second Language Instruction Make a Difference? A Review of the Research." *TESOL Quarterly* 14: 378–90.

————. 2001. "Focus on Form: A Design Feature in Language Teaching Methodology." In *English Language Teaching in Its Social Context: A Reader*, ed. Christopher Candlin and Neil Mercer, 180–90. London: Routledge.

Lozanov, Georgi. 1982. "Suggestology and Suggestopedy." *Innovative Approaches to Language Teaching*, ed. Robert Blair. Rowley, MA: Newbury House.

Macauley, William. 1947. "The Difficulty of Grammar." *British Journal of Educational Psychology* 17: 153–62.

Martin, Jim. 2001. "Language, Register, and Genre." In *Analysing English in a Global Context: A Reader*, ed. Anne Burns and Caroline Coffin, 149–66. London: Routledge.

Marzano, Robert, and Debra Pickering. 2005. *Building Academic Vocabulary: Teacher's Manual*. Alexandria, VA: Association for Supervision and Curriculum Development.

Maurer, Donna. 1996. *Annie, Bea, and Chi Chi Dolores*. Boston: Houghton Mifflin.

McLaughlin, Charles, Marilyn Thompson, and Dinah Zike. 2002. *Integrated Physics and Chemistry*. Columbus, OH: Glencoe/McGraw-Hill.

Medina, Jane. 1999. *My Name Is Jorge on Both Sides of the River*. Honesdale, PA: Boyds Mills Press.

Moll, Luis. 1994. "Literacy Research in Homes and Classrooms: A Sociocultural Approach." In *Theoretical Models and Processes of Reading*, ed. Robert B. Ruddell, Martha R. Ruddell, and Harry Singer. Newark, DE: International Reading Association.

Moustafa, Margaret. 1997. *Beyond Traditional Phonics: Research Discoveries and Reading Instruction*. Portsmouth, NH: Heinemann.

Nagy, William, Richard Anderson, and Patricia Herman. 1985. "Learning Words from Context." *Reading Research Quarterly* 20 (2): 233–53.

Nash, Rose. 1990. *NTC's Dictionary of Spanish Cognates Thematically Organized*. Chicago: NTC Publishing Group.

Opitz, Michael. 2000. *Rhymes and Reasons: Literature and Language Play for Phonological Awareness*. Portsmouth, NH: Heinemann.

Opitz, Michael, and Timothy Rasinski. 2008. *Good-Bye Round Robin*. Rev. ed. Portsmouth, NH: Heinemann.

Pallotta, Jerry. 1986. *The Icky Bug Alphabet Book*. New York: Scholastic.

Parish, Peggy. 1976. *Good Work, Amelia Bedelia*. New York: Avon.

Paulson, Eric, and Ann Freeman. 2003. *Insight from the Eyes: The Science of Effective Reading Instruction*. Portsmouth, NH: Heinemann.

Pearson, P. David, and M. C. Gallagher. 1983. "The Instruction of Reading Comprehension." *Contemporary Educational Psychology* 8 (3): 317–44.

Petitto, Laura. 2003. "How Children Acquire Language: A New Answer." Available at www.dartmouth.edu/~lpetitto/langAc.html.

Piaget, Jean. 1955. *The Language and Thought of the Child*. New York: Meridian.

Pinker, Steven. 1994. *The Language Instinct: How the Mind Creates Language*. New York: William Morrow.

Polk, Allison. 2012. "Paving the Way for Groundbreaking Research in Bilingualism." *Gaullaudet Today* (spring): 1–3. Retrieved from http://oes.gallaudet.edu/bl2/.

Prelutsky, Jack. 1986. *Read-Aloud Rhymes for the Very Young*. New York: Alfred A. Knopf.

Randell, Beverly, Jenny Giles, and Annette Smith. 1996. *Mom*. Crystal Lake, IL: Rigby.

Rasinski, Timothy, Nancy Padak, Joanna Newton, and Evangeline Newton. 2011. "The Latin–Greek Connection: Building Vocabulary Through Morphological Study." *The Reading Teacher* 65 (2): 133–41.

Read, Charles. 1971. "Pre-School Children's Knowledge of English Phonology." *Harvard Education Review* 41 (1): 1–34.

Rice, Joseph. 1897. "The Futility of the Spelling Grind." *Forum* 23: 163–72, 409–19.

Rice, Mabel. 2002. "Children's Language Acquisition." In *Language Development: A Reader for Teachers*, ed. Brenda Power and Ruth Hubbard, 19–27. Upper Saddle River, NJ: Merrill Prentice-Hall.

Rodríguez, Timothy A. 2001. "From the Known to the Unknown: Using Cognates to Teach English to Spanish-Speaking Literates." *The Reading Teacher* 54 (8): 744–46.

Samoyault, Tiphaine. 1998. *Alphabetical Order: How the Alphabet Began*. New York: Viking.

Scarcella, Robin. 1990. *Teaching Language Minority Students in the Multicultural Classroom*. Englewood Cliffs, NJ: Prentice-Hall Regents.

Schumann, John H. 1978. *The Pidginization Process: A Model for Second Language Acquisition*. Rowley, MA: Newbury House.

Schwartz, Alvin. 1972. *A Twister of Twists, a Tangler of Tongues*. Philadelphia: J. B. Lippincott.

Skinner, B. F. 1957. *Verbal Behavior*. New York: Appleton.

Smith, Frank. 1985. *Reading Without Nonsense*. 2d ed. New York: Teachers College Press.

Sober, Elliot. 1980. "Language and Psychological Reality: Some Reflections on Chomsky's 'Rules and Representations.'" *Linguistics and Philosophy* 3 (3): 395–405.

Stanovich, Keith. 1986. "Matthew Effects in Reading: Some Consequences of Individual Differences in the Acquisition of Literacy." *Reading Research Quarterly* 21: 360–407.

Swain, Merril. 1985. "Communicative Competence: Some Roles of Comprehensible Output in Its Development." In *Input in Second Language Acquisition*, ed. Susan Gass and Carolyn Madden, 235–53. Rowley, MA: Newbury House.

Terban, Marvin. 1982. *Eight Ate: A Feast of Homonym Riddles*. New York: Clarion Books.

Thompson, Denisse, and Rheta Rubenstein. 2000. "Learning Mathematics Vocabulary: Potential Pitfalls and Instructional Strategies." *Mathematics Teacher* 93 (7): 568–74.

Tompkins, Gail, and David Yaden. 1986. *Answering Students' Questions About Words*. Urbana, IL: National Council of Teachers of English.

Treiman, Rebecca. 1985. "Onsets and Rimes as Units of Spoken Syllables: Evidence from Children." *Journal of Experiemental Child Psychology* 39: 161–81.

Valdés, Guadalupe. 2001. *Learning and Not Learning English: Latino Students in American Schools*. New York: Teachers College Press.

Vygotsky, Lev. 1962. *Thought and Language*. Translated by Eugenia Hanfmann Gertrude Vakar. Cambridge, MA: MIT Press.

Wallerstein, Nina. 1987. "Problem Posing Education: Freire's Method for Transformation." In *Freire for the Classroom*, ed. Ira Shor, 33–44. Portsmouth, NH: Heinemann.

Weaver, Constance. 1996. *Teaching Grammar in Context*. Portsmouth, NH: Boynton/Cook.

———. 2008. *Grammar to Enrich and Enhance Writing*. Portsmouth, NH: Heinemann.

Wells, Gordon. 1986. *The Meaning Makers: Children Learning Language and Using Language to Learn*. Portsmouth, NH: Heinemann.

White, Thomas, Joanne Sowell, and Alice Yanagihara. 1989. "Teaching Elementary Students to Use Word-Part Clues." *The Reading Teacher* 42 (4): 302–308.

Wilbur, Richard. 1997. *The Disappearing Alphabet Book*. New York: Scholastic.

Wilkins, D. A. 1976. *Notional Syllabuses*. Oxford, UK: Oxford University Press.

Williams, Joan. 2001. "Classroom Conversations: Opportunities to Learn for ESL Students in Mainstream Classrooms." *The Reading Teacher* 54 (8): 750–57.

Wylie, Richard, and Donald Durrell. 1970. "Teaching Vowels Through Phonograms." *Elemenary English* 47: 787–91.

Index